State and Countryside

The Johns Hopkins Studies in Development
Vernon W. Ruttan and T. Paul Schultz,
Consulting Editors

State and Countryside
Development Policy
and Agrarian Politics
in Latin America

Merilee S. Grindle

The Johns Hopkins University Press
Baltimore and London

The Johns Hopkins University Press, 701 West 40th Street, Baltimore, Maryland 21211
The Johns Hopkins Press Ltd, London

Figure 3.1 is redrawn from William H. Durham, *Scarcity and Survival in Central America: Ecological Origins of the Soccer War*, with the permission of the publishers, Stanford University Press. © 1979 by the Board of Trustees of the Leland Stanford Junior University.

Figure 7.1 is reproduced here by permission of the Office for Public Sector Studies, Institute of Latin American Studies, University of Texas at Austin.

The paper in this book is acid-free and meets the guidelines for permanence and durability of the Committee on Production Guidelines for Book Longevity of the Council on Library Resources.

Library of Congress Cataloging in Publication Data

Grindle, Merilee Serrill.
  State and countryside.

  (The Johns Hopkins studies in development)
  Bibliography: p.
  Includes index.
    1. Rural development—Latin America.   2. Agriculture and state—Latin America.
3. Land reform—Latin America.   4. Latin America—Rural conditions.   5. Peasantry—
Latin America.   I. Title.   II. Series.
HN110.5.G75   1985   307'.14'098   85-8081
ISBN 0-8018-3278-0 (alk. paper)
ISBN 0-8018-2935-6 (pbk. : alk. paper)

To Stefanie and Alexandra

Contents

List of Figures and Tables

Preface

This book is a product of a decade of studying the problems of rural Latin America and the public policies that have ameliorated, exacerbated, or otherwise shaped those problems. The analysis has been strongly influenced by the many public officials in Latin America with whom I have discussed issues of agricultural and rural development. As is evident in my previous work, I have been impressed by the extent to which these concerned individuals have articulated coherent and logical explanations for national agrarian problems and the extent to which they have sought to design public policies to respond to their understandings of such problems. This book, seeking as it does to account for the influence of state elites in the policy process, owes much to the insights gained from discussions with such people and to the courtesy and patience with which my questions and concerns were addressed.

My interviews with public officials, as well as documentary research undertaken in the field, are basic sources that inform my analysis. In addition, I have reviewed official documents related to agriculture and rural areas and national economic plans for a variety of countries. Interviews in Washington, D.C., with officials of the World Bank and the Inter-American Development Bank also were conducted during the course of my research.

This book also relies on a wide range of monographs and case studies that have appeared in recent years. The issue of change in rural Latin America is complex and challenging and has, I believe, encouraged a large number of scholars to undertake difficult and time-consuming field research in selected countries, regions, and communities. This has frequently resulted in work of extremely high caliber and theoretical relevance. The insights and data I have derived from these sources have encouraged me to attempt to account for the patterns of change that seem to be occurring throughout the region.

It will become clear that I have adopted a broad definition of the term *peasant* in this book. For my purposes, the peasantry comprises the vast bulk of the rural poor, including smallholders, tenants, sharecroppers, and landless workers. I have adopted this term because of the difficulty of differentiating clearly among sectors of the rural population when economic and social conditions increasingly encourage families and individuals to engage in multiple income-generating activities. Differentiations among the rural poor do indeed exist and may well be increasing, but these distinctions derive more from relationships to the state, to each other, and to political and economic organizations than to inherent relationships to land, markets, or communities. As used here the term *peasant* corresponds closely to the Spanish term *campesino* and is often used interchangeably with phrases such as "the rural poor," "the mass of the rural population," or "the rural underclass" (Landsberger 1969, 1–5; Pearse 1975). I have also differentiated between policies for agricultural modernization and reformist policies—those having the explicit goal of rural development. Within the context of the development models adopted by state elites, the central goal of both types of policies is to bring about increases in production and productivity; reformist policies, however, also address the welfare of the rural poor, equity questions more generally, and rural development in the broadest sense.

Many basic statistics are taken from publications of the Food and Agriculture Organization of the United Nations (FAO), which provided the most complete information in a useful format, including the longitudinal data that are essential to an attempt to explain change (Paulino and Tseng, 1980). FAO data are based on official reports received from member countries. The FAO publishes data on crops and trade for consistent production years, while other data sources, such as the U.S. Department of Agriculture, report figures that vary by crop and country. FAO publications present data on a wide range of crops and livestock; USDA data are often limited to cereal production and trade. It should be noted, of course, that the proverbial grain of salt must be added to compensate for statistical data that are of variable quality and reliability. I have attempted to use reasonable caution in selecting data that demonstrate consistency in reporting over time and reliability when compared with other sources of information.

I was able to pursue this broad interpretation of development policy and rural Latin America because of the generous support of a Tinker Postdoctoral Fellowship. I also benefited greatly from a Charles Culpepper Postdoctoral Research Fellowship awarded by the Political Science Department at Brown University. I am particularly appreciative of these grants, and the institutions that awarded them, for the time they allowed me to do the research, the travel, and the analysis involved in this work.

Colleagues at the Harvard Institute for International Development—Dwight Perkins, Michael Roemer, John Cohen, David Cole, Christine Jones, Noel McGinn, Pauline Peters, John Thomas, Donald Warwick, and others—have been consistently interested in and supportive of my work, if not always in agreement with it. Similarly, John Montgomery of Harvard University has been helpful and influential in shaping my thinking about the problems of development. Robert Paarlberg of Wellesley College has added greatly to the book through his astute questions, probing, and suggestions. Students at Brown and Harvard universities have helped sharpen my presentation through discussions, questions, and well-defended critiques. Anders Richter of the Johns Hopkins University Press has been considerate, helpful, and responsive beyond the call of duty. Elizabeth Shaw at HIID has been a careful and concerned participant in the production of the manuscript, and on the home front, Nancy Walsh, Annalee Greenhalgh, and Gina Millward have assumed burdens and responsibilities that rightfully should have been mine and have therefore added immeasurably to this book. Steven Grindle and my children, Alexandra and Stefanie, have borne with tolerance and good humor the distraction, disorganization, and distress resulting from my travel and my writing spells. I am grateful to all these people for the generosity with which they have shared ideas, time, and intellectual and moral support with me. While they are in no way to be held responsible for errors of fact or interpretation in the following pages, I hope they will recognize how important their contributions have been.

1 | Introduction: Development Policies and Politics in Latin America

This book presents an interpretation of four decades of change in rural Latin America, exploring the relationship of capitalist expansion in agriculture to the plight of the rural poor and to the deepening problem of underdevelopment. It is centrally concerned with analyzing the role of state policies in stimulating capitalist forms of agricultural development and in managing the social unrest and dislocation caused by deteriorating conditions among Latin America's 100 million *campesinos*. It deals with the period from 1940 to 1980, with emphasis on the two most recent decades, the 1960s and 1970s. During this time, the region's rural economies underwent rapid change, presenting scholars with difficult questions to answer: What was responsible for the increase in conditions of underdevelopment? What role was assumed by the state in its interventions in the agricultural economy and in rural social relationships?

In 1971, Ernest Feder responded to these questions in *The Rape of the Peasantry: Latin America's Landholding System*. His work, based on data that became available in the 1960s, was a major attempt to account for the all-too-evident incidence of rural poverty. In it, he presented a persuasive statement of the need for massive agrarian reform throughout the region. Arguing that the "latifundio agriculture of Latin America is an unemployment agriculture," he located the causes of rural unemployment and underemployment in the highly inequitable structure of the region's landholding system (Feder 1971, 3). The result was underproductivity and static social and economic relationships. In order to end this stagnation and the rural poverty that limited the potential for national development, traditional landholding structures would have to be transformed and peasants would have to be allowed to accumulate agricultural surpluses from their land and labor and to invest them in more effective means of production and higher levels of consumption. These changes would not come easily, however, as Feder's review of a number of agrarian reform efforts demonstrated; in each case, traditional landholding elites placed major constraints on the extent of reform that was undertaken by the state.

1

However, by the time Feder's book was published, it was becoming evident that considerable change was occurring in Latin America's agricultural sector that could not be easily explained by *The Rape of the Peasantry*. Certainly Feder was correct in considering the distribution of land in rural areas to be of fundamental importance in accounting for inequitable social and political relationships in Latin America. And, as he argued, it is no doubt true that smallholders are often more efficient than large farmers in their use of land (Berry and Cline 1979; Griffin 1976). Moreover, it cannot be refuted that the maldistribution of income in rural areas has an impact on the national economy by perpetuating constricted consumer markets, low levels of health and education, high levels of population growth, burgeoning urban slums, and tense social relations. Nevertheless, while ownership patterns that concentrate land in a few hands are inevitably unjust and exploitive, they are not necessarily an impediment to increases in production or productivity, to the adoption of technical improvements, or to the development of capitalist forms of agriculture, as the experience of Latin America in recent decades indicates.

Particularly in the 1960s and 1970s, capitalist agricultural exploitation expanded rapidly. Important indicators of this change were the widespread adoption of green revolution innovations, increased investment in mechanization, expanded production for export markets, greater penetration of multinational capital in agribusiness enterprises, and utilization of wage labor as the dominant form of labor relations. This expansion was based on the very maldistribution of productive resources that Feder claimed was responsible for the sector's backwardness and stagnation. Indeed, increases in production and technical advances occurred even while the pattern of large and small landholdings continued to characterize the region, in some places in more exaggerated form than in the past. Between the 1940s and the 1980s, agricultural land was concentrated in even fewer hands in many countries, despite some official efforts at land reform and redistribution. The proportion of sharecroppers and tenants also fell among the rural poor, while the number of landless workers and those who engaged in two, three, or even more income-generating activities grew significantly. The motors of these changes are to be found in the expansion of capitalist agriculture, demographic growth, and state policies, not in the breakdown of archaic landholding patterns. In fact, the structure of landholding is a critical factor in explaining agricultural change, not its stagnation, because it has provided a small landholding elite with privileged access to state-provided inputs, infrastructure, markets, and support services.

A decade after the appearance of *The Rape of the Peasantry*, a major effort to account for the expansion of capitalist agriculture, increases in rural underdevelopment, and state-sponsored reformism was published. In *The Agrarian Question and Reformism in Latin America*, Alain de Janvry argued that underdevelopment in the agricultural sector is the result of "disarticulated accumulation," which occurs in peripheral states in the world capitalist system, and "functional dualism" in rural social class relationships, which is an integral part of dependent and uneven capitalist expansion in the periphery. He described an agrarian crisis characterized by "sharply uneven development among farms, crops, and regions and . . . massive rural poverty and political tensions," and he located the cause of this structural crisis in the global process of capitalist accumulation (de Janvry 1981, 3). He then interpreted a series of reformist efforts on the part of Latin American states to address this crisis—community development, technological diffusion, land reform, rural development, and basic-needs programs. According to his analysis, state policy is a result of "(1) the class structure and consequent balance of political forces in the social control over the state and (2) the objective and subjective contradictions of capitalism and the consequent crises of accumulation and legitimacy" (de Janvry 1981, 186). These factors place narrow constraints on the capacity of the state to resolve contradictions that are inherent in capitalist accumulation and class relationships.

In my own work on rural Latin America, which spans most of the 1970s and early 1980s, I have been deeply impressed by the conditions that de Janvry describes in his book. We both see an agricultural sector characterized by change rather than stasis, and agree that it is not the nature of these changes that needs to be explained so much as their causes and underlying dynamics. The expansion of large-scale, capital-intensive, export-oriented agriculture is a fact that can be demonstrated; increasing rural poverty and insecurity are evident; so too are grave balance-of-payments problems, a decline in the production of domestic food crops, massive rural-to-urban migration, and politically threatening levels of unemployment and landlessness. De Janvry and I differ, however, in terms of how we account for these facts and, in particular, how we explain the role assumed by the state. De Janvry begins with the logic of capitalist accumulation in the periphery; I begin with state policies and the "development ideologies" from which they are derived. As a result, we also differ in our interpretation of why state elites—those who are formal incumbents in decision- and policy-making positions—develop and pursue specific policies for agricultural and rural development, even though we generally agree on the outcome of these efforts.

De Janvry is correct in describing a form of capitalist agricultural expansion in Latin America that is profoundly affected by the global context of development. Moreover, it is also clear that state policies have consistently benefited a narrow agricultural elite and that reformist efforts have been limited and constrained by the political and economic power of this class. However, perspectives derived from research on the politics of policy making and implementation lead me to argue that the Latin American state does not merely reflect and reproduce class relationships in the society, assuming relative autonomy only when economic and legitimacy crises threaten the basis of capitalist accumulation. Rather, I believe, state elites have a variable capacity for autonomous decision making and often have specific interests in national development that cause the state to become active in shaping economic and social relationships with dominant-class interests in a society.[1] Thus, issues of policy choice, political leadership, and state expansion loom larger in my analysis than in de Janvry's book.

Far from becoming active only to resolve crises of an economic or legitimacy nature, the Latin American state in the period between 1940 and 1980 introduced conditions that made capitalist expansion feasible and it assumed an ongoing role of intervention, resource allocation, and conflict resolution. In this role it acquired an extensive administrative and political infrastructure in the countryside and promulgated a generous body of legislation that gave it the right to appropriate land and water resources and to intervene widely in markets for land, labor, and capital. The state was thus able to increase its power vis-à-vis specific social classes or alliances, and individual agencies acquired control over policy areas that they then used to build their own political and bureaucratic bases. The state developed an infrastructure that subordinated specific interests to what it defined as national economic interests and mobilized specific clientele groups. And it became increasingly central as a mediator in situations of rural conflict, utilizing repression, accommodation, and co-optation as tools for reestablishing social stability. So extensive and ongoing was the growth of the state's intervention and so varied was the use of its resources that its activities cannot be fully encompassed by an explanation that rests on capitalist dominance and crisis management alone.

In brief, I place four decades of rural change within an analytical perspective that stresses the role played by the state in defining the course of agricultural development in Latin America. Initially, the models of economic development that were accepted and pursued by state elites signaled the role that agriculture was to play in national development and prescribed the most efficient allocation of limited resources within the agricultural sector itself. As we shall see in subsequent chapters, legitimacy was accorded to the state apparatus to initiate these policies and to expand its presence in the agricultural economy and in rural areas. At the same time, these policies supported the emergence of a small class of capitalist entrepreneurs whose production was generally export-oriented and who subsequently developed both the economic and the political power to demand continued favorable treatment from the state.

Gradually, however, capitalist expansion within the context of a highly skewed distribution of productive resources brought increasing evidence of underdevelopment. By the 1970s, state elites became convinced that economic growth and social stability were being subverted by the private advantages accruing to the agricultural elite, and they began to consider policy alternatives that would address their concerns. Nevertheless, the range of options available to them was constrained by the growth of the economic and political power of the large-scale capitalist entrepreneurs; radical changes in the structure of agricultural production and capitalist accumulation were thus ruled out as economically and politically infeasible. Instead, a variety of policies were introduced to manage or compensate for the problems of poverty, underproductivity, and international dependence that capitalist expansion had brought in its wake. This stimulated further state penetration of the rural economy and social structures. Thus, over time, the state increased its capacity to address and manage protests of the rural poor arising from conflict over land and livelihood.

This general pattern of state expansion, capitalist development, and rural poverty and powerlessness in Latin American countries is explored in the following chapters. There are, however, significant variations among and within states in the region at various historical moments in terms of their relations with dominant-class interests and their capacity to manage rural protest. These are accounted for by differences among regimes and in how real power is distributed within them. Case study material from three countries that experienced a major expansion of capitalist agriculture and deepening conditions of underdevelopment provides evidence from five different regimes—a dominant-party authoritarian regime (Mexico), a personalist military dictatorship and a semicompetitive two-party oligarchic regime (Colombia), and a competitive multi-party semicorporatist regime and an exclusionary military authoritarian regime (Brazil). Broad policies were similar in all five cases, but significant differences in policy instruments were determined by the political and economic power relationships that confronted the respective state elites.

A BRIEF SUMMARY OF CHAPTERS 2–9

In Chapter 2, I consider a number of approaches to the question of state autonomy and argue for a definition of the state that does not posit a priori linkages to social class formations. A definition that focuses on the state as an executive and administrative apparatus for decision making and control makes it possible for me to consider the impact of state interests in national development on the formulation and implementation of specific policies. In the case of agricultural development in Latin America, the content of state policy can be linked to the development ideologies held by state elites. Moreover, the relationship of the state to the rural poor, as well as specific reformist initiatives, reflect both the expansion of the state and its role in regulating conflict and channeling protest behavior.

Development policies undertaken by Latin American states between 1940 and 1980 were not imposed upon a rural tabula rasa. Agrarian capitalism after 1940 was constructed on the base of a highly skewed distribution of basic agricultural resources that had deep historical roots. Chapter 3 traces the development of landholding patterns, rural social relationships, and market structures from the colonial period to 1940. During these four centuries, commercial opportunities—or the lack of them—were of fundamental importance in stimulating elites to acquire land and control over labor and to produce agricultural products for export, for domestic consumption, or for local subsistence only. Thus, in spite of the stereotype of a traditionally stagnant and backward rural sector, change, often in response to world demand for agricultural products, occurred intermittently after the colonization of the region in the sixteenth and seventeenth centuries and was an important characteristic of late-nineteenth-century development. It will be argued, however, that quantitatively and qualitatively the magnitude and duration of change in rural Latin America after 1940 was distinct from that of previous periods. Specifically, the role played by the state and by technological innovation will be seen to differ considerably.

After 1940 the state emerged as a more powerful conditioner of agricultural development. Chapter 4 examines the role of the state in stimulating capitalist forms of agricultural modernization and in deepening the gap between large- and medium-scale commercial enterprises on the one hand, and the bulk of subsistence and semisubsistence farms on the other. Development ideologies adopted after the collapse of the agricultural export economies in the 1930s and the concomitant expansion of the state were fundamental in encouraging the modernization of the agricultural sector after 1940 in a fashion that concentrated credit, infrastructure, mechanization, green revolution technology, and research and extension in the hands of a small agricultural elite. As this sector benefited from modernization, subsistence and semisubsistence farmers were increasingly unable to compete for access to the same kinds of resources and thus to remunerative and expanding markets. Evidence from Mexico, Colombia, and Brazil substantiates the major role of the state in seeking to stimulate a more productive and modern agricultural sector as well as in encouraging disparities among producers, crops, and regions. In the process, however, the state lost much of its capacity to impose its authority on the emergent elites, as the experience of specific regimes in these countries indicates.

Aggregate figures surveyed in Chapter 5 indicate that the agricultural sector remained highly underproductive and inefficient in spite of four decades of modernization efforts on the part of the state. This perspective is altered, however, when the figures on specific crops and specific regions are examined. Indeed, the data indicate that extremely high rates of growth were achieved in some instances, even though the performance of the agricultural sector as a whole was poor. Chapter 5 details the expansion of capitalist forms of agricultural production, from the increased production of a number of crops, to the extensive adoption of mechanization and green revolution inputs to boost levels of production and productivity, to the heightened presence of foreign capital in production, processing, and finance. These data suggest that large landowners responded to the stimulus provided by state policies, but that their very success generated problems for national development. A decline in the production of staple crops, rising food import bills, higher rates of rural unemployment and underemployment accompanied by massive rural-to-urban migration, the increased concentration of landholdings, and higher levels of international dependency—these were the costs of agricultural modernization in Latin America. The experiences of Mexico, Colombia, and Brazil confirm both the success of the large landowners and the widespread underdevelopment that confronted the states in the region.

Clearly, the modernization of Latin American agriculture under the auspices of the state furthered the vulnerability and exploitation of the rural poor. In Chapter 6, trends in the level of welfare and security in rural Latin America are surveyed for the period 1940–80. By the late 1970s, over 62 percent of the region's poor lived in rural areas, although only 37 percent of the total population was rural, and some data indicate that levels of income and welfare among these 100 million rural poor people deteriorated after 1960. Certainly life became more insecure for many. In most countries, 60–80 percent of the rural population was landless or nearly so by 1978.[2] Unemployment and underemployment increased even in the presence of massive rural-to-urban migration. Most of the agricultural population continued to live in conditions of poverty, illiteracy, malnutrition, and ill health.

Important to an understanding of the rural poor—who make up as much as 90 percent of the rural population of Latin America—is the fact that their condition and fate are inextricably linked to the expansion of large-scale capitalist agriculture. They are not isolated, backward, or "traditional" members of society who have simply been left behind in the process of development; they do not have to be forced, trained, or cajoled into "modernity" by government programs. The growth in their unemployment, underemployment, landlessness, wage dependence, subsistence orientation, and migration is a direct result of developments in the modern capitalist sector and of state policies, and as such cannot be understood or remedied without reference to these changes. Nevertheless, in the wake of these changes, the most significant of which have been imposed from without, these peasants have not remained passive. Instead, they have adopted a variety of strategies to ensure family subsistence in the face of deteriorating conditions. They have found income-generating possibilities in handicrafts and small-scale industry, in wage labor, and in labor migration, while at the same time attempting to retain small parcels of land for subsistence. These activities have allowed them to survive, but generally at the cost of greater insecurity.

Indeed, as the levels of security and conditions of life continued to deteriorate for the rural poor in the 1970s, the issue of ownership and access to land confronted Latin American states with the challenge to alter the structure of landholding in rural areas. With few exceptions, however, agrarian reform as a major public response to this challenge was not on the policy agenda of most countries in 1980 and was considered by many state elites to have become an inappropriate response to problems of agricultural and rural development. These countries had turned their attention from the agrarian reform efforts of the 1960s to other means of addressing rural underdevelopment—methods that would not touch upon the question of the distribution of land. In Chapter 7, various agrarian reform initiatives of the 1960s and 1970s are considered in order to explore why they came about and how they were superseded by other policies to address rural and agricultural problems. In this regard, the case of agrarian reform in Colombia is presented in detail, for it is a clear example of the limitations of redistributive policies under nonrevolutionary conditions. The sources and effects of reforms differed throughout the region, of course, but a consistent outcome in all countries was the increased influence of the state on economic and political conditions in rural areas. In large part, then, a major beneficiary of agrarian reform initiatives was the state itself.

Similarly, the state benefited from the pursuit of integrated rural development programs that were designed and implemented in the 1970s. As indicated in Chapter 8, these programs became a major alternative to redistributive agrarian reform and were eagerly adopted by states concerned about the increased evidence that rural areas were a bottleneck for national development. The PIDER program in Mexico, the DRI effort in Colombia, and the POLONORDESTE initiative in Brazil were characteristic of the formation and organization of integrated rural development schemes. In these three countries and elsewhere, the programs were based on the idea that two sectors of the agricultural economy would respond to two distinct types of public policies. That is, peasant agriculture would operate within a context and according to a rationality that was fundamentally distinct from the environment and rationality of large, capital-intensive agricultural enterprises. This "new dualism" ignored the relationship between the expansion of the large-scale capitalist sector and deteriorating conditions among the rural poor. Thus, the many problems encountered by rural development planners in the 1970s were related not only to the ambitious nature of the reforms that were undertaken but also to the fact that these programs did not address the root causes of rural poverty and underproductivity.

The failure of agrarian reforms to be widely implemented and the failure of integrated rural development programs to address the issue of land distribution are part of the reason why the level of conflict and violence in rural Latin America increased in the 1970s. Heightened insecurity among the rural poor clearly exacerbated social tensions, but this did not necessarily imply a threat to the stability of political regimes or economic systems. As Chapter 9 indicates, as the state expanded its role in rural areas through efforts to modernize large-scale agriculture and to address some of the needs of the rural poor, so too did it expand its potential to control the scope and destabilizing impact of rural protest movements. Thus, broadly organized collective action on the part of peasant groups, always a difficult undertaking, became even less likely as these groups were subjected to disaggregation, diffusion, and co-optation through the timely distribution of state resources and services and increased repressive capabilities. Major conflict over land in Brazil, guerrilla warfare in Colombia, and the formation of peasant organizations in Mexico indicate a general theme of this chapter: after 1940, the state emerged as the primary target of agrarian protest, the principal mediator of rural social class relations, and the central actor in containing the effectiveness of agrarian protest. Both the reformist and the revolutionary commitments of state elites offer some potential for addressing the deepening problems of rural underdevelopment and poverty. Ultimately, however, reform or the radical restructuring of rural economic conditions will be pursued primarily on terms defined by the state itself. Therefore, only through widespread and independent organization and mobilization of rural inhabitants can the needs of the rural poor be expected to gain high priority among state elites, whatever the characteristics of the regime they serve.

CAVEATS

This book does not pretend to account for the great variety of circumstances that characterize conditions of agricultural production and rural poverty in Latin America. If one is concerned with changes in agricultural productivity, for instance, a wide variety of factors must be considered, including climate, altitude, quality of soils, availability of water, appropriateness and accessibility of technological improvements, world and domestic market conditions, crop-specific requirements, location of markets, and infrastructure development. Added to this list of physical characteristics is a panoply of human factors that affect the behavior of those engaged in agricultural production—levels of health and nutrition, ethnic and cultural norms, degrees of wealth and poverty, person-to-land ratios, levels of knowledge, inheritance patterns, and land tenure relationships. To move beyond concern with agricultural production to a consideration of the political behavior of rural inhabitants raises many other factors as well, such as organization, leadership, linkages among social and economic classes, historical experience, and the responsiveness or repressiveness of government, all of which may differ over time and from country to country. Clearly, the enormous variations, idiosyncrasies, and experiences within and between countries are important to any explanation of change and continuity. While these will be discussed to some extent in the following chapters, this book deals primarily with significant patterns of change that have occurred in Latin America as a whole.

In an effort to capture some of the importance of the specific context of development and to help sort out general patterns and national or regional variations in historical experience, the book includes case studies from Mexico, Colombia, and Brazil. These countries were selected for a variety of reasons; central to their importance, however, is the extent to which capitalist expansion occurred during the four decades considered and the extent to which conditions of underdevelopment were created or deepened by this process. The three countries varied in terms of the capacity of the state to chart the course of national development and to control political mobilization. In Mexico, a strong government represented by a party-based authoritarian regime successfully incorporated low-status groups into the political system and then actively created and promoted a wealthy commercial agricultural sector that ultimately gained considerable power to influence official policies. In Colombia, a weak government was traditionally the creature of powerful landed interests, but a regime change in the late 1950s and a number of other events helped generate a political consensus that allowed for the legislation of agrarian reform measures that potentially threatened the interests of landowners. Ultimately, however, the movement for reform was inhibited by these landed interests, even while the state gained greater control over the rural economy and the means to deal with social unrest. In Brazil, a relatively strong government that emerged with the military authoritarian regime of 1964 eventually had to bow before an even stronger private sector, which was increasingly interested in investing in agriculture and in ensuring that public policies promoted its development. These three case studies show how state elites within specific regimes have defined and pursued agricultural development, and they indicate the limits of the state's capacity to establish policies in opposition to specific class interests. Moreover, they offer a range of experience from which to assess the causes and consequences of agrarian reform—the Mexican and Colombian cases are particularly important in this regard—and rural development initiatives in general.

2 | The State and Agrarian Change

In the period between 1940 and 1980, rural areas in Latin America were transformed. Traditional haciendas with stable resident labor forces gave way to large commercial farms using modern technology and wage labor. Commercial plantations also underwent change, becoming more mechanized and more reliant on temporary rather than permanent labor. Remote communal villages and individual smallholders became tied to urban markets and a money economy; their capacity to maintain subsistence levels of income was threatened, they were disadvantaged by the development of large- and medium-scale farms, and they were squeezed by population growth. Increasingly, landlessness and insecurity became characteristic of the rural poor. These changes, beginning gradually and accelerating noticeably in the 1960s and 1970s, cannot be separated from the emergence of active and continuous state involvement in rural economies and social relations nor from evidence of the deepening of conditions of underdevelopment.

The task undertaken in this chapter is to present a framework for an interpretation of these observable characteristics of the Latin American experience. A meaningful discussion of four decades of agrarian change must recognize the strong role of the state in determining the course of agricultural development; it must account for the relationships between capitalist expansion, public policy, and conditions of rural underdevelopment; and it must acknowledge the centrality of land to rural conflict and of the state to peasant political behavior. Each of these assertions raises a number of issues that must be addressed in order to understand the causes and consequences of change in rural Latin America.

THE STATE AND THE ORIGIN OF DEVELOPMENT POLICY

Data presented in this book demonstrate clearly that the state in Latin America had a formative impact on the development of the agricultural sector be-

11

tween 1940 and 1980 and, further, that it played an increasingly important role in the management of rural social conflict during the same period. Few analysts would disagree with the general proposition that the Latin American state was and in most cases continues to be strongly interventionist and that its activism in economic affairs dates at least to the 1940s and in many cases to the 1930s. In addition, most would agree that a wide variety of regimes have been similarly motivated to organize national political life with the intent of engendering and maintaining economic growth and social control.

There is much less agreement, however, on the question of the impetus to state action. The issue of who controls the state has therefore emerged as a significant focus of discussion among those who recognize its important role in the pursuit of economic development and the maintenance of social order.[1] Who shapes the issues and determines the outcome of the policy-making process? What must be explained is complex. On the one hand, it is quite clear that in almost all countries in the region, state development policies after 1940 consistently benefited a small group—the owners of foreign and national industrial, commercial, agricultural, and financial capital. Recognition of this has often prompted the assertion that a narrow alliance of domestic and foreign capitalists dominates the state and prescribes the nature and direction of state policy. The complex and even contradictory history of development policies in Latin America requires considerable elaboration and even a questioning of this simple assertion, however. At times, states have pursued reformist policies that have impinged directly on dominant-class interests. At times they have used a variety of policy carrots and sticks to shape the activities of these same groups—regulating foreign investment, expropriating underutilized landholdings, nationalizing financial institutions, developing public-sector enterprises that compete with those of the private sector, and imposing export and import control. At other times they have pursued policies to incorporate nonelite groups into national political and economic systems, in the absence of widespread unrest, and they have frequently acted in the absence of pressure or overt influence from dominant-class interests. Moreover, the states that have undertaken these actions are large, complex, pervasive, and expanding.

In more general terms, explaining the origin of development policy is made difficult by the fact that state policies are not consistent or even easily identified. While a given policy may benefit a specific group, others may infringe directly on that group's interests; the policies adopted may have unintended consequences or create their own contradictions; the policies may be adopted but not implemented; they may have both explicit and implicit goals; they may be pursued haphazardly, ineffectively, or incoherently; and they may increase or decrease the power of various groups or of the state itself. Linking policy content and impact to a clear understanding of the relationship between those who are formally charged with making policy—state elites—and the extent to which their decisions are shaped or controlled by domestic and international interests poses difficult conceptual issues. Indeed, in the ongoing discussion of the origin and nature of state actions, two distinct conceptualizations of the state have been adopted; each has implications for the degree to which the state is considered to have an autonomous capacity to shape development policy and through it, to direct the course of national development.

In the tradition of Marxist and dependency analysis, the state is defined as an alliance for social control which reflects and reproduces class relationships in the society; it takes the form of institutions to achieve legitimation and coercion; its purpose is to maintain the dominance of a given mode of production and the specific class relationships that this implies.[2] In capitalist society, the state reproduces the conditions for capitalist accumulation, including control of subordinate classes. In one development of this conceptualization, the dominant class intervenes directly in the policy process to achieve its ends; in another, the hegemonic class sets implicit limits on state policy through a given "social formation" of domination and subordination.[3] In terms of the Latin American state, it is often argued that the state and its policies represent not the interests of a specific hegemonic class, but rather an ongoing form of compromise and coalition among dominant classes and class fractions. Fernando Cardoso explains that at the most abstract level, the state is a " 'pact of domination' that exists among social classes or fractions of dominant classes and the norms which guarantee their dominance over the subordinate strata."[4] Important in this alliance is the power of foreign capital; among dependency theorists considerable debate has emerged over the extent to which nonnational capital dominates and shapes relations among domestic social classes and the state (Amin 1976; Cardoso and Faletto 1979; Evans 1979).

According to this general conceptualization, state policy is derivative of class relationships. Power to shape issues and determine decisional outcomes is located in social relationships of domination and control and in the concrete alliances among and conflicts within hegemonic classes or class fractions. When state policy changes, or when it infringes on the interests of dominant classes, explanation is sought in shifting coalitions and power relationships within the hegemonic class or class alliance. The empirical question that can be derived from this explanation is, therefore, How does state policy ensure the central interests of the dominant alliance? or, from the same perspective, How is the state absorbed into society (Hamilton 1982, 9; Skocpol 1979, 28; Stepan 1978, Chap. 1)?

In grappling with this question, Marxist and dependency scholars have had to address the problem presented by the activist nature of the state and the weak or fragmented nature of the bourgeoisie in late industrializing countries: Is the state under certan conditions independent of the class interests that dominate it? Many scholars, from Marx and Engels to contemporary analysts, agree that this condition potentially exists when societies are undergoing transition from one mode of production to another or during social revolutions

(Marx 1963, 105–6; Trimberger 1978). Some have argued that the emergence of an entrepreneurial state is linked to the development of a "state bourgeoisie," a class fraction whose specific interests may counter those of other fractions of the bourgeoisie but whose general interests coincide (Evans 1979, 43–50; Canak 1984). Moreover, it is acknowledged that from time to time—at moments of economic crisis and social instability—the state will acquire the capacity to act relatively autonomously, even against the interests of some sectors of the hegemonic class in a society, in order to manage and ameliorate the contradictions inherent in capitalist society (Miliband 1977; Poulantzas 1973). In a limited sense, then, state autonomy is asserted when actions are necessary to maintain conditions for continued capitalist accumulation and dominance, to save capitalist society as a whole, and to reinforce the legitimacy of a state apparatus dominated by the exigencies of capitalist accumulation. Indeed, the Latin American state has played a considerable role in the mediation of social conflict through co-optation, manipulation, and coercion, and this helps account for the complexity and conflict that exist within the bureaucratic apparatus of individual countries (Foweraker 1981; Hamilton 1982). Nevertheless, this relative autonomy is strictly limited. "In general terms . . . state autonomy is limited by the position of the state within a given social formation in which a particular mode of production and class may be dominant, and by the position of that social formation within the world capitalist system (Hamilton 1982, 24).

With regard to the agricultural economy and rural social relations, it is possible from this perspective to account for examples in which the state appears in the guise of populist reformer, promoting agrarian reform or development programs directed toward the rural poor (de Janvry 1981; Gutelman 1976; Bartra 1974). Such actions are pursued to end widespread social unrest and to ensure the production of commodities essential to the capitalist economy. "In its crisis management role, however, the state runs into narrow limits that derive both from reproduction of the essential contradictions of capitalism and from the state's fiscal, legitimating, and administrative capabilities" (de Janvry 1981, 186). Reformist experiments will therefore be short-lived and limited in scope, for their aim is to ameliorate threats to the dominant class alliance, not to restructure society or its economic base.

In the interpretation of agricultural development and state policies in Latin America between 1940 and 1980, a Marxist or dependency approach to the state holds considerable explanatory power, especially as it explores the implicit and explicit limits on state autonomy resulting from dependence on support from economically dominant classes or class alliances. Nevertheless, this conceptualization is not adopted here, for it tends to shift the focus of analysis away from the complex action of the state apparatus and the often conflicting rationales for such actions (Canak 1984). Moreover, it provides unsatisfactory explanations for a number of specific problems of agricultural development.

For example, the issue of the timing of state action is problematic. The state in Latin America began to pursue policies for agricultural modernization in the 1940s and 1950s. This activity generally preceded the emergence of a class of capitalist agricultural entrepreneurs and was often initially pursued in the absence of strong urban and industrial pressure for more efficient and modern agricultural production. Nor does the influence of foreign capital seem to have been overarching; the penetration of foreign capital in agricultural production, finance, and processing did not occur extensively until the 1970s; in fact, in most countries, foreign capital flowed away from the primary sector into the industrial sector during the period in which the official policy was to modernize agricultural production. Nor had foreign capital penetrated deeply enough into the industrial sector at that time to exert extensive influence over the formation of policy. That state policy was instrumental to foreign, industrial, and agricultural capitalists is clear, but this begs the empirical question of the origin of state policy.

There are also problems in accounting for the timing of agrarian reform and rural development initiatives; these are only weakly linked to evidence of crisis. In fact, such initiatives were frequently pursued in the absence of grave threats to social peace by mobilized groups of peasants and were generally not a result of strong urban or industrial demands for greater productivity in agriculture. Instead, they were often a result of considerable political entrepreneurship by state elites who held strong beliefs about the importance of agrarian reform and rural development or who wished to expand the influence of various political or bureaucratic entities.[5] Moreover, the penetration of the agricultural economy and rural social relations by laws, decrees, regulations, programs, and state agencies was so great in the period under consideration that it is difficult to tie such continuous presence and multifarious activity to moments of crisis or the specific needs of dominant classes. Once armed with legal, organizational, and legitimate presence, state agencies seem to have taken on their own rationales and orientations, which guided their subsequent activities and helped shape their relationships with elite and nonelite social groups. Moreover, their actions were in pursuit of a variety of goals and often worked at cross-purposes. Thus, issues of bureaucratic autonomy, conflict, and control might also usefully be explored from a perspective that does not assume that state policy necessarily originates in class relationships.

A second conceptualization, derived from Weberian tradition, makes such an approach more feasible. In this case, the state is defined as an enduring executive and administrative apparatus that makes authoritative decisions and exercises control over a given territorial entity.[6] In a number of recent discussions of the state and its autonomy, this is the perspective adopted. Thus, for Skocpol (1978, 28), the state is "no mere arena in which socioeconomic struggles are fought out. It is, rather, a set of administrative, policing, and military organizations headed, and more or less well coordinated by, an executive authority." Stepan (1978, xii) argues that the state is "the continuous administrative, legal, bureaucratic and coercive systems that attempt not only to structure relations between civil society and public authority in a polity but also to structure many coercive relationships within civil society as well."[7] Because this definition does not assume any a priori linkage of power between the state and social groups, those who adopt it do not agree on the origin of state policy or on the question of the extent of state autonomy. Thus, the pluralist, corporatist, bureaucratic politics, and state interest perspectives differ in responding to the question of who controls the state.

For those who follow a pluralist approach to political analysis, state policy is the result of conflicting group pressures and the competition for power they engender. Like the Marxist and dependency perspectives, then, the pluralist view is that state policy is derivative. The state itself merely provides a more or less neutral institutional and procedural framework in which conflicting groups form coalitions and do battle over policy output. For pluralists, the autonomy of the state is very low, perhaps even lower than that assumed by many Marxists, for even social and economic crises are only occasions for new or different coalitions of interests in society to attempt to shape state policy. Adherents of the pluralist perspective on Latin American politics generally adopt Charles Anderson's influential model of "power contenders," in which groups with differing "power resources" compete for entrance into the political system in order to be taken into account by the ruling coalition or to form part of it.[8] State policy is determined by the political compromises that are made by the power contenders who make up the ruling coalition. The state as an executive and administrative apparatus reflects these political bargains. As with the Marxist perspective, the problems of timing, leadership, development ideology, and state expansion are poorly accounted for by the pluralist viewpoint.

For those who have argued for a corporatist perspective, the state, through its legitimate claim to control the representation of interests, has considerable autonomy to structure and influence economic and social relationships (Stepan 1978, chap. 1 and 2). According to this perspective, power to shape issues and determine decisional outcomes is shared by the state and the organized groups that represent functional interests within the state. But, given the capacity to mobilize interests and intervene actively through coercion, legitimating organizations, co-optation, or accommodation, the state is considered to have a high degree of ongoing autonomy from domination by any given class, interest, or hegemonic group. In theory, at least, the state, particularly the political executive, has the right to grant legitimacy to various functional groups and to determine the legitimate scope of their demands, especially when these conflict with the rights or demands of other groups. The state may even parcel out its authority over specific policy areas to certain organized interests. The groups then become incorporated into the definition of the state.

In this case, the issues that are not fully addressed relate to the limits on state autonomy and the existence of conflict and division within the state itself.

For those who adopt a bureaucratic politics approach, state policy is the outcome of competing and conflicting activities among the bureaucratic entities of the state itself. In this case, linkages to society are left unaccounted for or are considered to be part of bureaucratic games in which public agencies acquire support groups to press organizational or suborganizational interests on formal decision makers. Thus, as Allison (1971, 162) explains,

> The decisions and actions of governments are intranational political resultants: *resultants* in the sense that what happens is not chosen as a solution to a problem but rather results from compromise, conflict, and confusion of officials with diverse interests and unequal influence; *political* in the sense that the activity from which decisions and actions emerge is best characterized as bargaining along regularized channels among individual members of the government.

The autonomy of the state is potentially very great, limited only by the diverse interests of the bureaucratic "players" themselves and by the influence of the regularized channels of interaction that are set by institutional frameworks. Once again, while this perspective is useful for exploring the conflict and division within the bureaucratic apparatus and the contradictions and anomalies of policy making and implementation, it is clearly unsatisfactory in accounting for the influence of foreign and national economic interests on the policy process.

A fourth approach also focuses on the role of state elites in the formulation and implementation of public policies. This perspective differs from the bureaucratic politics framework, however, in that it attempts to account more fully for the linkages between state and society in terms of the variable autonomy of the state. It accepts the possibility that the state, as an executive and administrative apparatus for decision making and control, has identifiable and concrete concerns about the definition and pursuit of "national development." These concerns are independent of, but not necessarily opposed to or different from, the immediate interests or welfare of any particular group, class, class fraction, coalition, or alliance in society.[9] This perspective is adopted in the following chapters because it provides a framework for focusing on the development belief systems (development ideologies) of policy makers and planners, on the formulation and implementation of specific decisions, and on the skills and influence of particular political leaders. Insights into these issues allow us to analyze the extent to which "the technocrats and public managers form an 'independent state' . . . and allocate resources in a way that expands their own power and wealth."[10] Such a framework also provides an alternative to understanding the state as little more than an arena for class, interest, or bureaucratic conflict. In addition, it encourages an analysis of the impact of what is perhaps the most important political phenomenon in Latin American countries in recent decades—the enormous expansion of the state apparatus itself.

According to this perspective, the state is not assumed to be either autonomous or monolithic. However, the relative autonomy of the state is assumed to be a desirable condition sought after by state elites insofar as it presents them with greater flexibility to pursue policies that will engender economic growth and social stability and thus help legitimize and prolong the life of the regime they serve.[11] Thus, one of the tasks of successful political leaders and policy makers is to create and take advantage of opportunities to expand the role of the state in shaping economic and social conditions in a society. To do this, they expound theories of development, attempt to put together supportive coalitions, legislate reforms, and create new bureaucratic entities. In attempting to achieve their goals, state elites use resources—law, legitimizing formulas, budget allocations, coercive organizations, information, and captive support groups—that increase their potential to influence policy outcomes. Their potential autonomy is clearly bounded by the characteristics of social groups that support or oppose the state, by the international context of state action, and by the historical development and efficacy of the state and regime in question. Moreover, the state interacts with society in a specific historical context in which previous policy, experience, ideology, and expectations must be considered. Thus, relative degrees of autonomy vary over time and across policy arenas, and state elites are always constrained to some degree by political and economic realities. Various regimes—characteristic formal and informal arrangements among political and economic elites that allocate power and establish the rules of competition for access to power—present generalized patterns of linkages between decision-making structures, state elites, and societal interests that have the capacity to influence the content of decisions.

At any given moment or for any given policy area, development policies may coincide with the interests of dominant groups in society. This may be a result of a weak state that is in fact dominated by societal interests, it may be the result of the conviction on the part of state elites that these policies are in fact the best (or most feasible) means of achieving national development, or it may be a result of interactions of bargaining, conflict, and compromise between state elites and social classes. The point, however, is that it is difficult to infer domination of the state from the content or impact of the policy itself. In the agricultural sector in particular, policies to promote agrarian capitalism, agrarian reform, and rural development in Latin American countries did not consistently result from clear domination of the state by specific interests, but were influenced by the development ideologies adopted by state elites, by the leadership ("political entrepreneurship") of specific individuals, and by the political accommodations and bargains that were struck between state elites and various social groupings. In particular, the concept of development ideologies provides some insight into how state elites have defined the task of national development and why particular policies have been chosen and pursued.

DEVELOPMENT IDEOLOGIES AND
THE CAUSES OF UNDERDEVELOPMENT

The motivations for state intervention in agricultural and rural economies are always complex, but of critical importance are the development models that were adopted by state elites in Latin America between 1940 and 1980. These models, or development ideologies, offered policy makers comprehensive and logical explanations for national underdevelopment and provided insight into the region's relationship to the international market economy and to more industrially developed countries. Development ideologies not only explained the causes of the economic problems suffered by the region or nation; they also proposed specific policy solutions to these conditions, thereby providing a concrete guide to state actions to change existing realities. Policy makers therefore had definite perceptions of how economic growth was to be achieved and they attempted to ensure that state policies actually conformed to their interpretations of cause-and-effect relationships in economic growth.

After 1940, import substitution and export promotion became the dominant ideologies for economic development within policy-making circles (see Chapter 4). Central to both was the imperative to industrialize the Latin American economies as rapidly as possible. These models for rapid industrialization stressed the importance of the modernization of the agricultural sector, a term widely accepted by state elites to refer to ideal characteristics of capitalist development. For them, modern agriculture implied a farming sector that adopted technological improvements in order to increase production and productivity; that was highly mechanized; that utilized an independent and mobile labor force; that responded to domestic and international market demand in a prompt and sophisticated fashion; that invested in capital improvements; and that sought to use land, labor, and capital efficiently to enhance the profitability of operations. Ideally, then, agriculture in Latin America would develop so that it closely resembled capitalist agriculture in the United States and the industrialized countries of Western Europe. However, policy makers believed that in contrast to the already modernized countries of Europe and North America, Latin America's international and historical context required that the state assume the role of the basic promoter of agricultural modernization.

While there was general agreement among state elites on the need to modernize agriculture through capitalist expansion, two different perspectives emerged on how this was to be accomplished. One school advocated strong incentives for investment and entrepreneurial behavior, the other argued for agrarian reform to break the hold of feudal institutions on economic behavior.[12] Both were influential in generating policies for the agricultural sector. The first perspective was most influential in the 1940s and 1950s and reemerged in the 1970s. The second was adopted as the economic rationale for agrarian reform efforts in the 1960s.

Clearly, the adoption of these perspectives on agricultural modernization was not isolated from the economic and political milieux in which they were put forth, nor were state elites either objective or isolated in the interpretations they adopted. The neoclassical and structuralist arguments were firmly rooted in the tradition of capitalist accumulation and were heavily influenced by development patterns and ideologies derived from advanced capitalist countries. Nevertheless, it is important to acknowledge that the models themselves played a key role in shaping the content of the policies actually pursued and in the particular form of capitalist expansion that emerged in the period in question, as will be explored in depth in Chapters 4, 7, and 8. From the perspective of a critique of agricultural and rural development, it is also important to acknowledge that modernization policies did not resolve problems of underdevelopment but instead contributed directly to their deepening.

Dependency theorists and Marxist scholars more generally have described the deepening problems of underdevelopment as a direct result of capitalist development in the periphery.[13] While they disagree about the nature of preexisting modes of production—were they predominantly capitalist or predominantly feudal?—all agree that the impact of capitalist expansion distorted national and rural development.[14] Initially they argued that incorporation of peripheral economies into the world capitalist system necessarily implied stagnation, boom and bust cycles, and the "functionality" of traditional relations of production in the periphery to capitalist development in the center.[15] In more recent discussions, however, they have allowed for the possibility of "associated dependent development," in which significant capitalist development can occur in both the industrial and the agricultural sector in the periphery , but at the cost of even greater dependence on the highly industrialized capitalist centers (Cardoso 1973; Amin 1976; Evans 1979). Thus, capitalist expansion in the countryside translates into transformation of the traditional haciendas and latifundios into capitalist enterprises utilizing extensive technological innovation and wage labor. As sharecroppers and tenants are thrown off the land to make way for its more efficient use, the rural poor are gradually proletarianized or semiproletarianized.[16] This perspective also points to the increasing penetration of transnational agribusiness in Latin America, which has led to the introduction of highly capital-intensive technology, stronger links to "controlled" international markets, the development of an often inappropriate food-processing industry in the peripheral countries, and an expansion of export production that has resulted in diminished production of domestic foodstuffs.

My analysis of the causes of underdevelopment focuses more specifically on the content and impact of development policies and on the tensions they create within the state and between the state and private-sector interests. Conditions of underdevelopment deepened because policies to encourage agricultural modernization were introduced into a rural context characterized by a highly skewed distribution of basic agricultural resources. This maldistribution of resources determined the relationship of social groups to the market economy and their ability to respond to the incentives provided by the state. At the outset of the period under consideration, large landowners not only owned most of the land in Latin America, they also owned land with the best soils, the most favorable climate, the greatest access to water, and the closest proximity to markets, transportation, and storage facilities. As policies were implemented and capitalist agriculture responded, the quality of land and infrastructure became even more important in advancing or constraining the fortunes of producers. Moreover, the expansion of modern agriculture, tied as it was to the international market economy and based on capital-intensive and land-extensive farming practices, created serious impediments to economic development. State policy was therefore centrally important in bringing about higher levels of inequality in rural areas and in encouraging conditions of underdevelopment. In turn, state elites fashioned new policies in an attempt to deal with these conditions. Of central importance in the development of such policies were the issues of rural poverty and the relationship of the state to the rural masses.

PEASANTS, RURAL CONFLICT, AND THE STATE

Peasants were clearly victims of the changes that occurred in rural Latin America between 1940 and 1980. There is considerable consensus in both theoretical and empirical work about the economic and social conditions confronted by a large proportion of peasant families during this period.[17]

1. The incorporation of peasant households into market relationships for acquiring urban industrial goods and selling agricultural commodities occurred on disadvantageous terms, often resulting in increased levels of debt, retreat into subsistence agriculture, continued utilization of primitive technologies, and the need to multiply sources of income.
2. Traditional forms of tenure relationships—renting, sharecropping, and labor service—diminished rapidly as land values increased and commercial farming became more capital intensive and as agrarian reforms encouraged the decline of these relationships.

3. Simultaneously, many peasant households faced greater constraints on their ability to maintain direct control over the land as a result of land concentration by large-scale farmers and land fragmentation due to population pressures and inheritance patterns.
4. Many households turned increasingly to wage labor as their hold on the land became more tenuous or as it was removed entirely; this wage labor tended to be overwhelmingly seasonal, migratory, temporary, and insecure.

Thus, the peasant population was increasingly composed of landless and insecure workers and those relying on agricultural production for only a share of their family's livelihood. In many studies of the rural sector, peasants have been described as increasingly proletarianized and semiproletarianized.[18] However, on the subjects of the destiny of the smallholding peasantry and the nature of rural conflict, there is less consensus among observers of the process of rural change. Some have argued that an increasingly marginalized peasantry is bound to disappear, forced off the land and absorbed into a rural or urban labor force, their numbers and insecurity serving to keep wages extremely low.[19] According to this perspective, tensions within the agrarian structure are the result of archaic and precapitalist modes of production among smallholders, tenants, or sharecroppers. The process of change, although painful, will result in a fully commercialized agricultural sector of large and medium landholdings worked by a rural proletariat whose size and availability promotes low wages. Those not accommodated by this change will be absorbed into the urban sector as an industrial proletariat. Moreover, rural conflict and class alliances will center increasingly on issues of organization, wages, and conditions of employment—not land—and alliances with urban wage laborers will become more frequent, given the commonality of interests and relationships to capitalist modes of production.[20]

Other analysts, however, have been impressed by the versatility, vitality, and persistence of peasant subsistence production, even in the face of deteriorating conditions. Their research often highlights the peasant household that maintains a tenacious hold on a plot of land, however small or poorly endowed, for subsistence production based on family labor, while members of the household also seek wage employment in agriculture or in urban and international settings.[21] In contrast to the "proletarianization" perspective, then, is the view that peasants are being slowly but never completely separated from control over the land, a process that is described as "depeasantization."[22] It has been asserted that the small-farm sector, though clearly disadvantaged in terms of its economic position, is an important underpinning to the expansion of capitalist and export-oriented agriculture.[23] Its persistence as a producer of basic food commodities for the domestic market and as a source of extremely low wage labor is essential in allowing the large and medium producers to respond to international rather than domestic demand. In this context, the semiproletariat actually underwrites capitalist expansion as peasant labor becomes available at prices below subsistence.[24] Subsistence production and rural poverty in general therefore become functional subsidies for the expansion of the capitalist sector, and rural conflict centers not only on issues of wages and organization (because of the growth of a large landless wage-earning component of the rural poor) but also on the issue of control over land and competition over access to public services.[25] Moreover, as the peasants' hold over land and means of subsistence becomes more insecure, rural protest activities tend to become more frequent.

Evidence presented in the following chapters tends to support the second perspective. However, it is suggested that what may be functional for the capitalist sector of the economy may come to be viewed as dysfunctional by state elites concerned about the process of national development. First, it will become clear that land remains a central focus of agrarian protest and demand making and that maintaining or gaining access to land is not clearly linked to objectively identifiable sources of income among the rural population. The land is a central component in increasingly complex income-generating strategies that involve entire households.[26] It is maintained through sacrifices that far exceed the market value of the land itself and is sought after for reasons that go far beyond its ability to sustain an adequate living for the family.

Thus, the terms *proletarianization* and *semiproletarianization* can be misleading if it is assumed (as it frequently is) that political and economic protest is primarily shaped by efforts to improve or sustain returns from the principal source of livelihood (Paige 1975). Many rural households in Latin America in the late 1970s received as little as 20 percent of their income from their own land, even taking into account the nonmarketed portion used for family subsistence; it frequently was less than 50 percent of total income, while wage labor, artisanry, and petty capitalism supplied the rest. Nevertheless, even for these semiproletarians, the value of the land itself is central as a minimal condition of survival for the household; it is a source of subsistence the household can retreat to when all other sources fail, even if in normal times it provides only a fraction of total family income.[27] Even the meaning of a large rural proletariat can be obscured by the importance of the household (not the individual or the community) as the basis of rural livelihood and of the land as a central component of this. For example, landless sons often contribute to maintaining the family and its plot of land through their wage labor; their behavior may be a response more to the total household condition than to their specific status as wage earners.

There is also evidence of heightened levels of rural conflict in the period under consideration. However, it is clear that the direction and scope of that conflict were fundamentally affected by the arsenal of responses available to the state. In this period, agrarian reform efforts bequeathed extensive legal power to the state to intervene in conflicts over the ownership of rural land. Through the various agrarian reform and support agencies that were created, the state gained considerable administrative capacity to deal with social unrest. This legislation and institutional framework were rarely used to change the structure of landholding in the countryside radically, but they did provide the state with the ability to respond to specific instances of rural protest with piecemeal land expropriations and entitlements to land. Similarly, minimum wage, social security, and other labor legislation provided the legal, procedural, and institutional rationale for intervening in disputes over wages and working conditions. Access to credit, infrastructure projects, education and health benefits, extension services, and technical inputs all placed resources in the hands of the state to co-opt rural dissidents and to manage the course of rural protest. Frequently, these same resources allowed the state to control the economic activities of the rural poor by creating dependence on credit, withholding legal title to the land, and other measures. State actions also stimulated the mobilization of peasants into organizations that were then carefully controlled and continuously co-opted. The state in Latin America therefore emerged as a "patron" of the rural poor in a way that allowed it to continue to encourage capitalist expansion on large landholdings. At the same time, the state attempted to use rural development policies to alleviate some of the economic and social problems created by the development of the large farm sector.

Through its expanded rural presence, the state also became a more efficient repressive force when rural protest could not be diffused or co-opted by other means. Military, police, and paramilitary organizations were professionalized after 1940 and were infused with the doctrines and techniques of counterinsurgency, especially in the period after the Cuban Revolution of 1959. While co-optation and piecemeal response to heightened demand-making and agrarian protest were increasingly in evidence, so also were the repressive forces of the state. Thus, in predicting the incidence and direction of rural protest activities, the continued centrality of land and the willingness or capacity of the state to intervene, mediate, or control conflict must be considered. We will return to this topic in subsequent chapters. However, before detailing the dynamics of agricultural development and agrarian conflict in post-1940 Latin America, it is important to place the agricultural and rural changes that occurred in the region within the context of their historical legacy, a legacy that encouraged the highly concentrated distribution of basic agricultural resources.

3 | Legacies of the Past

The changes that occurred in rural sectors of Latin American countries after 1940 were built upon a foundation of four centuries of agrarian history. Central to this experience was the formative impact of market forces on landholding patterns and the structure of rural social relationships. While rural areas have often been characterized as the static bulwark of a backward and traditional society, the historical record indicates recurrent modifications of agricultural practices and labor relationships in response to international and domestic economic conditions. It is noteworthy, however, that as far back as the early sixteenth century, booms and declines in world and local demand for primary commodities, changes in the availability of labor and capital, and technological improvements affected the highly skewed nature of the distribution of land and power in rural areas only by reinforcing it.

How this maldistribution of resources was created and subsequently maintained offers important clues to understanding the process of rural change in Latin America after 1940. The periods of conquest and colonial domination created patterns of commercial and subsistence agriculture based on large landholdings and an exploited and powerless peasantry. A period of capitalist expansion in the late nineteenth and early twentieth centuries left these characteristics even more firmly implanted as the region was deeply incorporated into the world market as a producer of primary commodities. By the 1940s, however, agriculture had come to be seen by Latin American state elites as a source of difficulty for the economic development of the region.

THE COLONIAL ERA: CREATING THE PATTERN

The huge agricultural estates that developed during the sixteenth and seventeenth centuries were not a goal of Spanish colonial policy. Instead, political domination and the extraction of wealth were primary motives behind the colonial venture. In the areas where the conquerors encountered populous Indian cultures that were capable of producing a surplus to support hierarchical and urban societies—in Mexico, Central America, and the highlands of the Andes in South America—imperial objectives were initially pursued successfully through the institution of the *encomienda*. In this initial phase of conquest and domination, private landholdings were of minimal importance.

The encomienda was not a land grant, but a unit of territory and Indian settlement to be administered by a Spaniard, usually as a reward for services to the crown.[1] The *encomendero* had the right to extract tribute from the Indian population in the form of goods and labor services, generally as traditional chiefs and priests had done within the Indian societies prior to the arrival of the Spanish.[2] The colonial power claimed ownership of the land; the Indian population and its wealth were "entrusted" to the colonizer through a system of indirect domination. Importantly, the encomienda was devised not to generate more wealth but only to extract and "redistribute" that which already existed (Keith 1976, 130). Initially, the encomienda system served the Spanish well: it allowed them to extend their control over vast populated areas without fundamentally altering the productive practices of the native societies; it enabled them to extract minerals—primarily gold—to enrich both crown and settlers; it provided the early colonists with food and servants; and it allowed the government to reward the efforts of the conquerors and to grow rich at the same time. By the middle of the sixteenth century, however, two circumstances weakened the economic viability of the encomienda in many regions. First, the initially vast reserves of gold were depleted and the amount of wealth to "redistribute" diminished. Second, wars, deprivation, savage exploitation at the hands of the Spaniards, and the introduction of European diseases caused a massive depopulation of the native Indian societies. Although estimates vary, it is likely that the native population of the highlands of Mexico and the Andes was reduced from an estimated thirty million to approximately two and a half million within a century of the conquest.[3] Elsewhere—in the Caribbean, for instance—the native populations were virtually annihilated. Without a large captive labor force and without a surplus of wealth to extract, the encomienda could not ensure the continued well-being of the colonizers; in the consequent search for income and security, large private landholdings became a principal means of satisfying colonial needs.

In the region's mineral-rich centers, where the encomienda system had emerged most fully, the development of mining offered a solution to the economic crisis of the empire in the late sixteenth century. Silver mining, begun in Mexico in the 1530s and in Peru in the 1540s, created a domestic demand for agricultural products and stimulated a more dynamic economy.[4] As a consequence, in Peru and Mexico in particular, encomenderos and other wealthy Spaniards sought, through a variety of legal grants and purchases from the crown and its administrative units in the New World, to acquire title to large tracts of land in the latter part of the sixteenth century and throughout the seventeenth century.[5] The haciendas that emerged in this period were generally owned by members of the Spanish elite, who typically lived in urban areas. Ecclesiastical corporations also acquired large tracts of land during this period. They utilized a labor force formally tied to the landowners through the legal requirements of the *repartimiento*—a system of forced labor—or informally bound to the land through paternalistic relations, debt peonage, and lack of alternatives for ensuring the subsistence of the family or community.

Through debt peonage and landownership concentrated in a few hands, many peasants were settled on large estates and forced to offer labor services—generally a certain number of days a week—in exchange for access to a small plot of land for subsistence cropping, some food rations, and an occasional "beneficence" from the landlord. Debt bondage, often transmitted across generations, was induced through estate stores, which sold basic necessities and other commodities in exchange for the scrip issued to peasant workers; this scrip could be redeemed only through the estate. Loans to meet family emergencies or community obligations, and charges for the use of animals or implements, were other means used by landlords to tie a work force to their estates. Similar mechanisms were employed to subordinate and indebt the smallholders and Indian communities whose land abutted that of the large estates. The landlord was thus able to encroach upon these lands and to further increase his power. Debt bondage also frequently characterized the experience of migrant laborers in later periods, especially those from highland areas who were recruited by labor contractors to work lowland plantations or haciendas. Such relationships of dominance and exploitation were strengthened by the capacity of the large landowners to control legal and police authorities at the local and regional level and to prevent the incursion of laws, policies, or officials seeking to alter their control over productive resources.

Frequently, paternalistic patron-client relationships between landlord and peasant developed to soften the appearance, if not the reality, of exploitation. Not incidentally, they were also fundamental in tying a stable and dependable —if underproductive—labor force to the land and were maintained at some cost to the *hacendado* because of the general scarcity of labor.[6] Depending on the geographic and economic characteristics of the region, as well as on the availability of an indigenous labor force, smaller farms and some subsistence plots also developed, often on the peripheries of the large estates or in close proximity to urban markets. In some cases also, where farming was particularly profitable and labor especially scarce, wage labor and forms of sharecropping and renting appeared that often allowed workers some power to negotiate conditions and rates of pay. In frontier areas, smallholders and squatters were able to establish considerable control over productive resources and thereby to ensure their subsistence. In addition, particularly in high and relatively inaccessible regions, Indian communities protected by colonial legislation retained control of communal lands and managed to eke out a marginal subsistence in relative isolation from the Spanish.

The desire to acquire land that led to the emergence of the hacienda system of large landholdings and exploitive labor relations was based primarily on the need of the Spaniards to provide an income for themselves; it was not primarily the result of a desire to ensure social status or to achieve an aristocratic life style, as is often claimed.[7] Land promised economic security because the mines stimulated a limited but important domestic market in corn, wheat, beans, livestock, hides, and other commodities; production was organized around the mining areas themselves and around the emerging urban centers that wealth from silver made possible. In addition, some of the new hacienda owners, favorably situated relative to ports and transportation, were able to exploit emerging European markets for dyewood, cacao, sugar, and even some silk.[8] In Chile, favorable conditions stimulated the export of goods to other parts of the empire. In general, however, the majority of the haciendas, exploiting Indian labor through various systems of coercion, paternalism, and debt peonage, remained creatures of the regional markets of the internal economy. Within this domestic market, a declining population, a limited money economy, and geographic realities were disincentives to agricultural development in terms of increased production or more efficient use of land, labor, or capital. The profits to be derived from hacienda production therefore tended to be low, which in turn tended to limit the purchase or acquisition of land to a small group of wealthy Spaniards who were interested in maintaining a steady income and a secure social status rather than in dramatically increasing their wealth through agriculture (Keith 1977, 9–20; MacLeod 1973).

While the hacienda, tied as it generally was to mining and domestic markets, developed as a response to the economic opportunities presented by regional markets, the plantation economies of Brazil and the Caribbean developed close ties with the European export markets. Where the native population was less dense, less urban, less wealthy, and less well organized than that in the central regions of Spanish conquest, adaptations of the encomienda quickly proved ineffective in ensuring either territorial domination or the provision of wealth to the colonial power. In these areas—primarily in the Caribbean and in the Portuguese colony of Brazil—commercially oriented plantations were rapidly established to provide agricultural products for a European market. In this development, the Portuguese crown was much more active than the Spaniards in stimulating production and investment, especially in sugar, and in ensuring an available labor supply through the African slave trade.[9] Importantly, technical developments achieved in milling in the Portuguese Atlantic islands prior to the Brazilian colonial venture proved critical to the economic viability of sugar production in the colony. By the early seventeenth century, a thriving export economy and a technically advanced plantation system had developed in northeast Brazil. The sugar plantations also stimulated large cattle-breeding enterprises and some agricultural production to supply the needs of the sugar estates, and smallholding peasants engaged in both commercial and subsistence farming settled on the peripheries of the plantations.[10]

It has frequently been observed that the haciendas of the Spanish empire and the plantations that developed in the Portuguese, British, French, Dutch, and some Spanish colonies differed greatly among themselves; in reality, the distinction between the two types of latifundio and the regions where they developed was often blurred.[11] Nevertheless, as prototypes of systems for the exploitation of land and labor, they differed in their response to markets, their use of technology, capital, and labor, and the income they generated for their owners (Wolf and Mintz 1957). The plantations were established to serve a European market and tended to utilize greater inputs of capital, technology, and labor than did the haciendas, which were characterized by lower profits, more absentee ownership, and lower levels of complexity and efficiency (see Table 3.1). It is clear, however, that both the haciendas and the plantations developed in response to opportunities for commercial agriculture. Equally, their development was constrained by the limitations of the markets available to them. This was apparent in the defensive pattern of the hacienda's development and in the "boom and bust" history of the export-oriented plantations.

The haciendas that developed in the central Spanish empire were successful economic enterprises only when they were close to their markets and when the regional economy was thriving. It is no accident that haciendas close to the mining or urban administrative and commercial areas tended to be limited in size and that hacendados tended to be entrepreneurial in outlook—land values were higher, profits greater, and competition for land more intense. On the other hand, landholdings in the most remote areas were among the largest, most backward, and most subsistence-oriented, if they were not simply abandoned to the remnants of the indigenous communities.[12] Similarly, where water or irrigation was available, smaller haciendas known as *fundos* or *chacras* developed and were relatively productive, while in distant arid zones, huge landholdings, dedicated to primitive livestocking, developed (Keith 1976, 134; Burns 1977, 36).

In general, however, after the population decline of the sixteenth century, the haciendas developed in an environment in which land was plentiful and the supply of available labor and capital was scarce. Markets were limited and unstable; economic recessions, such as that brought about by a decline in mining output at the end of the sixteenth century, led to reduced markets and profits for the haciendas that had supplied the mines. The response of the hacendados to this situation was to increase their landholdings as much as possible—in many areas the seventeenth century was marked by this movement—to limit alternative sources of employment to the Indian population, and to tie the peasantry to the estate through debt peonage or various tenancy arrangements.[13] In this way, the hacendados attempted to lower the

Table 3.1. Land, Labor, Capital, and Markets: Haciendas and Plantations

	Haciendas	Plantations
Markets	Relatively small and unreliable, regional, with inelasticity of demand; attempt to limit production to keep prices high.	Relatively large and reliable, European, with elasticity of demand; attempt to increase production to maximize profits.
Profits	Relatively low; highly concentrated in small group.	Relatively high; highly concentrated in small group.
Capital and Technology	Little access to capital, especially foreign. Operating capital often from Church. Technology simple, often same as that of peasant cultivators.	Availability of foreign capital for equipment and labor. Direct foreign investment late in nineteenth century. Relatively advanced technology, with expensive machinery for processing.
Land	Size determined by passive acceptance of indigenous groups. Attempt to monopolize land to limit alternative sources of income to labor force; much unused land. Relatively cheap. Unclear boundaries.	Size determined by availability of labor. Relatively valuable with carefully fixed boundaries.
Labor	Large labor force required seasonally; generally indigenous; informally bound by debt, provision of subsistence plot, social ties, payment in provisions.	Large labor force required seasonally; generally imported; slavery common; also wage labor.
Organization	Limited need for supervision; generally hired administrators/managers, absentee landlord.	Need for continual supervision and managerial skill. Generally resident owner/manager.

SOURCES: Keith 1977, 12–20; Mintz and Wolf 1957.

price of labor and to utilize additional labor rather than inputs of capital to ensure a steady income. Primarily producers of grain and livestock, the majority of the hacendados actually claimed far more land than they cultivated. Their well-known greed for land must therefore be understood in terms of their desire to ensure a minimally stable income in a context of declining population and limited demand (Duncan and Rutledge 1977; Keith 1977; Brading

1977). Thus, they often acquired land in order to limit production of commodities where prices might decline as a result of increased output, and to limit competition from other haciendas or from the Indian communities. Most centrally, monopoly over land made available a surplus labor force that served to subsidize low levels of production in a context of generally low prices for agricultural commodities.

In some areas, the lack of an available labor force limited the extent of the hacienda system. In Bolivia, for instance, the hacienda extended only as far as the indigenous population. "This meant the bleak altiplano . . . and adjacent valleys where the Indian population had been concentrated since pre-Inca days. . . . Large regions of the country never felt even the minimal organization of the hacienda system."[14] In Costa Rica, scarcity of labor and the poverty of the Spanish colonizers also severely limited the development of the hacienda (Seligson 1980, 7–9). Throughout Latin America, indigenous communities managed to survive by withdrawing to increasingly remote and inaccessible areas. In some places, the economic returns from hacienda production were so poor that peasants were able to establish some independence and claim the land belonging to absentee hacendados (Edelman 1982). Elsewhere, the scarcity of labor gave peasants the capacity to bargain for better conditions. Nevertheless, by the eighteenth century, when the indigenous population had begun to stabilize demographically, the monopoly of land achieved by the hacendados in most of Latin America was impressive. With this advantage, the landowners were able to increase their demands for rent and labor on the sharecroppers, tenants, and workers who had been settled on—and often bound to—the estates in earlier periods.[15]

In spite of such efforts to monopolize land and ensure a cheap labor force, many hacendados were not able to achieve a satisfactory income from their holdings. Technological backwardness, geographic isolation, the low productivity of an informally captive labor force or an inability to retain sufficient labor, and lack of markets often meant that the primary motivation of the hacienda became self-sufficiency. In times of depression, landowners attempted to extract a profit by charging rents for access to land rather than by producing a marketable surplus. Whenever possible, the hacendados attempted to extract enough profit from their holdings to maintain an aristocratic urban existence, but frequently they turned to commerce or mining for a more assured income. Where neither was possible, as in parts of Central America, the hacendados, far from achieving wealth and distinction to support their urban life, "retired to a rather squalid self-sufficiency on their chacras and bohíos, supported by a few mules and a handful of peons" (MacLeod 1973, 291).

The hacienda system of the colonial period was complex and varied and the operation and motivation of the productive enterprises clearly differed by locality, type of crops produced, and owners. There were certainly haciendas and ranches that produced competitively for fairly remunerative markets; the majority of landholdings, however, approximated the stereotype of a backward, often marginal, and repressive system that made scant contribution to the economic advancement of the colonies or that of the colonial power.[16] It is important to stress that this backwardness was more a response to the limited opportunities available for profitable enterprise than it was a reflection of an aristocratic cultural pattern imported from Spain or a reluctance on the part of the hacendado to soil his hands with labor.[17] The pattern followed by the majority of the haciendas was in fact a defensive response to limited and unstable markets. In this way, the hacienda system is somewhat similar to the peasant economy in which smallholders engage selectively in commercial or subsistence production, depending on the prices and risks involved. Thus, the slogan "maximization of security and minimization of risk" that has been attributed to peasant productive rationality may also apply to many of the haciendas of the Spanish colonial period.

In contrast, the potential profitability of the export-oriented plantations was much greater and their capitalist characteristics were much more in evidence, although the use of slave labor was generalized. Of course, the high gains they promised were matched by high levels of risk in a competitive export system. Consequently, the history of agricultural development in Brazil and the Caribbean, and later in Central America and other parts of Latin America, is a saga of boom and bust as one primary product succeeded another in the drive to serve the European markets.

Brazil offers graphic evidence of the dependence of plantations on international market conditions. The thriving sugar economy of the sixteenth and first half of the seventeenth centuries was a result of European demand, Portuguese technology, Dutch and Flemish entrepreneurship, favorable soil and climate, and the massive importation of slave labor. These advantages were destroyed in the mid seventeenth century, however, when Dutch entrepreneurs, who had financed much of the sugar expansion in northeast Brazil, turned to the Caribbean—applying the expertise they had developed in observing the Portuguese colony—and stimulated sugar production that was more efficient and geographically closer to Europe (Stein and Stein, 1970, 39; Furtado 1963, pt. 1). Prices fell dramatically and both the Brazilian plantations and the cattle enterprises they had spawned declined accordingly throughout the latter part of the seventeenth and most of the eighteenth century. As in the case of the haciendas, economic decline stimulated a retreat into subsistence. "In this way, the Brazilian Northeast became converted from a highly productive economic system into an economy in which the major part of the population produced only what was necessary for its bare existence" (Furtado 1963, 70).

Often, areas engaged in export production experienced a succession of booms and busts. In the early colonial period, for instance, a developing European taste for cocoa led to the emergence of a cacao-based export economy in Guatemala. In the seventeenth century, however, cacao production was diverted by crown fiat to Venezuela and Ecuador, and Guatemala's agricultural economy reverted to subsistence farming. In the later seventeenth and the eighteenth century, a burgeoning textile industry in Europe stimulated the export of indigo; the development of alternative dyes led to a decline of this export and to economic stagnation until a boom in the export of cochineal occurred in the early and mid nineteenth century. Inexorably, demand for this export fell, but by 1860 the settlement of California had stimulated a boom in sugar production, and the U.S. Civil War a boom in cotton, both of which were followed by declines in demand and by economic contraction. The later nineteenth century saw the development of European and U.S. demand for coffee, and this crop—along with its international price—came to dominate the economy. In each case, the international market largely determined not only the conditions and type of agricultural products, but also the state of the domestic economy (Jonas 1974; Woodward 1976). Thus, wherever plantation economies developed, regions became extensively dependent upon conditions external to the region itself, conditions over which they had no control. The profitability of the plantation enterprise during boom periods tended to encourage monoculture and to deepen even further the impact of periods of bust on the domestic economy.

During the emergence of the hacienda and plantation systems, the colonial state both facilitated and constrained the pattern of economic development. From a legal perspective, the colonial powers enabled private individuals to buy or be granted large holdings and facilitated the appropriation of lands inhabited by indigenous groups. Less successfully, they attempted to regulate the treatment of the Indian population—generally brutal and at times genocidal—and to limit the emergence of a powerful landed elite that could challenge royal authority. Both the Spanish and Portuguese crowns were energetic in inhibiting the production of crops or livestock that competed with items produced by the home economies.[18] In addition, the Spanish, entranced by the allure of the easy wealth of the mines or desirous of extracting as much wealth as quickly as possible from the colonies, established extensive regulations and imposed taxes on alternative economic enterprises, especially those oriented toward the export economy.[19] The Portuguese government, on the other hand, took an active role in stimulating exports, at least where sugar was concerned.

The privilege bestowed on the grantee, whereby he received exclusive rights to manufacture cane crushers and water mills, reveals that the specific purpose [of state policy] was to develop sugarcane farming in the colony. Later, special concessions were made—such as tax exemptions, guarantees against court attachment of production facilities, honorary recognitions, titles, and so on—to those prepared to install sugar mills. (Furtado 1963, 43)

Nevertheless, the Spanish and Portuguese colonial policies were probably most notable for their failures—their inability to prevent the emergence of a small landowning elite that virtually monopolized productive (and much unproductive) land and their inability to protect either the Indians or the slaves from the depredations of their masters and owners.

The colonial period was thus responsible for establishing the pattern of large landholdings and an exploited peasant or slave underclass throughout much of Latin America. The availability and reliability of commercial opportunities clearly had much to do with the location and characteristics of the productive systems that emerged. During this period, economic and demographic changes had direct consequences for the use of land, labor, and capital in the region. Underlying these changes, however, was a striking uniformity in the unequal distribution of land and the dependent position of labor, whether in areas dominated by domestic production or in those dominated by export production. In the nineteenth century, commercial expansion changed the nature of many agricultural enterprises in the region. Export markets came to dominate production, foreign money flowed into the sector, and export profits stimulated national economies. If anything, however, these changes further cemented the nature of landholding and rural power relations that had developed in the colonial period.

THE EXPORT BOOM, 1850–1930: THE PATTERN IS REINFORCED

The social structure inherited from the previous centuries provided only a tiny market for agriculture. Much of the population either grew its own food or received food rations in exchange for services performed on the estates. . . . Only the cities of Santiago and Valparaiso, the northern mining districts and people in road or bridge construction gangs offered any outlet. . . . Landowners knew that the possibilities of growing rich by supplying this market were obviously limited to those farms on the outskirts of Santiago.[20]

Latin America's rural sector in the mid nineteenth century is often characterized as a static reminder of conditions in the seventeenth and eighteenth centuries. Production for the domestic market remained tenuous and a limited export agriculture developed and declined in response to changing European demands and technology. Already, however, expanding world trade in the first half of the century had begun to stir a response in some Latin American countries.[21] Between the 1850s and 1930, agriculture in Latin America was to change radically as a result of industrial expansion in Western Europe and the United States. During this period, in country after country, the domestic economies came to depend on the export of one or two primary products to major industrial centers—primarily Britain, and later the United States—and the region became more firmly linked to and dependent upon international demand for a limited number of primary commodities and their own demand for manufactured goods from the industrial countries (Cortés Conde 1974). These economies also became even more susceptible to the boom-and-bust cycles that characterized primary-commodity export systems. This period, then, witnessed the widespread emergence of an agrarian capitalism characterized by greatly increased investment, some technological innovation, changing relations of production, and increased international dependency.

As the nations of Western Europe and North America industrialized, they also urbanized, grew substantially in population, and became more prosperous. The increased demand for coffee, sugar, grain, cacao, tobacco, cotton, beef, bananas, rubber, wood, and other products would not have reached Latin America, however, had it not been for important technical developments in transportation and communication.[22] Primary among these was the use of steam in maritime transportation, an innovation which made it possible to ship perishable and bulky foodstuffs at greatly diminished prices.[23] Between the 1850s and the 1880s, the building of railroads and improved port facilities also stimulated production for the export markets, as did the expansion of domestic road networks. In the latter part of the century, the telegraph speeded communication of world prices for commodities and thus influenced production patterns.[24] In addition, specific improvements aided individual products. Beef production in Argentina, for example, was greatly stimulated by the development of the refrigerator ship in the 1870s, and the coffee-processing machinery introduced at mid century played a role in greatly increasing production of that crop in Costa Rica (Burns 1977, 130; Cardoso 1977, 187; Seligson 1980, 19). Finally, the impetus to export production involved important domestic determinants such as the availability and utilization of capital and labor and the development of an internal market, and these caused patterns to differ from one country, region, or crop to another. (Cortés Conde 1974).

The extent of the boom in primary commodities is impressive. Argentina exported fourteen times as much in 1893 as it did in 1854; by the end of the century, Mexico, another principal beneficiary of the export boom, had increased its exports fourfold in less than twenty-five years. Chilean wheat found a ready market in California and Australia in the 1850s and later in Argentina and England; exports of this crop increased fourteen times between 1845 and 1895. In Brazil, Colombia, and Central America, a greatly increased demand for coffee caused this crop to account for the great majority of export earnings received by these countries. Brazil's coffee earnings increased thirteen and a half times and Costa Rica increased its exports almost five hundred times between 1832 and 1870. In Peru, sugar plantations in the coastal region expanded production sevenfold between 1887 and 1930, while in the same period the value of sugar exports increased ten times. In the Caribbean, Cubans introduced technical improvements and expanded the production and export of sugar over nine and a half times between the 1840s and 1910. Wool exports from Argentina increased impressively between the 1840s and the 1880s.[25] The thriving export economies were at times reinforced by mining and urban commercial developments that increased demand for local products. Generally, however, the export boom absorbed much land that had previously been dedicated to domestic or subsistence production.

The economic developments of the nineteenth and early twentieth centuries were also aided by important domestic social and political changes. The population of Latin America recovered definitively from its decline and stasis during the colonial period, growing from approximately twenty million in 1800 to sixty million at the end of the nineteenth century. In addition to creating sizable urban areas, this increased population also enabled landowners to expand the area under cultivation and to impose increased production demands on sharecroppers, tenants, and workers because of the greater competition for access to land and employment opportunities controlled by them. During this period the state became active in improving transportation and communication networks and, in some countries, in establishing banking and credit facilities to serve rural landholding interests and in ensuring favorable conditions for foreign investors.[26]

Political stability, achieved early in Chile and Brazil, became more notable in other countries toward the end of the century as the long periods of anarchy, violence, and civil war that followed the independence movements of the 1810s and 1820s came to an end. Strong presidents such as Porfirio Díaz in Mexico (1876–1910), Guzmán Blanco (1870–88) and Juan Vincente Gómez (1908–35) in Venezuela, and Augusto Leguía (1919–30) in Peru centralized power, carried out internal reforms, and involved the state more in stimulating export-oriented development. In a large number of countries, agricultural export elites came to dominate national politics and to shape influential policies. These leaders and elites were important figures in inviting increased foreign investment into the region. Central to the development of agrarian capitalism in the region, however, were the liberal reforms that spanned the period from mid century to the 1880s and that opened up the commercial market in land by weakening the ability of the Church and the Indian communities to retain their hold over it. The land concentration that accompanied the export boom of the late nineteenth and early twentieth centuries was a direct result of these laws, as was the emergence of higher levels of conflict over land ownership.[27]

The development of export-oriented agrarian capitalism in the last quarter of the nineteenth century was characterized by the opening up of the Latin American economies to greatly increased foreign investment, especially from the United States. Investment was made directly in agricultural enterprises, in the processing and shipping of commodities, and in the development of infrastructure such as railroads and communication, which stimulated the growth of export-based economies. Between 1883 and 1911, British and American investment in Mexico increased from 193.5 million dollars to 1,494.6 million. In Cuba, investment from the United States increased from about 50 million dollars in 1894 to 919 million in 1929. In 1892, foreign investment in Argentina was 833.8 million pesos; by 1913, it had expanded to 3,520.0 million pesos (Cortés Conde 1974, 112, 46, 137; Wolf 1969, 38–39). Enterprises such as W. R. Grace and Company, the South Puerto Rico Sugar Company, and United Fruit Company bought up huge expanses of land to produce sugar and fruit, established mills, ports, and company towns, and reaped lucrative profits, generally in close alliance with the commercial and export elites of the countries where they invested. In northern Mexico, "by 1902, U.S. firms held more than a million hectares in Sonora; in Sinaloa they owned 50 percent of the productive deltaic plain and 75 percent of all irrigable land, where sugar, cotton, and fresh vegetables were raised for the market."[28]

Peru's experience with agriculture from the late nineteenth century until 1930 is illustrative of the impact of foreign demand and investment on the use of land and labor. In the northern coastal region of the country, for instance, sugar production after 1883 was progressively organized into modern corporate plantations dominated by foreign companies that acquired enormous landholdings. The expansion of the sugar estates resulted from the consolidation of a large number of haciendas and some indigenous reserves that had been engaged primarily in subsistence production. The technical requirements of sugar processing made large-scale production more efficient, and this, along with the monopoly on irrigation achieved by the plantations, forced most small and medium producers out of the market by the early twentieth century.

In one valley in the region, sixty-five haciendas were absorbed into seven large plantations between the late nineteenth century and 1918. During World War I, three large corporations, two of which were foreign-owned, came to dominate coastal production. By 1918, these three companies controlled virtually all the land in the Chicama Valley, with the largest accounting for over 11,000 acres. By 1927, only two corporate giants remained, and the largest controlled over 21,000 acres in the valley (Klarén 1973, 17–18). Where the sugar plantations absorbed smallholdings or haciendas with resident tenants or sharecroppers, they also absorbed this labor into a landless wage-earning work force that helped meet the high labor requirements for sugar production. Labor was also obtained through the importation of Chinese coolies (until the 1870s) and the recruiting of highland Indians. In 1912, approximately 20,000 wage laborers were engaged in sugar production and processing; by 1928, the number had reached 30,000.[29] The expansion of sugar production also encroached upon an emerging class of relatively prosperous peasant smallholders that had grown foodstuffs for the domestic market, and the hold of the plantations on both labor and water resources was strengthened (Klarén 1977, 239–40).

By contrast, in cotton production on the coast during the same period, increased output was achieved largely by cultivating unused land that had already been incorporated into the haciendas; smallholdings were generally not at risk. Nevertheless, the haciendas of the region had long before monopolized the best land available, in addition to most sources of water, and they were therefore in a favorable position to respond to foreign market demands, while smallholders, unable to compete, were forced into subsistence production, into offering their labor on the cotton estates, or into migration to coastal cities. In addition, the liberal reforms of 1847 weakened the position of tenants and sharecroppers on the cotton estates, and as they lost customary and contractual rights to hacienda lands, they acquired the characteristics of a landless rural labor force (Paige 1977, 150–56; Klarén 1977, 231). In the sierra region of Peru, demand for wool and beef in the early twentieth century also enabled some large landowners to increase their holdings at the expense of the indigenous communities and to reinforce the traditional dominance of the landlord over the peasant and the peasant community (Cotler 1970, 36). Indian communities that were favorably situated to deliver wool to coastal markets, however, also prospered from the export boom (Paige 1977, 209–10).

Other areas of Latin America underwent similar processes of land concentration and changes in labor force utilization, the degree of change often being determined by the technical requirements of the export crop and the characteristics of the population engaged in agriculture. In much of Mexico, the liberal reforms of 1855–57, in addition to the expanding export markets for cotton, sugar, henequen, coffee, wood, vanilla, and chicle, led to wholesale appropriation—by fair means and foul—of lands belonging to Indian communities; by 1910, 90 percent of the rural population was landless, and only 15 percent of the indigenous communities retained possession of their traditional communal lands.[30] In Bolivia, too, haciendas expanded at the expense of the Indian communities in the early twentieth century; even lands that were marginally arable were absorbed into the large landholdings, and Indian communities were forced onto the very poorest lands (Malloy 1970, 31). In parts of Colombia, haciendas grew by appropriating both Indian communities and Church lands that were forced onto the market by the liberal reforms of 1861, and by expanding onto virgin territory.[31]

In Chile, where indigenous communities had not been an important factor in inhibiting large landholdings during previous periods, wheat production grew by expanding cultivation to unused or grazing lands already belonging to the haciendas (Bauer 1975). In Argentina, another region unencumbered by populous indigenous communities, wheat and cattle booms of the late nineteenth century led to large landholdings, but these were unusual in the extent to which they utilized modern technologies and a large immigrant labor force (Scobie 1964). In Brazil, the expansion of coffee production in the south was dominated by a wealthy planter class that acquired large landholdings on a moving frontier to the west and south of Rio de Janeiro, Minas Gerais, and São Paulo, and that adapted to the abolition of slavery in 1889 by encouraging massive immigration from Europe and the use of wage labor (Furtado 1963). The expansion of coffee cultivation in Guatemala and El Salvador also resulted in the consolidation of landholdings and a weakening of the position of smallholders, tenants, and sharecroppers, as did the foreign-dominated expansion of banana production in Central America (Durham 1979, 40–49). The enclosure of open range in Costa Rica turned many formerly independent peasants into wage laborers (Edelman 1982). The expansion of sugar processing in the Dominican Republic had similar consequences: "A society formerly composed of a few wealthy landowners and a mass of independent peasants engaged in herding or primitive farming was fast becoming a society made up of landless laborers, a group of wealthy, often foreign, entrepreneurs and a small number of independent professionals and merchants" (Calder 1982, 1).

There were, however, significant exceptions to this pattern of land concentration, most notably in the coffee regions of Costa Rica and Colombia and in central Chile. In Costa Rica, the coffee boom began in the 1830s and was characterized by the expansion of smallholdings onto virgin and public lands, often facilitated by public policies for land acquisition. With the gradual disappearance of virgin territory, the expansion of coffee production by the late nineteenth century was taking place on smallholdings through the conversion of lands from the production of other crops, a pattern which led the country to develop a monoculture economy that was almost completely dependent on international market prices for coffee.[32] However, the scarcity of labor and the labor-intensive nature of coffee cultivation drove wages extremely high in the 1860s and 1870s, and the most marginal smallholders were often forced to sell their lands and to become wage laborers on larger farms. Seligson (1980, 23) reports that by 1883, over 70 percent of the rural population of Costa Rica was landless. The increased production of coffee in the central highlands and the new wealth it brought also stimulated concentration of landholding in other areas of the country as cattle haciendas increased their production as well, responding to the new domestic demand for beef (Edelman 1982).

In Colombia, major population movements to colonize lush mountain areas in the central regions of the country led to a prosperous coffee economy based on relatively small holdings.[33] In Chile, the number of landowners in the central region increased as a greater market orientation developed in the late nineteenth century, but in the country as a whole, extensive monopolization of land was clearly evident by the early twentieth century, as indicated in Table 3.2 (Bauer 1975, 117). In Mexico, the number of ranches and haciendas increased in a region north of Mexico City between 1882 and 1910, the same period in which indigenous communities in the south were being deprived of their communal holdings (Brading 1977, 54).

Table 3.2 and Figure 3.1 present data on land distribution in three countries

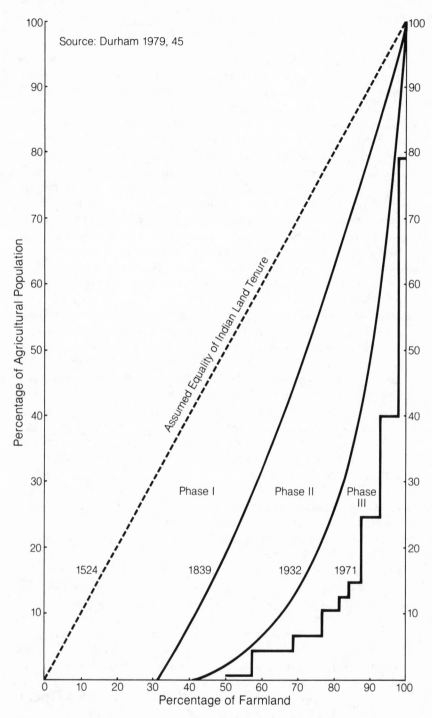

Figure 3.1. Land Concentration in El Salvador, 1524–1971

40

Table 3.2. Distribution of Landholdings, Brazil and Chile, Early
Twentieth Century

Size of Holding (hectares)	Percentage of Total Properties	Percentage of Total Area
Brazil, 1920		
under 10	0.0	0.0
10–100	71.4	9.0
100–1,000	24.4	27.6
1,000–10,000	3.8	37.4
10,000–up	0.3	26.0
Chile, 1924		
0–5	42.5	0.28
6–20	23.3	1.10
21–50	12.7	1.80
51–200	11.5	5.02
201–1,000	7.3	12.80
1,001–5,000	2.0	16.70
5,001–up	0.7	62.30

SOURCES: For Brazil, see Forman 1975, 45; for Chile, see Loveman 1974, 52.

for the early twentieth century. The pattern of concentration is striking, with 3–4 percent of the landowners often controlling as much as 70–80 percent of the land. Patterns of landholding varied, but the dominant dynamic during the period was one of consolidation of land into large estates with individual and corporate owners seeking to monopolize productive land, available labor, and water resources in order to benefit from the growing export economy. Often, the land-rich haciendas continued to maintain a resident labor force of tenants and sharecroppers but drastically increased the rents or labor requirements extracted in return for access to land. This clearly varied in terms of the availability of labor and the effectiveness of coercion; in some areas, landowners were forced to offer greater incentives to workers in order to attract or keep them, and some evidence suggests considerable capacity on the part of workers in such situations to negotiate the terms of employment (Bauer 1979).

While the period between 1850 and 1930 witnessed great expansion in the agricultural export economy, increased utilization of technology was not a general characteristic of the times, except on the large sugar plantations, where processing was integrally linked to production. Most expansion resulted from the extension of production to previously uncultivated regions, often through slash-and-burn techniques, as occurred in Costa Rica, Colombia, and Brazil, or from the conversion of land from the production of other crops or livestock, as occurred with wheat in Chile and with cotton and sugar in Peru and Mexico. This increase in production through more extensive use of land was accompanied by an increase in the amount of labor employed to produce the crops. Importantly, throughout the region land continued to be cheap, whereas capital continued to be scarce and expensive, reinforcing a pattern of production based on extensive landholdings and intensive control over labor in order to depress wages. Even with expansion, however, vast areas remained uncultivated, and underproductivity was the norm for agriculture. In a few areas where land values rose significantly and where labor was scarce, as in Costa Rica, greater investment of capital in modernizing techniques of production and processing were more apparent (Cardoso 1977, 182). In the pampas of Argentina, technical improvement was encouraged by labor scarcity and the high level of demand for both beef and wheat (Gallo 1977). As Bauer argues in the case of Chile, however, limited investment in modernizing production was an understandable strategy to follow, given the costs and risks involved in increasing the productivity of either land or labor.[34] The importation and repair of machinery was difficult and expensive, and owners were conscious that world prices for the goods they produced were unstable; they were therefore reluctant to invest heavily in modernizing their estates. In addition, the introduction of capital improvements frequently required considerable change in agricultural practices and land conditions, such as educating a work force and leveling and clearing fields.[35] In general, then, technological innovation to increase production was limited during the export expansion period. Tractors were a rare sight in the region before 1940, and even plows often were not standard equipment; as late as 1940, fully 75 percent of the farms in Brazil relied only on the use of the hoe for cultivation (Burns 1977, 197).

The expansion of export-based agrarian capitalism had significant consequences for politics and public policies in the region. The later nineteenth century witnessed the emergence of a politically powerful landed elite interested in using the power of the state to advance its goals.[36] At times emerging from the colonial land-holding elite, at times competing with it, this elite was instrumental in discouraging initiatives to tax landholdings or to intrude in the regulation of rural labor relations. It sought instead to encourage public investment in infrastructure, to establish official subsidies for agricultural inputs and services, and to facilitate credit. By limiting the availability of these resources to large landowners, the agricultural elite was able to increase its hold on land, labor, and capital and to deny these to smallholders, tenants, and sharecroppers.[37] The landowners found ready allies in a powerful commercial export elite, whose concerns included the expansion of free trade as a stimulus to the export of primary commodities. Both groups were intimately linked to foreign investors and commercial agents dealing in primary commodities. In the interests of these two groups, government services benefited export-oriented production, and agricultural production for domestic consumption was largely ignored by official policy makers.[38]

The concentration of land and the dispossessed or weakened position of many peasants did not occur without resistance or reaction. The most notable example of rural unrest in this period, of course, was the agrarian uprising of 1910, which was a central impetus to the Mexican Revolution. Social banditry was evident in some areas, as well as recourse to legal and political authorities. Elsewhere, especially in areas of plantation production, labor unrest and some labor organization emerged and created the basis for later rural mobilization in politics. Tension between wage workers and the corporate plantations on the Peruvian coast erupted in violence in 1910 and again in 1921; strikes were common in the region by the early 1920s. Highland areas in Peru and Mexico had a long history of resisting landlord dominance (Klarén 1977, 246–47; Warman 1980). In El Salvador, uprisings among dispossessed peasants occurred repeatedly between the 1870s and 1900. Where large coffee estates had developed in Colombia, rural unrest developed among resident workers in the late 1920s. Agrarian tenant syndicates, whose purpose was to resist the demands of the landlords and to organize production on a commercial basis, were mobilized throughout that country in the same decade. Rural violence lasted into the 1930s and was responsible for forcing the enactment of legislation to protect the status of tenants and sharecroppers. The 1930s also witnessed rural unrest in the Brazilian northeast and in El Salvador. In spite of considerable evidence of mobilization, much of the unrest and incipient organization was quashed by the state and the landholders, and was not a notable feature of rural politics again until the 1950s and 1960s, although it remained a vivid memory in the rural areas affected.[39]

In summary, it is clear that the development of the agricultural export economies between 1850 and 1930 had a number of significant consequences for the region. The pattern of large landholdings that had characterized Latin American rural areas since colonial times became even more marked as small and medium landowners, sharecroppers, and tenants were absorbed by the haciendas and plantations. In a related development, a large rural wage-labor force made its appearance at this time. But as the landowning elite grew wealthier and more powerful politically, it spent more time and money pursuing urban and continental lifestyles, and the economic and cultural gap between city and countryside tended to widen noticeably. Moreover, regions that had long been poor and "uncivilized" emerged as important economic centers—Argentina, southern Brazil, and Costa Rica are good examples of this. In addition, as more production was oriented toward foreign markets, domestic provision of food declined and was exacerbated by rising urban demand; the importation of food for domestic consumption increased after the turn of the century.[40] Finally, with the move toward monoculture, Latin

American economies became highly vulnerable to the long-term decline in world prices for primary commodities and to short-term fluctuations in international prices. The weakness of this system became apparent with the economic collapse of the 1930s.

COLLAPSE AND INDUSTRIALIZATION: THE PICTURE IN 1940

The difficult years emphasized once again to the Latin Americans the dependency and vulnerability of their economies. Cuba's economy broke down: foreign trade in the early 1930s was 10 percent of the 1929 figure. Uruguay's exports dropped 80 percent in the early 1930s. Brazil's exports plummeted from U.S. $445.9 million in 1929 to U.S. $180.6 million in 1932, while Argentina sold 40 percent less in the 1930–34 period than it had in the previous five years. In short, by 1932, Latin America exported 65 percent less than it had in 1929 (Burns 1977, 177).

The crash [in Chile] was led by the mining sector, the output of which fell by 70 percent in three years; it spread rapidly to other sectors of the economy, however, such that total output fell by 46 percent between 1929 and 1932. (Stallings 1978, 28)

When the international economy collapsed in 1929 and 1930, the agricultural and mining-based export economies of Latin America collapsed also. The next ten years brought intense political, economic, and social adjustments to this crisis, and by the 1940s, while many of the characteristics of the previous rural structure remained intact, a more urban and more industrial society had emerged that was to alter the role of agriculture and the rural sectors in national development.

The crisis of the Depression was notable in many countries for it spurred the emergence of active nationalists who were intent upon increasing industrialization and centralizing power in their countries. In 1930, governments were overthrown in Argentina, Bolivia, Brazil, the Dominican Republic, Guatemala, and Peru. In the following three years, Chile, Ecuador, El Salvador, Honduras, Peru, and Uruguay experienced forceable takeovers of power. The initial policy objective of the leaders of these movements and the political forces that surrounded them was to protect the economies from the worst aspects of the Depression through import and exchange controls and higher tariffs. In addition, however, most of the new governments sought to create the bases for industrial economies that would be less dependent on international conditions and less disadvantaged in the exchange of primary commodities (whose prices tended to decline over time) for industrial products (whose prices tended to rise). The first steps toward import substitution as a means of industrialization were taken, with the state acting as both promoter and guide. Clearly, some countries embarked on this developmental process before others, and some countries were in a better position to move toward industrial growth. Mexico, Brazil, Argentina, Colombia, Chile, and Uruguay achieved considerable advances in the 1930s; not until the 1940s and the 1950s, however, were other countries able to embark on similar import-substitution policies.

Political consolidation, often supported by urban-based movements of workers or the middle classes, enabled the state in many countries to begin to exert a much stronger influence on economic development. Investment of private capital in industrial activities was encouraged through large state-funded infrastructure and heavy-industry projects that would provide and subsidize electrical power, steel, communications networks, and petroleum. Public corporations and agencies to finance industrial development were created. Nacional Financiera was established in Mexico in 1934. Peru (1936), Venezuela (1937), Chile (1939), Colombia (1940), Argentina (1944), and Brazil (1952) soon followed suit with industrial development banks that played a large role in providing funds for private-sector investment and in the construction of basic infrastructure and services essential to industry. Moreover, the governments of the 1930s and 1940s can be credited with the introduction of a large number of social welfare programs that helped subsidize and control urban workers so that wages could remain low and industrial strife could be mediated by the state.[41] Economically, then, the 1930s were a critical period for attempts to break with external dependency based on the export of primary commodities.

Socially, during this period, the most advanced Latin American countries became significantly more urbanized. For the region as a whole, in 1920, 14 percent of the population lived in urban areas; in 1940, the proportion had risen to 20 percent. In Argentina, Chile, and Uruguay, it had reached 35–45 percent of the population. This population shift was in part responsible for the emergence of the middle sectors into political prominence, followed by the urban workers in the years after 1920. The hold that the landholding elite had maintained over politics in Chile, Argentina, Brazil, Venezuela, Uruguay, Peru, Colombia, and Mexico was significantly weakened, if not definitively broken, as a result of the increased importance of urban sectors in national politics.

The picture in 1940, then, is of conditions that had changed considerably for agriculture and the landed and export elites, if not for the rural poor. A more centralized state, new political forces, and a self-conscious drive toward industrialization meant that the landed and export elites would no longer be able to determine, almost single-handedly, the course of national politics. These changes would become apparent after 1940. Nevertheless, the extent of change to the agricultural sector should not be overemphasized. Many countries continued to rely on the export of a single primary commodity—the Central American and Caribbean countries are notable in this regard, but Brazil, Argentina, and Colombia can also be cited—and the pattern of extensive rather than intensive farming on large landholdings continued to be the modal one. Although weakened, the landed elite continued to exert enough power in national politics to prevent reform of either the landholding system or rural power relations. Large sectors of the rural population were still small-holding peasants, tenants, and sharecroppers; the emerging class of landless rural laborers had increased in size and proportion of the rural population, but it remained a minority. After 1940, then, agricultural change and development would proceed from the basis of the highly unequal distribution of land and power that had characterized rural areas since the early colonial period.

4 | The State and the Ideology of Modernization

Agro-export elites, both domestic and foreign, gained renewed prominence during the rapid expansion of agrarian capitalism in the nineteenth century and often dominated state decision making through the 1920s. But in the 1930s and 1940s, they first experienced a weakening of their economic position and then a serious undermining of their national political power (although they remained dominant at the local level) due to the rise of populist movements, military nationalism, and demands for centralization of power, bureaucratic expansion, and statist approaches to economic development. With the hegemony of the landowners and exporters broken, with the new populist working-class movements firmly in the control of political leaders intent on using them to enhance their own power, with an indigenous industrial class that was weak or nonexistent, there was considerable room for political leaders and bureaucratic officials in a number of Latin American countries to promote new definitions of economic development.[1] For state elites in the period after 1940, development became synonymous with industrialization, and industrialization required agricultural modernization.

The theoretical underpinnings of Latin America's drive for industrialization emerged after 1949, when the U.N. Economic Commission for Latin America (ECLA) was created. Prior to this, specific policy instruments to promote domestic manufacturing were widely adopted in the 1930s, when drastically declining exports significantly reduced the foreign exchange available for importing industrial goods.[2] Later, ECLA economists, under the guidance of Raúl Prebisch, clearly identified development with industrialization and added a theoretical and nationalist rationale for the move away from reliance on the export of primary products.[3] Terms of trade, they asserted, were inherently biased against primary products in the world market. Prices for these products were erratic in the short term and consistently declined in the long term in relation to prices for manufactured goods. Without industrialization, they reasoned, Latin American economies were doomed to suffer from their peripheral status in the world capitalist economy and to remain underdeveloped.

Importantly, the ECLA prognosis promoted and legitimized a strong role for state management and leadership of the economy. According to Prebisch, the process of industrialization in Latin America was inherently distinct from that experienced by early industrializers because of changes in the nature of the international capitalist economy. Because of this, the state would have to assume much of the role that private-sector entrepreneurs had performed in other countries. To facilitate economic development, the state should have control over important industrial infrastructure like public utilities and basic industries, and strict control over the importation of all commodities should be maintained in order to exclude those not considered to be central to industrial expansion. Moreover, wage and price controls and economic planning should be undertaken by the state. These instruments could then be used to cajole, regulate, protect, or entice the weak domestic private sector into assuming a more active part in industrialization. Planning and management as means toward economic development subsequently emerged as important emphases within Latin American bureaucracies.[4]

INDUSTRIALIZATION STRATEGIES AND
THE AGRICULTURAL SECTOR

Perspectives and policies to stimulate import substitution had a great impact on the development of agriculture in the region. Stimulated by a range of state policies, manufacturing surpassed agriculture for the first time in its contribution to the gross domestic product in Argentina, Brazil, Chile, Mexico, Uruguay, and Venezuela in the 1940s and enjoyed a modest spurt of growth in a number of other countries (see Table 4.1). In all countries, agriculture's share of the gross domestic product steadily declined as the manufacturing sector became more dynamic.

Within the policy-making apparatus of Latin American states, the first result of the promotion of rapid industrialization was the relegation of agriculture to a secondary position in national development plans. From the 1940s on, it was explicit policy that agriculture's role was to support and finance industrial development; the prosperity of the agricultural sector would cease to be the principal focus of planning and decision making.[5] Within the context of the import-substitution model, agriculture would underwrite industrialization by providing (1) foreign exchange from exports for the purchase of capital goods abroad; (2) capital for urban and industrial expansion; (3) cheap food for an expanding urban work force; (4) a pool of cheap labor for newly created industries; (5) raw materials for manufacture; and (6) a market for domestic manufactures.[6] For policy makers, these functions implied that the agricultur-

Table 4.1. Agriculture and Manufacturing as Share of GDP, 1940–79 (Percentages)

Country and Economic Sector	1940	1950	1960	1970	1979
Argentina					
Agriculture	23.2	16.2	14.9	13.1	13.0
Manufacturing	22.7	23.7	26.5	30.2	29.9
Bolivia					
Agriculture	NA	25.4	24.5	16.8	16.3
Manufacturing	NA	12.2	11.6	12.9	15.8
Brazil					
Agriculture	21.4	16.8	13.4	10.0	7.4
Manufacturing	15.0	21.2	26.3	28.4	30.3
Chile					
Agriculture	13.0	11.6	9.8	7.8	8.5
Manufacturing	11.8	23.1	24.8	27.2	24.0
Colombia					
Agriculture	44.7	37.7	32.7	28.6	25.8
Manufacturing	8.3	14.5	16.7	17.5	18.8
Costa Rica					
Agriculture	NA	38.4	29.4	25.0	18.5
Manufacturing	NA	11.5	12.5	15.1	18.0
Dominican Republic					
Agriculture	NA	34.5	33.9	25.8	18.5
Manufacturing	NA	12.4	14.6	16.7	16.2
Ecuador					
Agriculture	38.3	42.1	39.0	29.8	22.8
Manufacturing	16.0	16.0	15.7	17.5	21.7
El Salvador					
Agriculture	NA	40.9	36.0	30.6	27.5
Manufacturing	NA	12.9	13.9	17.6	17.5
Guatemala					
Agriculture	NA	35.5	33.4	30.1	28.4
Manufacturing	NA	11.1	11.9	14.6	15.1
Honduras					
Agriculture	50.5	44.8	32.8	34.5	28.3
Manufacturing	6.8	9.1	15.3	14.0	15.8
Mexico					
Agriculture	19.7	19.4	16.2	11.8	9.0
Manufacturing	16.9	18.8	19.3	23.4	24.9
Nicaragua					
Agriculture	NA	36.6	29.5	27.0	33.5
Manufacturing	NA	10.8	13.0	19.2	20.0

Table 4.1—*Continued*

Country and Economic Sector	1940	1950	1960	1970	1979
Panama					
Agriculture	NA	32.6	26.1	20.7	17.7
Manufacturing	NA	8.2	11.8	15.9	11.9
Paraguay					
Agriculture	49.2	40.8	NA	34.3	29.3
Manufacturing	16.0	15.9	NA	17.3	16.3
Peru					
Agriculture	NA	25.5	24.4	18.8	14.9
Manufacturing	NA	14.2	17.1	20.6	21.5
Uruguay					
Agriculture	16.3	13.5	11.0	12.6	9.9
Manufacturing*	17.3	20.3	24.3	24.2	26.7
Venezuela					
Agriculture	19.2	9.2	7.9	7.5	6.5
Manufacturing	13.6	11.2	14.0	15.0	12.9
Latin America					
Agriculture	25.1	19.7	17.1	13.8	11.9†
Manufacturing	16.6	18.7	21.3	24.3	25.2†

SOURCE: *SALA* 1980, 265–83; 1983, 289–98.

* Includes mining and quarrying.

† 1975.

al sector would have to become more efficient and generate a surplus that could then be transferred to the emergent industrial and urban sectors.

Thus, a second impact of the adoption of the import-substitution model was the identification of agricultural development with increases in production and productivity, as distinct from questions of equity, distribution, and rural welfare (Voll 1980, 25). According to development planners, such increases would be achieved through a process of agricultural modernization, that is, through the spread of technological innovation and more extensive capitalization of farm enterprises, and the termination of precapitalist forms of labor relationships. Although some state elites in the 1950s and 1960s stressed land distribution as an important stimulant to modernization, in general, policy makers were not hostile to large landholdings per se, only to inefficient and "traditional" ones. From this perspective, large holdings offered great potential for the consolidation of modern agriculture through mechanization, application of modern technology, and wage labor.[7] Central to the modernization of agriculture was the importance of foreign technology and capital to the transformation of the sector.

Third, it was asserted that the state should assume a strong role in bringing about agricultural modernization through investment in infrastructure, extension, research into new agricultural technologies (especially those associated with the development of "miracle" seeds and the utilization of fertilizer), subsidies on agricultural inputs, credit, the import of machinery, and marketing channels. And, in accordance with the general development strategy, most governments expanded their investments in these specific services for agricultural modernization during the 1950s, even though public investment during these years clearly reflected the secondary function of the sector.[8] Overall, agriculture received only about 5 percent of total government expenditures; in specific countries—Argentina, Brazil, Chile, Costa Rica—it was often much less (see Table 4.2). But because of the rapid expansion of the state in the national economy during this period, absolute amounts earmarked for agriculture actually grew considerably, as is evident in the indices reported in Table 4.3.

To oversee these investments, a plethora of public agencies and enterprises was created. Almost all countries established agricultural credit banks, some of which were to provide services for a single product or a limited range of products or producers—cattlemen's banks, coffee credit institutes, small farmers' banks, and the like. Special research and extension agencies or offices within the ministry of agriculture were often joined by state firms that produced and marketed inputs such as improved seeds and fertilizers. Frequently their activities were to be coordinated through official credit institutions so that those who

Table 4.2. Government Expenditures on Agriculture as a Percentage of Total Government Spending, 1950–78

Country	Average Annual Percentage					
	1950/ 1955	1956/ 1960	1961/ 1965	1966/ 1970	1971/ 1975	1976/ 1978
Argentina	3.5	2.6	2.7	2.9	2.6	2.4
Bolivia	NA	4.2	12.0	22.4	20.6	28.4
Brazil	4.9	4.7	2.9	2.0	1.3	1.5
Chile	3.3	2.5	4.7	6.2	3.7	2.4
Colombia	4.9	5.7	8.8	12.6	11.1	6.4
Costa Rica	NA	1.9	1.7	2.7	2.9	2.1
Mexico	12.0	7.1	6.9	6.8	8.6	5.2
Peru	5.8	4.7	4.2	6.0	8.6	9.6
Venezuela	5.0	5.6	7.2	7.1	7.7	7.5

SOURCE: Elías 1981, 25–26.

NOTE: Figures are based on Ministry of Agriculture expenditures plus the expenditures allocated to agriculture by other ministries and decentralized agencies. Argentina, Brazil, and Mexico also include expenditures of state governments. Figures exclude foreign grants and loans. See Elías 1981, 15–16.

Table 4.3. Index of Real Government Expenditures on Agriculture, 1950–78 (1960 = 100)

Country	1950	1955	1960	1965	1970	1975	1978
Argentina	87.6	106.8	100.0	116.8	198.0	149.1	177.3
Bolivia	NA	NA	100.0	531.8	1103.4	1402.8	2900.6
Brazil	NA	77.7	100.0	133.7	166.3	225.7	670.1
Chile	51.6	32.4	100.0	154.9	256.3	339.3	206.6
Colombia	52.9	71.6	100.0	429.6	766.1	396.3	NA
Costa Rica	NA	NA	100.0	125.0	320.3	410.0	593.8
Mexico	124.2	110.9	100.0	148.0	347.3	931.8	1125.8
Peru	NA	231.2	100.0	412.2	676.7	1390.5	1037.0
Venezuela	26.1	35.5	100.0	107.9	125.3	320.2	260. 4

SOURCE: Elías 1981, 17.

obtained loans would have priority access to modern inputs. In addition, irrigation agencies were developed throughout Latin America. Regional development agencies, such as those established in Brazil in the 1940s and 1950s, also became a common phenomenon. Similarly, governments all over the region established marketing agencies to control prices, regulate imports, and distribute commodities. Some, like Mexico's powerful CONASUPO, became involved in all aspects of food production, processing, and distribution (Grindle 1977). And, in the 1950s and 1960s, agrarian reform institutes were established in practically every country, often in tandem with public agencies charged with the oversight of indigenous affairs. While often accused of inefficiency, waste, duplication of function, and corruption, these agencies nevertheless expanded the presence of the state in agriculture, giving it greater leverage to shape the sector's development.

Fourth, while import substitution as a development ideology emphasized agricultural modernization, specific policies to promote industrialization discriminated heavily against the rural economy. The generalized use of an overvalued exchange rate, for instance, meant that exports of primary products diminished in profitability for producers. Similarly, export taxes often discouraged production of traditional exports. Tariff barriers and inflation raised the prices of domestic manufactures, thus decreasing the rural markets' access to them. The terms of trade affecting the relationship of manufactured and agricultural products effectively transferred resources to the urban and industrial sector, the price often being paid by the rural poor.[9] Policies to maintain cheap domestic food for urban consumption—a large and often growing component of the wages of the low-income working population—also discouraged agricultural production in countries such as Ecuador, Chile, Uruguay, Guatemala, and Venezuela. Inflation was a major disincentive to food production, especially when coupled with these consumer-oriented food price policies. As a result of these conditions, agricultural production lagged in the 1950s and 1960s in almost all countries (see Chapter 5).

A fifth aspect of import-substitution policies with consequences for the agricultural sector was the encouragement they gave to rapid urbanization and rural-to-urban migration. In 1940, approximately 20 percent of Latin America's population lived in towns of 20,000 inhabitants or more; by 1960, this proportion had increased to 33 percent; by 1970, to 41.5 percent; by 1975, to 63 percent; and projections for the year 2000 placed 73 percent of the population in urban areas. Already-large cities grew to encompass one-third or more of national populations between 1940 and 1980.[10] Deteriorating terms of trade between rural and urban areas forced many to leave villages and haciendas in search of work. Mechanization, changing tenure relationships, and the concentration of landholdings attendant upon the modernization of large farm enterprises were other factors that forced people, especially the poor, from rural areas (see Chapter 5). At the same time, cheap food and state-subsidized housing, health, and education facilities that were available only in urban areas attracted many, as did the promise of job opportunities. Although such benefits often proved illusory because industry failed to absorb the mass of available workers and the state failed to expand services rapidly enough, they were nevertheless important stimulants to altering the rural-urban distribution of population in the region. While the rural population continued to grow, its rate of expansion was far outdistanced by that of the cities, and the centralization and urban-industrial emphasis of political and economic decision making was reinforced.

In the 1940s and 1950s, therefore, the adoption of import substitution as a development ideology had clear ramifications for agriculture in Latin America. But import substitution itself generated grave problems for further industrialization in the region. By the late 1950s in many countries and during the 1960s in most others, the "easy phase" of import substitution, emphasizing light consumer industry, was fully developed and the second phase, emphasizing the creation of industries to produce capital goods, was embarked upon. Emphasis on heavier industry led to mounting balance-of-payments deficits and foreign-exchange shortages as industrial products, raw materials, and foreign loans were imported for the newer, more expensive, and technologically complex industries. The situation was particularly severe in the more economically advanced countries such as Brazil, Argentina, Chile, Mexico, and Colombia (Baer 1962; O'Donnell 1973; Kaufman 1979).

Gradually, as these economic problems mounted during the 1960s, development planners began seriously to consider a return to an outward-oriented development strategy, now emphasizing the increased export of manufactured goods in which specific countries had "comparative international advantage." In a process that accelerated during the 1970s, import substitution was supplemented or replaced by a new development model of export promotion, or "opening up to the exterior."[11] As a development ideology, however, this model continued to visualize the future of Latin American countries in terms of their industrial capacity.[12] Like import substitution, export-promotion policies generally emphasized a strong and managerial role for the state. Appropriate state policies should provide incentives to entrepreneurial groups, encourage greater efficiency in industrial production, determine the conditions under which foreign capital would be involved in domestic enterprises, attempt to establish and maintain price stability, maintain control over the labor force, and dismantle a number of impediments to export growth that had developed under import substitution.[13]

The new development emphasis on exports, evident by 1966 in Brazil and in Colombia in the late 1960s, in Mexico by 1970, in Chile and Uruguay after the military takeovers of 1973, by 1976 in Argentina, and by the late 1970s in Peru, was accompanied by a reappraisal of the role of agriculture in national development. Within policy-making circles, the sector was singled out as one that, without greater investment from private and public sources, would continue to be an impediment to industrial growth.[14] In addition, after international food shortages in the early 1970s, there was renewed interest in the long-term profitability of certain export crops, often of a nontraditional nature, that figured importantly in world trade. Moreover, exports of agricultural commodities offered possibilities for offsetting the high cost of importing fuel.[15] Added to this, of course, was heightened concern over the failure of the agricultural sector to supply sufficient food for domestic consumption. In a period of mounting expenditures for imports and increased balance-of-payments deficits, the more efficient production of domestic food crops came to be emphasized as a means to reduce external dependency. Potential political tensions also added to official concern. Inflation was particularly severe in the mid 1970s, and poor people were expending increasing portions of their income on food for subsistence; concern about the possibility of urban unrest mounted among policy-making elites.[16]

Clearly, according to the new development ideology, if agriculture continued to be the orphan of industrialization, national economic development would be sacrificed to external dependence or domestic political unrest. Thus, as a result of renewed attention to agriculture, public investment in rural areas increased noticeably after 1965 in a number of countries (Elías 1981). Tables 4.2 and 4.3, for instance, show the increase in expenditures on agriculture that occurred from the mid 1960s to the late 1970s. Trends for Mexico, Colombia, and Brazil are illustrated in Figure 4.1. With export promotion, therefore, agriculture remained supportive of the general drive toward industrialization but moved into a more prominent position in development policy making, one in which its problems were treated with greater urgency.

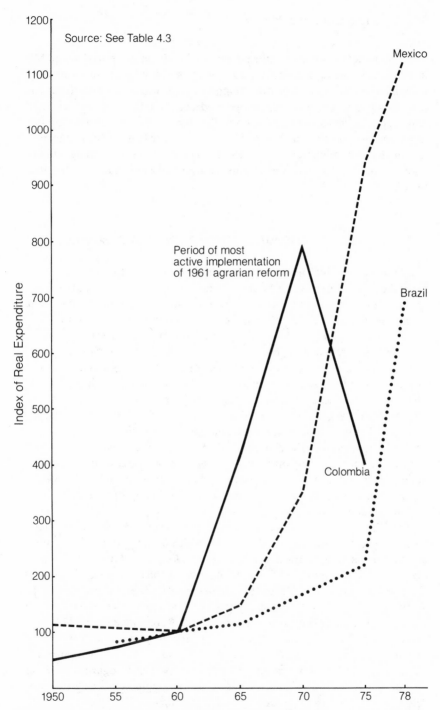

Figure 4.1. Government Expenditures on Agriculture in Mexico, Colombia, and Brazil, 1950–78

Development ideologies in the period after 1940 did much to shape public investment in the agricultural sector and to establish agriculture's place in overall national economic growth. Importantly, as will become evident in the following pages, policies to encourage modernization in the sector facilitated and supported increased bifurcation of the rural economy. Moreover, while large landowners generally lost power to emerging urban industrial interests, the impact of development ideologies stressing modernization in agriculture allowed them to increase their influence over policy making for the rural sector.

THE POLITICS OF UNEQUAL AGRICULTURAL DEVELOPMENT

Until the 1970s, advocates of modernization anticipated that most farmers, given the proper incentive structure and education, had the potential to adopt new technologies and to increase production, regardless of the scale of their enterprise (Berry 1975, 253). Some farmers, of course, would be at the fore-front of the movement to modernize production and labor relations, perhaps because of natural advantages related to the quality or location of their land, or because of personality characteristics favoring risk-taking and innovation. When consideration was given to who would or should benefit from the limited funds or services available, the logic of rapid modernization indicated the advisability of targeting aid toward those who had the greatest potential for increased production with the least amount of "prodding." Policy makers generally believed that the demonstrable payoffs of increased efficiency and modernization on priority farms and among the most entrepreneurial person-alities would trickle down to the rest of the rural economy in terms of better prices, yields, and markets, and more available knowledge, research, and mechanization.

As we saw in the previous chapter, however, the distribution of basic agri-cultural resources was highly skewed when the state began to play a more entrepreneurial role in rural areas. At that time, 1–5 percent of the landowners often controlled as much as 85 percent of the land, and had control over essen-tial water resources. In addition, this small elite was generally in a position to set the terms of access to land, employment, and livelihood for the rest of the rural population. Peasants, on the other hand, were settled on land of poor quality, often lacked access to water, and generally lived in the most remote and unproductive regions of the country or were bound to the large estates. As a result, state action to improve production and spur technological innovation discriminated heavily in favor of those who monopolized basic agricultural resources. This is clear in assessing the distribution of official credit, research and extension, infrastructure, mechanization, and green revolution inputs.

Credit

Throughout Latin America, policy makers considered credit to be a primary ingredient for encouraging agricultural modernization. Consequently, between the 1930s and 1950s, agricultural credit institutions were widely introduced. These official banks generally assessed the credit-worthiness of loan applicants on the basis of the availability and suitability of conventional collateral—land value, value of constructions and machinery on the land, and indebtedness. They also weighed factors such as the applicant's ability to utilize modern inputs to increase productivity. In addition, the banks often favored the producers of certain crops, either as a result of officially established priorities or the political power of producer organizations. They offered subsidized credit, often at negative real terms of interest in the region's highly inflationary economies, to those producers who met these criteria, both for short-term production loans or for longer-term investments.[17] In addition, organizational constraints limited the reach of bank outlets to major provincial cities, where farmers were generally required to go to undertake lengthy and complicated application procedures for loans.[18]

Within the context of a highly skewed resource base in agriculture, competition for subsidized loans was actually limited to a small sector of the agricultural population, specifically to those who controlled large amounts of land; to those who had substantial constructions on their property; to those who owned or could acquire expensive agricultural machinery; and to those who had access to information and supplies of green revolution technology and who were able to sustain the economic risks involved in their application. These individuals were also more likely to be able to undertake the travel and bureaucratic procedures required of loan applicants and to be adept at establishing the personal or pecuniary relationships with bank personnel that enabled them to cut through red tape and delay. Peasants, who had land and constructions of low value (or who rented or sharecropped) and no agricultural machinery, few animals, and little potential for utilizing expensive inputs, remained outside the eligibility requirements for most official credit. Given the built-in bias of lending policies and practices, the rural poor could acquire credit only through traditional informal channels at highly usurious rates, or through official programs that set up special loan funds for them. Even in the latter case, however, banking practices often meant that credit was available only to a small portion of the rural poor.

Examples from several countries suggest the extent of the bias in credit provision. In Peru, between a third and a half of the credit made available by the Agricultural Development Bank between the 1940s and the mid 1960s was granted to cotton growers, who were among the wealthy coastal agricultural exporters. Food crop producers—generally peasants—were largely ignored by the bank's activities (Frankman 1974, 292–95; Durham 1977, 14–15). In

Ecuador, approximately 75 percent of public agricultural credit was absorbed by large coastal producers; only 12 percent of the loans went to peasants until the early 1970s, when the government became more concerned with broader issues of rural development. In this later period, the proportion directed to low-income producers—who formed 70 percent or more of all farmers—rose to 35 percent (World Bank 1979, 163–64). In Costa Rica, 88.2 percent of credit allocations made in the early 1970s were made to farms and ranches over 200 hectares in size producing for export. Farms producing for domestic markets received only 11.8 percent of the credit (Guess 1979, 43). In Bolivia, agricultural loans made after 1956 went primarily to large sugar producers in the Santa Cruz region (Thorn 1971, 190–91). In Colombia, most credit advantaged barely 10 percent of the farm units (Grunig 1969, 22). In the mid 1960s, 90 percent of official credit in Guatemala was allocated to three export crops, which were grown by large landowners—coffee, cotton, and sugar (Griffin 1976, 162). Credit programs financed by the World Bank and other international lending organizations were also highly skewed toward owners of large agricultural holdings.[19]

Research and Extension Services

Research and extension services in Latin America also benefited large landowners disproportionately in the period under consideration. Frequently financed by foreign public or private aid, institutions for research and extension concentrated their efforts on expanding production of highly remunerative crops and were primarily concerned with the adoption of internationally acclaimed technologies and crops; conversely, until the 1970s, they showed little interest in indigenous crops or in problems specific to peasant agriculture (Hewitt de Alcántara 1976). Trained abroad or in urban settings, researchers and extensionists themselves found it easier to deal with large producers, who were able to experiment with technical innovation with a minimum of risk, than with the "backward," "traditional," or "illiterate" peasants, who often rejected innovation because of the risk it implied to precarious family security. Moreover, the limited number of official research and extension agents further justified the concentration of effort on the large producers.[20] Incidentally, of course, the large landowners were also those receiving state subsidized credit to encourage them to innovate with agricultural technologies and, as we will see, those benefiting most from publicly financed irrigation projects that lessened the risk of adopting new methods, inputs, and crops. The interest of these farmers in the profitability of certain crops also skewed investment in the types of crops and techniques that would be promoted.

The history of agricultural research in Mexico is a good example of the impact of state programs on the distribution of wealth in rural areas. A joint venture between the Mexican government and the Rockefeller Foundation was initiated in 1943 to bring technical innovation to the country's agricultural sector. Utilizing technologies that had proved effective in the United States, researchers concentrated first on corn and wheat, expanding their concerns to beans, potatoes, vegetables, other grains, and livestock in later years. The research and extension effort was concentrated on lands where irrigation was available. According to Hewitt de Alcántara, basic assumptions about the international transferability of agricultural techniques were the cause of the biased impact of the research program.

> At that time, there was no question as to whether the social and economic requirements of the farming techniques then in use in the United States were compatible with the agrarian structure of Mexico; there was no mention of the uneconomically small size of many subsistence holdings, their isolation and subjection to local money-lenders, the low quality of their resource base, or any number of other factors which fundamentally distinguished the Mexican countryside from the United States (Hewitt de Alcántara 1976, 23).

Consequently, she comments,

> Commercial wheat farmers, aided by numerous government programs . . . , were able to make maximum use of this new technology; but the great majority of subsistence farmers who dedicated their land to corn and who were largely ignored in official investment were not. Therefore, twenty years after the initiation of the joint technical assistance programme in 1943, Mexican wheat yields were the highest in Latin America, while average yields of corn were among the lowest (Hewitt de Alcántara 1976, 26).

The Mexican experience was repeated throughout Latin America in the postwar years as official research and extension services expanded.

Infrastructure

State-financed infrastructure, especially in terms of transportation networks and irrigation, also strengthened the position of the large-scale producers. For one thing, these investments raised the value of land and, unless special provision was made, encouraged wealthy and entrepreneurial producers to acquire or maintain control over it. Irrigation often meant access to credit that enabled farmers to expand the amount of land they cultivated through mechanization. Research, extension, and input programs were also geared to areas where lands were fertile and irrigation was available. Transportation networks that made markets more accessible encouraged innovation and greater production in the most promising agricultural areas, most of which came under the control of large landowners. In Bolivia, for instance, heavy government investment in road construction in the Santa Cruz area stimulated significant investments in sugar and rice, the concentration of landholding in the area, and the prosperity of a very small portion of the rural population (Wennergren and Whitaker 1975, 41–43; Thorn 1971, 190–91). In Guatemala, public investment in agriculture was concentrated in the construction of irrigation systems, storage facilities, and roads, all of which benefited large, export-oriented farmers (World Bank 1979, 142). Similarly, in the 1970s, the value of land in Ecuador's irrigated zones doubled in five years, excluding many peasants from the land market (World Bank 1979, 141).

Mechanization

In pursuit of agricultural modernization, public policies encouraged the mechanization of croplands, in spite of an increasingly idle or underemployed agricultural work force and the failure of industry to absorb it, and in spite of a tradition of extensive rather than intensive use of land, which mechanization frequently only emphasized. Exemptions from import duties were generally granted for agricultural machinery such as tractors, harvesters, and trucks, and state-financed loans were made available to qualified applicants who wished to mechanize, applying the credit-worthiness standards that were discussed earlier. In addition, subsidized fuel prices encouraged the replacement of labor with machinery, especially during periods of rural unrest or relative labor shortages. Those landholders benefiting from infrastructure programs in irrigation and transportation facilities were also more able to utilize the modern equipment and to increase the profitability of their holdings. Moreover, mechanization of farm units was not scale neutral, and under most conditions it offered greater advantages to large farmers than to small ones. As a result of these factors, mechanization became concentrated in the most agriculturally dynamic regions. For example, Abercrombie reports that in the early 1970s the pampas in Argentina accounted for 70 percent of all machinery in the country; 95 percent was located in the east and south of Brazil; 70 percent was found in about a third of Colombia's departments; and in Uruguay, 80 percent was located in the south and west (Abercrombie 1972, 19). In Mexico in 1970, mechanization affected 25.7 percent of the crop area for private farms of more than 5 hectares; it affected only 4.3 percent of the crop area on private farms under 5 hectares in size and 13 percent of the area in ejidos (Yates 1981, 200).

Green Revolution Inputs

Beginning in the 1940s and expanding rapidly in the 1960s, official programs were introduced to increase the use of fertilizer, insecticides, pesticides, and high-yielding varieties of seeds. Often produced by state-owned industries or distributed through state agencies, these inputs were most readily available at subsidized prices to those who could acquire credit to purchase them, those who owned land near major transportation networks, those who were clients of government research and extension services, those who could purchase them in large quantities, and those who could manage shipping costs. Thus, although much green revolution technology is relatively scale neutral in its application, its availability was generally restricted by inequitable income and credit distribution. Moreover, successful use of the green revolution inputs, highly sensitive to the availability of water and to climatic conditions, was generally limited to those with good access to water resources. To the extent that large landowners monopolized the benefits of modern technology for crop production, the peasant population was further marginalized from the process of economic modernization.

This general pattern of unequal development is readily observed in Mexico, Colombia, and Brazil, where a variety of regimes pursued policies for agricultural modernization. The political context of development policy making is important in these three countries, for it indicates how state elites, in pursuit of regime goals, were influenced and constrained by the beneficiaries of the state's modernization policies.

AGRICULTURAL MODERNIZATION IN MEXICO

In few countries of Latin America has the impact of the state on agricultural modernization been as great as in Mexico. In the years after the Revolution of 1910, and especially after 1940, consciously constructed policies shaped an agricultural sector composed of large capitalist enterprises, small private commercial and subsistence minifundios, and subsistence- and semisubsistence-oriented communal holdings known as ejidos.[21] These policies, formulated and pursued through the mechanisms of an authoritarian dominant-party regime, promoted increased differentiation between large landholders and the peasants who became the orphans of the country's impressive economic growth. By the early 1970s, massive rural poverty, very high levels of rural-to-urban migration, lagging production of basic food crops, and rising import bills could be clearly linked to state policies that promoted agricultural modernization.[22]

The Revolution of 1910 and its aftermath largely destroyed the power of the traditional landed elite in Mexico and initiated a still unresolved conflict between private commercial agricultural interests and the mass of the peasant population—both small private farmers and *ejidatarios*—over access to land, water, and state support and protection. The revolution eventually brought into existence a regime manned by political executives, bureaucrats, and party officials with strong statist orientations toward economic development, men who had, by the 1940s, acquired an impressive capacity to maintain social control. Until 1935, in spite of the promises for massive agrarian reform found in the Constitution of 1917, the revolutionary politico-bureaucratic elite actively promoted and participated in a form of agricultural development based on large private landholdings and capitalist accumulation. Land distribution, in the form of ejido grants, was undertaken only under pressure from organized groups of peasants or in response to de facto situations involving peasant possession of ancestral land. Often the claims of peasant groups were embroiled in legal and bureaucratic processes for generations as the state attempted to mediate individual and group demands and to maintain its commitments both to the sanctity of private property and to the necessity for social peace.[23] Throughout the country during this period, former landowners asserted their claims and revolutionary political figures correctly identified control over land as a fundamental basis for building economic and political power. Large landholdings were continuously consolidated, while peasants persisted in pressing their demands for land. As a result, rural conflict was endemic in the country long after the principal actors in the revolution had made their peace with each other in 1929 (Craig 1983; Esteva 1980; Sanderson 1981).

With the election of Lázaro Cárdenas to the presidency in late 1934, the impact of state development policies in rural Mexico changed significantly. This period witnessed a genuine attempt by an energetic sector of the politico-bureaucratic elite to create a rural society based on an equitable distribution of both land and water resources, and to reorganize peasant economic, social, and political behavior through collective and communal efforts (Cornelius 1973; Esteva 1980). Cárdenas, capitalizing on the legal power of the state and the support of a reorganized and centralized agrarian political force, confronted the new landed elite with a massive agrarian reform and a concerted effort to strengthen the role of the state in agricultural development. Between 1934 and 1940, Cárdenas promoted the distribution of more than twenty million hectares of land, twice as much as his predecessors had consigned in the preceding twenty years. By 1940, ejido grants accounted for half the cultivated area of the country and 51 percent of the value of production; the number of landless laborers declined from 68 percent of the rural work force in 1930 to 36 percent in 1940 (Hewitt de Alcántara 1976, 4). Land distribution under Cárdenas heavily emphasized the productive and social importance of the collective ejido, which the president envisioned as the key to the future greatness of Mexico. To strengthen this subsector of the agrarian economy, Cárdenas stimulated peasant organization and then actively sought to incorporate ejidatarios into the official party as supportive pillars for state action.[24] His administration also attempted to channel agricultural credit to the ejidos and was notable for its commitment to infrastructure programs, especially irrigation works that were to benefit the ejido sector. Health and education expenditures in rural areas also expanded significantly in this period.

After 1940, however, state policy toward agriculture rapidly moved away from commitment to the economic development of the ejidos. The "developmentalists" who assumed office after Cárdenas identified the future of Mexico with rapid industrialization and with the creation of a strong and entrepreneurial private sector supported and tutored by a dominant state-party apparatus that could establish the conditions they thought necessary for rapid economic growth.[25] Import substitution, informally promoted in the 1930s, was accorded official recognition, and agricultural modernization was to be stimulated through support and services provided to those who owned more than five hectares of land.[26] According to official perspectives, the development of private agriculture would be the "foundation of industrial greatness," and administrations after 1940 sought the means both to encourage its development and to transfer much of its surplus to the industrial economy.[27] In consequence of these policies, the state explicitly turned its back on the promotion and support of the collective ejido, especially during and after the presidency of Miguel Alemán (1946–52), preferring to see ejido lands cultivated by individual members. The potential political power of collective peasant productive units was to be broken because they were considered to present a threat to private property and to the dominance of the state.[28] Ironically, the incorporation of the peasantry into a centralized party apparatus under Cárdenas created the potential for controlling rural protest and demand-making even while policy was being fundamentally altered.

Land distribution slowed during these years, and became more clearly a measure taken to resolve local situations of rural unrest or to reward the loyalty of government supporters. Public investment in agriculture demonstrated a clear trend toward modernization and capital accumulation. Similarly, belief in peasant-based agriculture was abandoned and peasants were stigmatized for being unproductive and technologically backward, a characterization that took on increasing reality as support was rechanneled to the commercial sector and as peasant organizations were destroyed or emasculated by state policy. The 1940s and 1950s were therefore important years for increasing the gap between commercial agriculture—largely centered in the north and northwestern regions of the country, where much of Mexico's political elite originated—and subsistence agriculture—largely made up of the ejido sector and small private farmers who were unable to compete with private commercial interests.

The promotion of modernization on private holdings is evident in the destination of government expenditures for agriculture. Credit for the ejido sector between 1940 and 1970 grew at about 5.4 percent a year, while financing for the commercial sector grew much more rapidly during the 1940s and then more modestly; overall, the growth of financing for commercial agriculture averaged over 25 percent a year and came to account for 45 percent of all state-financed credit for agriculture by the 1960s.[29] While ejidos accounted for the largest number of loans, private farmers received larger loans on average, even though they accounted for only a quarter of all farm families (Yates,

1981, 207–8). Credit for ejidatarios was further encapsulated by bureaucratic procedures and official regulations that stipulated onerous terms for its utilization and repayment.[30] Often credit was tied to the purchase of specific inputs that peasants were ill-prepared to use or that arrived in adulterated form or on schedules with little connection to the agricultural cycle. Irrigation programs, which continued to receive 75–85 percent of all investment in agriculture through 1970, were directed toward large farmers and became the defining characteristic of zones where state-subsidized green revolution research and extension were introduced. In fact, irrigation districts became the focus of agricultural development policies after 1950 and were the areas where the fewest minifundios were located.[31]

Credit, research, extension, distribution of inputs, mechanization, and marketing facilities were all heavily concentrated in these areas, and the productive center of the agricultural economy shifted to the northern parts of the country. Thus, irrigation districts accounted for 93 percent of all official credit and 70 percent of all mechanized farming by 1970. In a survey conducted in the late 1960s, it was discovered that a hectare of irrigated land in Mexico received from five to twelve times the value of green revolution inputs as did a hectare of nonirrigated land (CDIA 1974, 1:362–63). Not incidentally, the ejido sector, which accounted for 57.4 percent of the land in irrigation districts in 1940, controlled only 49.1 percent of that land in 1970. In addition, not evident in these figures are the numerous ejidatarios forced by economic necessity and lack of government support to rent their plots illegally to more prosperous farmers. Moreover, because there were far more ejidatarios than private farmers, there was much more irrigated land per private farmer than ejidatario. Nationally, 24.4 percent of private land was irrigated, while only 15.1 percent of ejido land benefited from irrigation (Yates 1981, 70–71). Public investment in regions dominated by ejido and minifundista agriculture was virtually ignored. By 1970, 12 percent of the country's agricultural units accounted for 42 percent of its productive land, 48 percent of its irrigation and government investment, 73 percent of its machinery, and 61 percent of its green revolution technology, but supplied only 20 percent of its agricultural jobs.[32]

The 1970s witnessed both a resurgence of official interest in agriculture and renewed conflict over policies to shape its development. Under the presidency of Luís Echeverría (1970–76), agricultural development achieved higher priority in national economic planning, due largely to concern for the international ramifications of lagging production and the domestic consequences of a highly skewed distribution of income, especially in rural areas (Grindle 1977; Sanderson 1981). While industrial expansion continued to dominate development plans, state elites became convinced that stimulating the agricultural sector was essential to further economic growth in the country as a whole. Moreover, in the early 1970s, the peasant population was "rediscovered" as an important sector of the agricultural economy, one whose output was to be stimulated and whose social condition was to be improved (see Chapter 8).

During the Echeverría years there was an unusual attempt to return to the agrarian populism of the Cárdenas period by increasing investments in rural development, strengthening the economic position of the ejido sector, and emphasizing the potential for collectivization. According to official plans, much of this was to be accomplished by increasing even further the state's role in rural economic relations. Rural development would be achieved by lessening the dependence of the peasant population on exploitive middlemen and local-level bosses (known as *caciques*), in effect by replacing their activities with those of the state in providing credit, better prices, storage and transportation facilities, infrastructure, extension services, and access to fertilizer and other inputs (Grindle 1977). At the same time, collectivizing the ejido would allow peasant producers to accumulate and invest greater amounts of capital and thus expand their production potential.

Echeverría's policies were pursued by expanding official investments in rural development. By the mid1970s, agriculture accounted for 15 percent of all government investments, compared with the 10 percent or less of Echeverría's predecessors.[33] In addition, absolute amounts of state investment in the sector increased considerably due to renewed efforts to expand the state's presence in the economy.[34] In spite of Echeverría's populism, however, there was not a concerted effort to divert the flow of resources from the large-farm sector to peasant agriculturalists. The irrigation districts continued to receive their lion's share of investment and services, and export-oriented agriculture continued to enjoy its traditional benefits. In cases where the emphasis on peasant agriculture did clash with the interests of the now powerful capitalist farmers, the stage was set for a confrontation between the state and the agricultural entrepreneurs who were in fact creatures of previous state policy.

Throughout 1975 and 1976, land invasions and peasant mobilization occurred in the northern states of Sinaloa and Sonora. Groups of organized peasants, demanding land and government protection, at first followed Echeverría's lead and then increasingly acted independently in the confrontation. Large landowners in these two agriculturally important states declared a strike that required presidential intervention to resolve.[35] Just prior to leaving office in late 1976, Echeverría expropriated 100,000 hectares of land in the state of Sonora and redistributed it to 9,000 peasants, plunging the northwest into a serious political crisis. A federal court subsequently ruled the expropriation illegal. After that, considerable efforts were required to pacify the peasants and landowners involved and to avoid similar unrest elsewhere. Having witnessed the turmoil created by the Echeverrista approach, the succeeding administration, that of José López Portillo, consistently discouraged the use of land distribution as a feasible solution to rural and agrarian problems. In the 1970s, the best land of the nation was rented or owned by a powerful group of entrepreneurs, so thoroughly integrated into the commercial and banking elite of the country that any attempt to expropriate their holdings (at times surpassing the legal limit by thousands of irrigated hectares), or to challenge their position as commercial intermediaries between countryside and city, was likely to bring on a national economic and political crisis. Crisis was also implicit in any effort to promote the kind of local political organization of the peasantry required to increase the productivity, and to defend the bargaining power, of those already in possession of a workable piece of land. Both expropriation and organization implied, to many, an open turn towards socialism; and the traditional concomitant of such fears was the flight of capital. As private capital flowed out of the country, international borrowing became the only way to obtain the considerable resources required to set new development programmes in motion. But borrowing increased indebtedness, which led to monetary instability; and monetary instability hurt everyone. (Hewitt de Alcántara 1980, 34)

It was clear to the regime's politico-bureaucratic elite that the importance of the modern capitalist sector to the national economy in the 1970s was too great to permit the kind of rural instability that accompanied the redistributive efforts of the 1930s. In essence, under the Echeverría administration, the state maintained its long-enjoyed ability to initiate policy, but when opposed by private agricultural interests, it was unable effectively to pursue policy (Bennett and Sharpe 1982).

This constraint became more evident in the late 1970s. By 1980, almost 25 percent of all federal investment was directed toward agricultural and rural development in Mexico, in accordance with development priorities established by the state. Policy makers continued to locate the cause of rural underdevelopment in the previous stimulation of export production, the skewed distribution of government resources toward zones of high potential for such production, the urban bias of pricing policies for basic commodities, and the lack of official support and resources available to peasants. As with the Echeverrista analysis, the state was expected to take an even more active role in the agricultural economy in an effort to redress these imbalances. However, according to the development logic of the López Portillo administration, the role of the state would be to introduce technological change into traditional agriculture, not to substitute for exploitive middlemen. With provision made for differences in peasant production practices and the rationale behind peasant risk-taking, the government would set about stimulating the modernization of peasant agriculture, as it had worked to modernize the large-scale capitalist sector in previous decades.

At the same time, the government maintained and strengthened its commitment to the capitalist farmers, whose economic importance to the country increased steadily. In late 1980, the López Portillo administration passed the Law for Agricultural Development, which was viewed by many as an effort by state elites to reestablish political peace with the large farmers. Among other things, the law, which became effective in 1981, made it possible to establish contracts for land and labor between private and ejido organizations, a measure that amounted to legalizing for the first time the renting of ejido plots and the sale of ejido labor to private farmers. This measure strengthened the ability of medium and large private farmers (both national and transnational) to expand at the expense of the ejidos and to turn ejidatarios into wage laborers. In fact, even while stressing the importance of rural development the government of the late 1970s returned to a model of agricultural modernization that had been dominant since 1940. Technological change, not structural transformation in rural areas, continued to be defined as the key to agricultural development. The large-farm sector would continue to be the primary beneficiary of state development aid, its position ensured by the political and economic threats it could invoke against any signficant policy changes. The Mexican state had, through its own development policies, limited its capacity to alter subsequent policy directions.

In sum, then, agricultural development in Mexico was largely shaped by the extensive role of the state in promoting conditions for increased production. Its efforts included policies to achieve greater equity in rural areas in the 1930s and, after 1940, policies for agricultural modernization targeted for specific regions and groups. The power of the state, which remained considerable over the period in question, was ultimately constrained by that of the capitalist agricultural interests and by the inability of the state itself to affect fundamentally the conditions of peasant agriculture (see Chapter 8).

THE MODERNIZATION OF COLOMBIAN AGRICULTURE

In the four decades between 1940 and 1980, the state played a less decisive role in agricultural development in Colombia than in Mexico; policies specifically intended for the agricultural sector were generally undertaken in response to the political pressure of organized interests—coffee growers, cattlemen, sugar producers, rice growers, cotton producers, or the peak organization of large landowners, the Colombian Agricultural Society. Nevertheless, when state elites did enunciate policies for agricultural development, their rationale was consistently to raise output and stimulate the modernization of what was regarded as an inefficient and backward rural economy (Berry 1975, 258–59). Even the agrarian reform effort undertaken in the 1960s, to be discussed in greater detail in Chapter 7, was justified on the grounds of the need to increase efficiency and productivity in the sector by attacking the traditional and unproductive latifundios and encouraging the development of capitalist forms of production and labor relationships (DNP 1960; Havens, Flinn, and Lastarría-Cornhill 1980). In the 1970s, the emphasis on encouraging growth and capitalist modernization in agriculture intensified as policy makers became newly conscious of the impact that policies to promote industrialization had on the sector and as agricultural organizations themselves promoted technical innovation as the key to greater production and profits.[36] Despite changes in regimes over this period, the dogma of modernization and capitalist expansion was rarely questioned.

Even prior to the 1940s, the state in Colombia was interested in promoting a modern agricultural sector. In the 1920s, for instance, expansion of coffee cultivation at a rate of 10 percent a year encouraged policy makers to assume a large role for the state in the development of infrastructure—communication channels, roads, and ports—in order to link the countryside to international markets. The state began to assume the role of primary provider of credit to the agricultural sector with the creation of the Caja Agraria in 1932. But it was in the 1940s that state elites began more actively to stimulate the modernization of agriculture. Policies to maintain high agricultural prices, to provide ample and cheap credit, to continue to develop basic infrastructure, to improve marketing facilities, and to promote mechanization were pursued with the intent of turning landowners of all descriptions into capitalist entrepreneurs (Kalmanovitz 1978, 28). This phase of activism was cut short by the period known as La Violencia (1946–53), when partisan conflict, especially in rural areas, brought about the paralysis and practical collapse of the state.[37] In the late 1950s, however, the state again became concerned with efforts to modernize the agricultural sector, and budgets for the Ministry of Agriculture and related entities increased considerably (see Tables 4.2 and 4.3).[38]

The 1960s are a notable period for official action toward the agricultural sector because of the agrarian reform initiated in 1961. The legislation of the reform, in the absence of widespread pressure from the peasant population, and the more vigorous pursuit of its measures between 1968 and 1970 under the leadership of President Carlos Lleras Restrepo, indicated the desire of some sectors within the state apparatus to challenge the status quo in rural areas. Nevertheless, the reform itself was effectively stymied by the large landowners, first when they participated in drafting and approving a cumbersome and emasculated reform law, and then when they acted as a serious impediment to its implementation.[39] In the early 1970s, the large landowners, organized into the powerful Colombian Agricultural Society, were able to call a halt to the reform and to the state-promoted peasant mobilization that accompanied it. The Chicorral Agreement, entered into by the state and large landowners in 1972, then initiated a period in which land redistribution was officially disclaimed except when social conditions necessitated it (DNP n.d., 27; Grindle 1980, 28). At the same time, the state promised greatly increased aid to large landowners, primarily in the form of credit on highly favorable terms.

Modernization policies of the 1970s continued to echo efforts of earlier periods, emphasizing credit, infrastructure, and technical innovation for large- and smallholders alike. A large rural development program, DRI (Desarrollo Rural Integrado), which was introduced by the López Michelsen administration in 1976 and adopted by the succeeding Turbay Ayala administration, had as its primary goal the modernization of peasant agriculture through credit, infrastructure development, and the rapid adoption of green revolution inputs. Even when peasant-based agriculture received official concern, however, poverty and low levels of production were defined as technical problems, not redistributional ones. Moreover, administrations of the late 1970s firmly repressed independently organized peasant groups (Bagley and Edel 1980). They also made a commitment to curtail many of the other activities of the state in the sector and to deregulate it, a trend that became apparent in the declining proportions of total expenditures earmarked for agriculture in the late 1970s.

Thus, the military dictatorship of 1953–57 and the semicompetitive oligarchic regime established in 1958 were consistently characterized by the weight of the large landowners in official policy making for the agricultural sector.[40] Numerous semipublic entities, such as the Coffee Growers' Federation and the Cattlemen's Bank, whose responsibilities included the regulation of specific products, were in fact largely free to set their own policies in the name of the state. The Coffee Growers' Federation controlled coffee exports, set prices, and regulated credit and foreign-exchange matters for its members. Similarly, representatives of organized interests sat on the boards of decentralized agricultural agencies and commissions and took an active part in policy making, even for the agrarian reform. When indicative plans for various crops were drawn up by the government in the late 1970s and early 1980s, drafts of the plans were circulated to the peak producer organizations for approval and revision before they were finalized and released by the government.[41] Representatives of the state in turn were invited to serve on the boards of organizations such as the Coffee Growers' Federation and the Colombian Agricultural Society.

More generally, official policy sought to ensure food self-sufficiency by prohibiting the import of foodstuffs except on an emergency basis. Domestic production of both manufactured and agricultural goods was protected, and domestic prices for a number of agricultural products—rice, wheat, and barley, for instance, but not subsistence crops like potatoes—were maintained far above international prices to encourage their production. The political importance of the coffee growers was sufficient to maintain high support prices for this crop, despite the large surpluses and falling international prices that occurred during this period.

By the 1950s, a modern capitalist agricultural sector had begun to emerge. Initially, it represented about 15 percent of the total value of agricultural production. By the 1960s, it had grown to answer for 32 percent of the value of agricultural production, a proportion that rose to 65 percent by the late

1970s.[42] By the late 1960s, state elites had begun to abandon their perspective that the entire rural sector was backward and inefficient. Instead, they began referring to the "modern, efficient" practices of the commercial farmers and to the "inefficiency" of the traditional sector, composed of both latifundios and minifundios (Berry 1975, 270; Grindle 1980). In the 1970s, development plans consistently pointed to a capacity for growth in the modern sector if adequate resources for technical innovation, credit, and infrastructure could be called upon. Originally, peasant farm production had been considered important for its contribution to domestic self-sufficiency, but by this later period peasants had come to be important to the government primarily for "social" reasons (DNP 1980, 2:265).

Policies based on these perspectives were instrumental in encouraging a greater bifurcation of the agrarian economy. Agricultural credit, often at negative real interest rates, was perhaps the most frequent instrument used by state elites to favor the commercial sector. The Fondo Financiero Agrario, a fund set up by the government to loan money for crops and livestock to commercial farmers, disbursed one-third of all private and public credit available for agriculture in the late 1960s and early 1970s.[43] On the other hand, INCORA, the land reform agency, disbursed only 7–15 percent of the available credit, and this went to middle-sized farmers and to smallholders (Kalmanovitz 1978, 357). Even in this institution, half of the available credit was directed to the most economically secure 10 percent of the low-income target population (Vallejo 1977, 97). In the 1970s, the proportion of credit available through the Caja Agraria, set up to respond to smallholders, decreased, while the Fondo showed considerable dynamism, increasing its lending five times between 1974 and 1981 (Colombia 1980; Junguito 1978, 36). INCORA credit resources also declined. Overall, it was estimated that 10 percent of those obtaining credit accounted for 52 percent of the total funds available (Grunig 1969, 22; Araya and Ossa 1976, 15).

Moreover, credit was generally linked to the use of technical inputs like fertilizer, improved seeds, and technical assistance. Three-quarters of all institutional credit was tied to technical assistance, whereas in the case of noninstitutional credit, on which most peasants relied, technical assistance was generally not available. As a result of such credit policies, by 1971 all the cotton and sorghum areas in the country used improved seeds, 60 percent of the sesame, barley, and soybean areas were sown with improved seeds, while only 23.5 percent of the corn areas (the portion of the crop that was grown on flat valley land) and 0.3 percent of the potato areas utilized improved seed (Kalmanovitz 1978, 234; Junguito 1978, 36). This suggests that those with greatest access to official credit—the large landowners, who controlled about 70 percent of the land—were also the beneficiaries of most of the government's emphasis on green revolution innovation, research, and extension.

Credit policies were important in stimulating the mechanization of Colombian agriculture. Loans were easily and cheaply available for agricultural machinery, an overvalued exchange rate encouraged the importation of such machinery, and research and extension services were organized around its utilization.[44] Until 1970, the state financed credit for approximately 30 percent of the value of imported machinery for agriculture; over 65 percent of the tractors in the country were found on plots larger than 50 hectares. By 1980, 35 percent of Colombia's agricultural land was mechanized, principally the flat valley land suitable for machine use; and most of the country's export crops—cotton, soybeans, oil palm, and sugar—were grown on these large mechanized plots.[45] Although the state attempted to program the available credit for specific crops or specific uses in order to assign priorities among them, in fact, organized groups of cultivators and ranchers consistently altered the allocation of resources through their representation in the Fondo. As explained by an expert on the Colombian economy in 1981,

> In fact, the government here doesn't have that much impact on the agricultural sector. Certainly it has much less influence than it thinks it has. . . . The government uses its biggest instrument, credit, as a response rather than as a regulator or director. That is, the amount of credit available for different crops is a response to their profitability. That is, if the price of cotton goes up, the cotton growers pressure the government to extend more credit and the government responds to this.[46]

The green revolution was also channeled primarily to large-scale capitalist agriculture. Official experiment stations were developed in the 1950s and were extended considerably in the 1960s, when commercial farming was developing rapidly. But in the 1970s, research and support activities diminished, after the green revolution had affected large commercial farms but before it had been programmed to reach small farmers (Junguito 1978, 47–48). In addition, research for a number of crops systematically benefited the large landowners. For instance, a national rice research program, established by the government in 1957 and supported in part by the Rockefeller and Ford foundations, the United Nations, the World Bank, and the Interamerican Development Bank, achieved remarkable success in raising rice output in the 1960s and 1970s. The Colombian rice growers association, FEDEARROZ, which represented large growers, collaborated closely with the government in developing and disseminating varieties of rice appropriate for irrigated areas, and the association later took part in determining marketing and price-regulation policies. The upland rain-fed areas of the country, where peasant production predominated, were unable to participate in this technological innovation, and as a result, their output fell from 50 percent of the national total in 1966 to 10 percent in 1974.[47]

Similarly, advances in coffee production technology benefited those who had enough land and capital to obtain credit to purchase new varieties of coffee plants and the fertilizer needed to assure their maximum output (Hall

1978). Moreover, government irrigation projects affected approximately 250,000 hectares between 1950 and 1965; 50 percent of this land was held in parcels larger than 200 hectares, indicating that the majority of state aid for irrigation went to medium and large landowners.

In sum, state policies that were specifically oriented toward the agricultural sector in Colombia treated with approval and support the development of the capitalist sector while increasingly considering the subsistence and semisubsistence sector—or 60 percent of all farm units—to be residual.

MODERNIZING BRAZILIAN AGRICULTURE

Rural Brazil in 1980 was marked by notable differences among regions, by a highly visible maldistribution of resources and wealth in the sector, by the penetration of urban industrial and multinational capital into agribusiness enterprises, and by policies that systematically discriminated among crops, producers, and regions. In all cases, state policies had been central to creating these conditions, but only to the extent that specific regimes supported the welfare of powerful private interests. Significantly, the modernization of Brazilian agriculture was pursued with little regard to issues of equity, poverty, distribution, or employment.

As was the case in many other Latin American countries, the role of the state in Brazil expanded noticeably in the 1930s, closely tied to the process of incipient industrialization. The collapse of the international economy initiated a period of import substitution in Brazil that by the 1940s had become established government policy. In a classic pattern, the state imposed import and exchange controls and assumed a leading role in providing basic infrastructure and industries for industrial development—roads, railroads, banking facilities, public utilities, steel, and energy. At the same time, the coffee-based export economy of the pre-1930 period was saved from collapse by strong state intervention. In contrast to later experience, much of the state's activity in this period was initiated independently of organized political pressure from industrial or agricultural groups, a testimony to the political and economic weakness of these groups in the early period of industrialization (Faucher 1981). At the same time, previously independent coffee producers of the south and sugar producers of the northeast became progressively more dependent as state agencies were developed to regulate the production, distribution, and export of crops (Alcântara de Camargo 1979, 104). In addition, in the 1930s and 1940s, much of the urban working class was mobilized through populist and nationalist programs and incorporated into a competitive regime, after which its capacity for independent action was curtailed.[48]

Brazil's entry into World War II encouraged more state efforts to industrialize the country and to protect the domestic economy. Similarly, the 1950s were noted for the impetus given to industrialization by official policies. During this period, the process of industrialization stimulated the emergence of economically powerful and politically influential groups of industrialists and financiers, in addition to the managers and technocrats of the expanding state bureaucracy. After the military coup of 1964, the accretion of centralized authority to the state accelerated and was accompanied by the development of a close linkage between the military regime, large private-sector interests, especially those located in the São Paulo area, and multinational investors.[49]

Cheap food, agricultural exports, and raw materials for the industrial sector were clearly established as the goals of the state's policy of agricultural modernization in the postwar period. However, Brazil's rural areas were notably less important politically to both regimes in power in this period than the expanding urban and industrial sectors and the elites who dominated them.[50] Until the 1960s, the state restricted most of its efforts to modernize agricultural production to marketing and infrastructure development. After the change to an export-promotion perspective in 1966, the military regime sought to stimulate the production of export crops and their processing, if any, within the country, as well as the manufacture of agricultural equipment. Export incentives, credit, extension, and the stimulation of domestic production of machinery and green revolution inputs were the instruments chosen to achieve these goals. Import preferences and tariff exemptions for agricultural inputs were phased out from the late 1960s to the mid 1970s while protectionist policies were established to stimulate local supply. In general, controls on the prices of domestic food crops served as a disincentive to their production, even while export crops were receiving favorable treatment through government subsidies (Mendonça de Barros and Graham 1980, 5; Skidmore 1973). Nevertheless, these policies were frequently interrupted by stop-gap measures when specific crises, especially food shortages in urban areas, arose.

Among the regions of Brazil, the east and south offer great contrasts to the northeast.[51] After 1940, the east and south rapidly became the most dynamic centers of industrial growth in the country. In seeking to modernize the rural economy to underwrite this industrialization process, the state channeled the vast majority of its limited resources for agriculture to these regions. By the 1970s, modern capitalist agriculture had been adopted in the east and south while the northeast had become increasingly marginalized and was described as a traditional and inefficient agricultural region.

The regional allocation of state investments is clear in a number of cases. Policy makers in the 1950s, for example, considered marketing structures to be fundamental to the modernization of Brazilian agriculture. As a result of investments in infrastructure between 1952 and 1965, the road network in Brazil expanded over two and a half times, and the use of railroads, highways, and shipping increased rapidly, a process that in fact lowered food prices and made staples more readily available in the south. Moreover, while transportation facilities in the country as a whole remained poor and irregular, the east was the primary recipient of state investment (Smith 1969, 221–24; Schuh 1970, 311). Storage facilities to improve marketing, financed in part by the Economic Development Bank (BNDE), also disproportionately benefited the south and east.

In addition, the promotion of green revolution technology reinforced a skewed pattern of regional development. Fertilizers were extensively promoted in the 1950s and 1960s, and consumption became heavily concentrated in the east, where two-thirds of Brazil's total fertilizer was utilized; most of the rest was consumed in the south (Adams 1971, 55). In the early 1970s, the south accounted for 81 percent of the plows in the country (Sorj 1980, 28). The same distribution pattern characterized research and extension services. Historically, 60 percent of all agricultural research was centered in São Paulo, with another 26.7 percent being carried out in the east. In contrast, the north and northeast received 13.3 percent of the total funds allocated for agricultural research from the 1930s to the late 1970s (Mendonça de Barros and Graham 1980, 13). As the number of extension workers expanded fourfold between the 1960s and the early 1970s, the advantages of the east and south were further reinforced. Moreover, by 1960, 89 percent of the tractors in the country were concentrated in two commercial agricultural states, Rio Grande do Sol and São Paulo. The east and south accounted for 95 percent of the country's agricultural machinery by the early 1970s. In contrast, in 1960, the northeast accounted for only 3.7 percent (Clements 1969, 42; Abercrombie 1972, 19). In addition, in 1970, the south accounted for 65 percent of government loans to promote export production (Gomes and Pérez 1979, 68–69).

Within these regions, the distribution of state aid was heavily skewed to the advantage of large-scale producers. For instance, in the programs that sought to ameliorate the endemic drought and deprivation in the poverty-stricken northeast, relief and preventive measures were consistently tailored to the interests of agricultural elites in the region. From the late 1960s to the 1980s, large irrigation works were constructed by a variety of public agencies to alleviate the impact of drought on production and to ease the massive periodic displacement of the rural population. The result of this irrigation policy was to concentrate income among the 1 percent of the northeastern population that controlled 40 percent of the land and most of the water resources; consequently, not only could production be increased on such land, but the owners also benefited from higher land values where the irrigation works existed (Hall 1978). Programs to benefit drought victims—the "work fronts" adopted as a means of crisis control—were managed and controlled by the large landowners, who then used their political and economic influence with displaced peasants to ensure loyalty to the regime. Interestingly, neither irrigation nor the work fronts offered an effective response to the impact of periodic drought.

A number of other alternatives existed for dealing with the drought syndrome of the northeast, but failures of the past continued to be pursued through the 1970s because of the power and advantages they concentrated in the hands of agricultural elites and bureaucratic implementers alike.[52]

The overall structure of agricultural modernization efforts benefited only a few, however, regardless of region. For example, the value of agricultural credit made available at negative real rates of interest doubled between 1950 and 1960 and doubled again from 1960 to 1970. By the late 1970s, official credit programs in Brazil were the fastest growing among developing countries and it was estimated that 1 percent of the landowners laid claim to 40 percent of all loans; conversely, 80 percent of all farmers were excluded from loan activity. Producers of five crops—soybeans, coffee, sugarcane, cotton, and wheat—received 60 percent of the available credit.[53] Much of this money was provided for the purchase of agricultural machinery, which in turn was heavily concentrated in the most dynamic regions of the country.

Loans were also promoted to expand the use of fertilizer. In the 1960s, subsidized loans with negative real interest rates as high as 25 percent achieved wide adoption. Fertilizer was generally distributed without the accompanying technical assistance that would make it more accessible to low-income small farmers; consequently, less than 20 percent of all farms used fertilizer by the early 1970s (Sorj 1980, 28; G. Smith 1969, 226–38). Similarly, official price-support programs were estimated to affect only 10 percent of all producers (G. Smith 1969, 262). After 1966, when the state began to emphasize the domestic production of agricultural inputs, prices for machines and green revolution products rose appreciably, further restricting the use of these inputs to the small number of producers who had access to subsidized credit. So great were the disparities between the agricultural elites and the rest of the rural population that one observer of the allocation of state aid in this country commented, "Perhaps no where [*sic*] in the world are large farmers as coddled as they are in Brazil by generous government subsidies in the form of tax incentives, extremely soft loans, and price supports" (Lassen 1980, 103).

Indeed, the interests of the landowners were rarely challenged in Brazil. In the period before 1964, the control over the rural masses that was traditionally maintained by the landed elites was centrally important to the regime's power.[54] After 1964, the capitalist farm sector gained organizational power and became intertwined with the military regime's favored industrial sector; it was then able to increase its impact on policy making and implementation. Except for a brief period in 1963 and 1964, agrarian reform, or indeed any restructuring of the latifundia system in the country, was never seriously considered.[55] Even the reform efforts of the Goulart government in 1963 and 1964 were powerfully resisted by elements within the military and by the landowners; the threat posed by the reforms is important in explaining the military coup of 1964 (Cehelsky 1979). An extensive agricultural frontier, of course, helps account for the ease with which colonization and migration were chosen as alternatives to structural reform (Hall 1978, chap. 7). Moreover, the developmentalist perspective of the military regime was sympathetic to the modernization of large landholdings and the progressive development of traditional latifundios into modern capitalist enterprises. The 1964 agrarian reform law of the Goulart government was in fact an effort to discourage large unused agricultural properties, not large commercial ones (Cehelsky 1979, 206–7).

The power of the private sector in Brazilian agricultural development is especially evident in efforts to exploit the vast Amazon region. Until the 1940s, the Amazon was viewed by policy makers as a resource to be exploited for the benefit of other regions of the country, a perspective that enhanced the underdevelopment and dependence of the region. Gradually, in the decades that followed, greater emphasis was placed on the capacity of the Amazon to support a modern agricultural sector and to ameliorate some of the grave social and ecological problems of regions like the northeast. By the second half of the 1960s, policy makers were attempting to stimulate the industrialization of the region and the expansion of cattle ranching through the Amazon development agency, SUDAM (Mahar 1979, 28–29; Davis 1977, 36–37). Both industrialization and ranching were encouraged by means of liberal credit and tax incentives and foreign private capital. Thus, the process of development was left largely to the private sector; much of the initiative for it was expected from the São Paulo industrial area (Mahar 1979, 11–12; Davis 1977, 36–37).

In the early 1970s, the state attempted to assume a more assertive role in the region's development, as part of an effort to use the Amazon to absorb excess population and poverty in the northeast and to stimulate colonization of the interior. With this goal in mind, an east-west highway was constructed through Amazonia. Credit, additional infrastructure, subsidized green revolution inputs, support prices, and other mechanisms were to be used to stimulate crop production and colonization. According to development plans of the early 1970s, half a million people were to be settled in the areas between 1972 and 1974, and each family was to receive 100 hectares of land. By 1980, over five million people were to have been settled on the land bordering the highway (Mahar 1979, 18–22). The state was eager to attract private capital to this development effort but was also divided within itself in terms of the specific content of policies. Thus, for example, some agencies (the Ministry of the Interior, the Ministry of Planning, and SUDAM) favored policies that would encourage large investors to utilize advanced technologies, while others (the Ministry of Agriculture and the agrarian reform institute, INCRA) were convinced of the need to pursue a policy that would alleviate social pressures in the region.[56]

In the end, peasant interests and organization were held firmly in check while large foreign and national capitalists were allowed to organize and represent their interests to the state, and the policies that were eventually pursued favored the wealthy few. In fact, when it became apparent that both industrial and agricultural entrepreneurial groups in the São Paulo area desired to expand into the Amazon region to engage in extensive livestock production, some state agencies, eager for their participation, abandoned their earlier preference for crop production and began to speak of the " 'natural vocation' for cattle raising" of the Amazon region (Pompermayer Malori 1980, 10; Foweraker 1981, 155–58). Investors were attracted by cheap land, the low labor requirements of cattle ranching, and a growing domestic and international market for beef. In 1966, a tax incentive program was initiated that provided free financing for up to 75 percent of the costs of cattle production in the region. Eventually, $900 million was made available to 355 ranches, or an average of $2.5 million per ranch.[57] Moreover, what began as plans for state-controlled colonization projects became policies for state-promoted private colonization efforts in the hands of the southern economic elites. Thus, in 1974,

> there occurred a virtual reversal of the policy of occupation of the Amazon's open spaces for the purpose of resolving social and economic problems of the northeast. Instead it was asserted with growing force, the alternative should be "selective economic colonization" of the region, utilizing the small producers from the minifundia of the south of the country. Moreover, colonization should be carried out by private colonization enterprises and not official state agencies.[58]

Renewed official efforts to provide infrastructure for the region in the latter half of the 1970s were expected to create conditions even more suitable for private investment. In summarizing the state's development policy for the northeast and the Amazon, Mahar (1979, 88) notes:

> Since the early 1960s, regional policies in Brazil have clearly been a joint venture of the public and private sectors. In general, the role of the public sector has been to improve the preinvestment conditions of the poorer regions through infrastructure development, colonization, research, and other programs. The private sector, on the other hand, has been entrusted with the establishment of directly productive activities in industry, agriculture, and the services. In this latter endeavor, government has further enhanced the "investment climate" through an impressive array of fiscal incentives.

And, as resources were concentrated in their hands, the elites that benefited from these policies grew stronger and were better able to articulate their interests within policy-making and implementing structures, as the development of the Amazon region suggests.

THE CONSEQUENCES OF IDEOLOGY AND POLICY

The cases of Mexico, Colombia, and Brazil indicate that policies for agricultural modernization were not neutral instruments within the rural economies of these countries, but were in fact frequently decisive in encouraging the concentration of resources in the hands of large landowners and in creating extensive regional disparities. Effectively, the state subsidized the adoption of capitalist forms of production for a small sector of the population while reducing the availability of capital, technology, and infrastructure to the remainder. In the process, it contributed decisively to the emergence of politically and economically powerful interests that became central to subsequent policy making. In the following chapter, we will explore the capitalist agricultural sector to consider what use was made of the advantaged access large landowners had to resources of land, capital, and public services, and what the consequences of this expansion were for overall national development.

5 | Private Advantage and Public Consequences

The expansion of modern capitalist farming in Latin America after 1940 is not apparent in many statistics for the region; instead, the picture that emerges is one of underproductivity, inefficiency, and backwardness in the agricultural sector. In the region as a whole in 1980, approximately 37 percent of the economically active population was found in the agricultural sector, ranging from a low of 14 percent in Argentina to over 50 percent in Bolivia, the Dominican Republic, El Salvador, Guatemala, Haiti, Honduras, and Paraguay (IDB 1980–81; *SALA* 1980, 40). In spite of this large labor force, agriculture contributed less than 11 percent to the gross domestic product of the region in the same year, a figure that varied between 6 and 40 percent by country. In the decade between 1970 and 1980, the gross domestic product of Latin American countries grew by 5.6 percent while the agricultural product increased by 3.5 percent annually (López Córdovez 1982, 8).

Between 1950 and 1975, overall agricultural production increased by an average of 3.2 percent each year.[1] At the same time, the population continued to register a 2.8 percent annual growth rate, which largely negated modest gains in production. Table 5.1, providing indices of agricultural growth, indicates the failure of the sector to grow significantly on a per capita basis. Growth rates actually declined for much of the 1960s and 1970s in Venezuela, Uruguay, Peru, Mexico, Ecuador, the Dominican Republic, and Chile.[2] Moreover, in many countries, agriculture failed dismally to achieve the rates of growth anticipated in government development plans, as is apparent in Table 5.2

But while agricultural production in general grew slowly and in many countries was unable to keep up with the rapid rate of population increase, spectacular growth in the production of specific crops was registered in many countries, especially in the 1970s. Table 5.3 presents data for a number of the more notable success stories in the region for these years. The production of sugar increased by over 200 percent in El Salvador, Guatemala, and Honduras be-

Table 5.1. Indices of Total Agricultural and Food Production in
Latin America, 1948–80

Year	Agricultural Production	Food Production	Per Capita Agricultural Production	Per Capita Food Production
		1952–56 = 100		
1948–52	87	87	97	97
1953	95	95	98	98
1954	100	100	100	100
1955	103	102	100	99
1956	107	109	102	103
1957	111	111	102	102
1958	117	116	105	104
1959	118	114	102	100
1960	120	117	101	99
1961	128	123	105	102
1962	128	125	103	100
1963	132	131	103	102
1964	133	136	101	103
1965	143	140	105	103
1966	140	142	100	101
1967	147	150	102	104
1968	146	151	99	102
1969	153	157	100	103
		1969–71 = 100 (South America only)		
1970	100	102	100	102
1971	102	101	99	99
1972	103	102	98	97
1973	105	106	97	99
1974	114	114	103	103
1975	117	119	103	105
1976	121	127	104	109
1977	126	130	106	109
1978	130	133	106	108
1979	137	139	109	111
1980	139	144	108	112

SOURCE: FAO, *Production Yearbook*, 1970, 1980.

Table 5.2. Growth of Agricultural Production Compared with National Development Plan Goals

Country	Plan Period	Rate of Growth of Agricultural Production	
		Planned	Actual
Argentina	1965–69	4.2	4.3
Bolivia	1962–71	6.3	3.8
Chile	1967–71	3.5	0.6
Colombia	1970–73	5.4	2.4
Costa Rica	1965–68	7.1	7.7
Dominican Republic	1962–69	5.6	1.4
	1970–74	5.6	4.4
Ecuador	1964–73	6.6	1.7
	1973–77	5.3	0.4 (1973–74)
El Salvador	1973–77	5.0	5.3
Guatemala	1971–75	4.8	4.9
Honduras	1965–69	4.6	5.4
Nicaragua	1965–69	6.4	0.6
Panama	1969–72	5.3	1.6
Paraguay	1971–75	5.3	3.9
	1972–74	5.0	5.5
Peru	1961/63-1970	5.6	2.1
	1971–75	4.0	−1.0 (1971–74)
Venezuela	1970–74	6.1	4.3

SOURCE: FAO, *The State of Food and Agriculture*, 1975, 59.

tween the mid1960s and the late 1970s; it increased by over 150 percent in Nicaragua, Panama, and Bolivia in the same period. Beef production in the Dominican Republic grew at an annual rate of 7.6 percent between 1969/70 and 1977/79. Sorghum, practically uncultivated in Brazil before 1970, averaged 253,000 metric tons annually in that country in the late 1970s. In Chile, 46,000 hectares were planted with various fruits in 1973; by 1978, 60,000 hectares were dedicated to the same crops. Similarly, the production of soybeans in Paraguay, which accounted for an average of only 8,000 hectares in the late 1960s, expanded to an average of 287,000 hectares a decade later. By the 1970s, it was estimated that commercial agriculture, largely centered in the large-farm sector, accounted for half of all agricultural production, utilized nearly a third of the cultivated area, and employed a fifth of the work force in Latin America as a whole.[3]

Most of this growth was oriented toward international markets. In the 1940s, rising domestic demand led to increased production of a number of basic foods and a decline in the export of crops other than rice and sugar (FAO, *The State of Food and Agriculture*, 1948, 64–65, 67). Although domestic demand continued to grow rapidly during the subsequent three decades,

Table 5.3. Production of Selected Crops in Latin America, 1962–79

Crop	Country	Average Annual Rate of Increase (%)	
		1962/66–1969/71	1969/71–1977/79
Wheat	Brazil	21.2	4.7
Rice	Colombia	3.0	8.5
	Venezuela	3.2	13.9
Barley	Mexico	3.2	9.8
Sorghum	Argentina	325.9	7.6
	Brazil	—	125.5
	Colombia	—	20.4
	Mexico	32.3	6.0
	Venezuela	—	68.9
Soybeans	Argentina	16.0	63.9
	Brazil	30.0	59.0
	Mexico	39.8	10.5
	Paraguay	30.6	83.3
Cottonseed	Guatemala	9.8	9.6
Cotton	Guatemala	0.3	10.2
Palm oil	Brazil	—	10.0
	Colombia	—	9.1
	Ecuador	—	29.6
	Honduras	—	8.4
Vegetables and melons	Honduras	—	4.9
	Mexico	—	4.6
	Venezuela	—	7.0
Fruits (excl. melons)	Brazil	—	7.0
	Colombia	—	3.9
	Mexico	—	6.2
	Nicaragua	—	10.2
Sugarcane	Bolivia	2.2	14.2
	Brazil	1.5	6.5
	Colombia	−0.7	7.2
	El Salvador	5.2	10.9
	Guatemala	5.7	11.4
	Honduras	11.6	6.4
	Nicaragua	9.5	3.9
	Panama	3.5	10.9
Coffee	Bolivia	29.6	12.4
	Colombia	0.5	3.8
	Nicaragua	3.4	4.5
Tobacco	Brazil	1.5	6.1
	Colombia	−1.2	5.0
Cattle	Argentina	1.3	2.5
	Colombia	3.5	2.5

Table 5.3—*Continued*

Crop	Country	Average Annual Rate of Increase (%)	
		1962/66–1969/71	1969/71–1977/79
	Dominican Republic	1.8	7.6
	Paraguay	−2.1	2.6
Poultry	Bolivia	8.3	10.4
	Brazil	−0.7	5.3
	Costa Rica	11.8	4.1
	Ecuador	3.7	24.0
	El Salvador	1.3	13.9
	Guatemala	8.2	3.5
	Honduras	−4.9	5.5
	Nicaragua	3.7	5.1
	Panama	3.6	4.7
	Peru	−1.1	9.0
	Venezuela	−3.6	8.1

SOURCE: FAO, *Production Yearbook*, 1967, 1979.

price policies that favored urban consumers limited the profitability of production for the mass domestic market. Export production, on the other hand, was frequently encouraged by higher international prices and the growing nexus between Latin American suppliers and markets in the United States.[4] While crops such as coffee, sugar, cotton, and bananas continued to dominate as the exports with highest volume for Latin America, other products showed higher rates of growth: fruits and vegetables from Mexico, Central America, Brazil, Chile, Colombia, and Uruguay; soybeans from Brazil and Argentina; beef and poultry from Mexico, Brazil, Nicaragua, Costa Rica, Argentina, and Venezuela; and cut flowers from Colombia. In the 1970s, the value of agricultural exports from Latin America increased by 95 percent, while volume grew by 28 percent (IDB 1979, 17–18). In addition, domestic demand for higher-priced luxury foodstuffs such as meat, fruits, and vegetables grew as the middle and upper classes expanded in size (FAO, *The State of Food and Agriculture*, 1978, 2/37). After decades of stagnation or decline, the rapid development of livestocking in the 1970s also fueled domestic demand for feed crops such as sorghum, which registered high rates of growth.

Production of these crops expanded hand in hand with the increased use of technology. Tables 5.4 and 5.5 indicate rapid growth in the use of fertilizer and mechanization (tractors). Table 5.4 underscores the importance of the 1960s for the rapid adoption of fertilizer. In that decade, fertilizer consumption grew by 21 percent a year, a trend that continued at a rate of 26 percent a year in the 1970s in spite of greatly increased prices, which were especially onerous for countries that had to rely primarily on imports to satisfy domestic demand.

Table 5.4. Fertilizer Consumption in Latin America, 1940-79
(1,000 Metric Tons)

Country	ca. 1940	ca. 1950	ca. 1960	ca. 1970	1978/79
Argentina	0.5	12.5	12.3	79.7	86
Bolivia	—	—	0.4	2.8	4
Brazil	1.9	31.5	181.9	601.3	3,222
Chile	16.6	37.6	93.5	145.4	127
Colombia	—	8.0	29.3	157.7	273
Costa Rica	—	0.8	5.1	53.0	80
Dominican Republic	—	0.4	10.8	24.5	62
Ecuador	—	1.4	6.7	54.3	70
El Salvador	—	0.8	41.3	61.5	112
Guatemala	—	5.8	10.4	24.1	100
Honduras	—	2.0	7.1	22.5	23
Mexico	2.8	9.4	172.5	533.7	1,067
Nicaragua	—	—	0.5	33.5	48
Panama	—	1.0	—	14.3	23
Paraguay	—	—	—	2.9	3
Peru	43.1	51.1	54.2	81.6	128
Uruguay	0.5	1.7	6.0	46.2	58
Venezuela	—	2.2	16.3	47.0	197
Total	65.4	166.2	648.3	1,986.0	6,127

NOTE: Nitrogenous, phosphate, and potash fertilizers.

SOURCES: FAO, *Production Yearbook*, 1950, 1960, 1970; *SALA* 1983.

The application of fertilizers was a fundamental cause of the rising yields that became more important as opportunities for land extension declined.

Taking advantage of easy long-term credit programs, agricultural entrepreneurs increased the number of tractors in use sixfold between 1950 and 1981. The use of tractors in agriculture increased most rapidly in the 1950s, as is evident in Table 5.5. Estimates indicate that in Latin America as a whole there were approximately 20,000 tractors in use in 1930; 35,000 by 1940; and nearly 400,000 by 1960. There were more than 600,000 tractors in use by 1970, and this figure rose to over 800,000 by 1981.[5] In the early 1970s, it was estimated that there was approximately one tractor for every 50–100 cultivated hectares in commercial agricultural zones.[6] The use of improved seeds, herbicides, and pesticides also expanded impressively in the 1960s and 1970s. For example, use of pesticides grew by 8.4 percent annually in the 1970s (López Córdovez 1982, 17). Irrigated cropland, essential in most cases for the proper utilization of both chemical and biological innovations, also increased markedly (see Table 5.6). Overall, there was significant growth in the expendi-

Table 5.5. Tractors Used in Agriculture in Latin America, 1947–81

Country	1947	1958	1961/65	1969/71	1981
Argentina	18,777	82,000	150,000	171,450	158,900
Bolivia	579	20	—	355	740
Brazil	4,672	48,773	56,803*	168,257	340,000
Chile	4,143	14,966	22,307	21,523	34,650
Colombia	2,795	19,599	27,600	22,780	29,000
Costa Rica	392	548	4,454	5,100	6,000
Dominican Republic	298	—	2,330	2,510	3,220
Ecuador	549	1,517	1,611	3,133	6,844
El Salvador	—	1,200	—	2,510	3,320
Guatemala	631	—	—	3,167	4,020
Honduras	248	—	348	1,693	3,280
Mexico	17,035	39,000	64,800	91,318	125,000
Nicaragua	255	2,400	—	—	2,250
Panama	268	1,643	—	2,414	4,050
Paraguay	55	—	—	2,200	3,300
Peru	2,343	6,350	7,168	10,902	14,300
Uruguay	2,890	23,200	24,695	26,659	28,400
Venezuela	4,403	10,171	13,115	19,200	39,000

SOURCE: FAO, *Production Yearbook*, 1950, 1960, 1970, 1982.
*1959.

tures on modern inputs on medium and large landholdings between 1960 and 1980 (see Table 5.7).

In addition to increased production of specific crops and the utilization of modern inputs, the expansion of capitalist agriculture was affected by the penetration of foreign capital in agribusiness enterprises. As both domestic and international demand for luxury foodstuffs grew, food-processing corporations expanded their facilities in Latin American countries. Between 1966 and 1978, U.S. investment in this industry grew from $365 million to $1.04 billion, expanding from 15 percent to 21 percent of total U.S. direct foreign investment in Latin America.[7] This investment was heavily concentrated in Argentina, Brazil, Mexico, and Venezuela, where the growing middle and upper classes accounted for increased consumption of snack and convenience foods. Moreover, as demand grew for fertilizer, pesticides, herbicides, and improved seeds, companies such as du Pont, W. R. Grace, Monsanto, Exxon, and Allied Chemicals were increasingly in evidence. And as tractors were more widely utilized in Latin America, corporations such as International Harvester, John Deere, Massey Ferguson, and Ford not only increased their imports to Latin America, they also opened assembly and production facilities (Burbach and Flynn 1980, pts. 2–3).

Table 5.6. Irrigated Cropland in Latin America, 1950–78 (1,000 Hectares)

Country	ca. 1950/55	ca. 1960	1979
Argentina	1,500	1,555	1,560
Bolivia	64	64	125
Brazil	141	462	1,700
Chile	1,363	1,103	1,252
Colombia	505	226	305
Costa Rica	15	26	26
Dominican Republic	135	110	145
Ecuador	24	463*	520
El Salvador	5	—	102
Guatemala	32	32	66
Honduras	33	66	80
Mexico	2,504	3,515	5,100
Nicaragua	2	29†	78
Panama	8	14	28
Paraguay	12	9	55
Peru	1,212	1,078‡	1,180
Uruguay	26	42‡	70
Venezuela	246	218	310

SOURCES: *SALA* 1960; FAO, *Production Yearbook*, 1970, 1982.
* 1968.
† 1967.
‡ 1966.

Foreign capital became widely involved in the actual production of crops and livestock and also participated more in the financing, processing, and distribution of agricultural commodities.[8] In the state of Sinaloa in northern Mexico, for instance, 20–40 percent of the credit for agricultural production came from foreign sources in the 1970s. In some cases—beef in Argentina, for instance—the amount of foreign capital decreased in production while it increased in the packing and processing industries. In Mexico and Central America, contract production linked national producers with transnational capital. Agricultural capital from foreign bank loans often competed with capital made available by the state, as in the case of the Bank of America in Guatemala, which was heavily involved in major projects and nontraditional export loans (Nairn 1981). As might be expected, most of the foreign investment, especially that connected with mechanization and green revolution technology, was concentrated in the countries with the largest commercial agricultural sectors.

Table 5.7. Expenditures of Medium- and Large-sized Crop-raising and Livestock-raising Farms, Latin America, 1960–80 (Percentages)

Type of Expenditure	Percentage of Expenditure				Rate of Growth (%)	
	1960	1970	1980		1960/70	1970/80
Capital expenditure						
Buildings, irrigation works, and soil preparation	5.4	6.3	6.7		4.6	5.0
Plantations, market gardens, and vineyards	2.6	2.9	3.0		4.2	5.2
Machinery, equipment, implements, means of transport	6.2	8.2	11.4		6.5	7.9
Breeding animals and draught animals	6.8	5.6	4.9		2.3	2.9
Subtotal	21.0	23.0	26.0	Average	4.5	5.7
Operating costs						
Wages	31.6	24.6	18.1		1.0	1.2
Seeds, fertilizers, and pesticides	19.4	21.6	23.0		4.7	5.1
Fuels, lubricants, hire of machinery	5.1	7.1	9.5		7.0	7.5
Leasing of land, water, and working animals	3.3	3.9	3.8		5.3	4.2
Animal feedstuffs, vaccinations, and medicines	12.8	13.1	13.0		3.8	4.4
Interest and other financial costs	3.8	3.8	3.5		3.6	3.8
Other	3.0	3.2	3.1		3.2	4.2
Subtotal	79.0	77.0	74.0	Average	3.2	4.0
Total	100.0	100.0	100.0	Average	3.5	4.4

SOURCE: López Córdovez 1982, 22; based on national agricultural censuses and additional data.

Table 5.8. Area Planted and Production of Selected Staple Crops, 1969–80

Crop and Country	Area Planted (1,000 Hectares)		Production (1,000 Metric Tons)	
	1969–71	1978–80	1969–71	1978–80
Beans				
Costa Rica	22	21	9	11
Ecuador	78	45	36	24
Mexico	1,789	1,523	904	893
Panama	16	14	5	4
Peru	77	73	62	56
Venezuela	97	69	34	40
Cassava				
Argentina	26	21	296	188
Bolivia	18	16	223	219
Ecuador	35	22	382	179
Venezuela	39	38	317	345
Corn				
Argentina	3,880	2,624	8,717	8,203
Colombia	684	637	856	848
Costa Rica	50	39	56	64
Dominican Republic	27	22	46	62
Ecuador	312	204	239	209
Guatemala	671	621	751	968
Mexico	7,412	6,647	9,025	10,045
Nicaragua	260	188	238	217
Panama	77	66	66	64
Peru	373	351	605	565
Uruguay	194	130	161	121
Venezuela	606	494	698	745
Potatoes				
Argentina	190	110	2,212	1,618
Brazil	214	198	1,557	2,032
Ecuador	47	28	560	286
Peru	293	253	1,877	1,636
Uruguay	22	21	135	137

SOURCE: FAO, *Production Yearbook*, 1982.

UNANTICIPATED CONSEQUENCES OF MODERNIZATION

Increased production of specific crops (especially those for export), rapid capitalization in terms of mechanization and green revolution technology and irrigation, and increased penetration of foreign capital were intimately related to the accumulation of wealth and power in the hands of a small agricultural elite. As we saw in Chapter 5, the state was central to the emergence of this elite. Subsidized credit was frequently available to encourage innovation on larger landholdings; market information and guaranteed prices or markets permitted further risk-taking and more aggressive entrepreneurship; transportation networks and storage and marketing facilities greatly decreased the chances of crop loss and spurred more responsiveness to domestic and international markets. At the same time, direct linkages between financial institutions and food processors, distributors, and retailers increased at the regional, national, and international levels. However, the prosperity of the agricultural entrepreneurs was not the central goal of the state policy makers who sought to encourage modernization. Within the context of the development ideologies they had adopted, Latin American policy makers wanted capitalist agriculture to expand in order to resolve a number of severe problems in their countries—underproductivity, economic dependence, rural backwardness, and a variety of impediments to industrial development. Instead, however, a series of conditions was generated that state elites came to believe was actually detrimental to the achievement of national and rural development.

Staple Crops, Food Imports, and Dependency

Agricultural modernization, in the form it assumed in Latin America, resulted in the substitution of highly remunerative crops for humbler ones such as corn, beans, potatoes, and cassava, which were the staples of national diets. As the urban population grew and as domestic demand for high-priced goods such as meats, fruits, and vegetables rose, production of these commodities promised higher profits than could be earned from basic crops, whose prices were generally controlled by state policies. International demand for sugar and commodities such as coffee, cotton, livestock, and tobacco also encouraged those with the necessary technical, managerial, and financial ability to switch from less remunerative to more profitable crops. In some cases, the close association between growers and processors or distributors and contract agriculture stimulated shifts in production.[9]

Table 5.8 indicates the decline in the amount of land devoted to several basic crops that occurred in a number of countries in the 1970s. In some cases, as with corn in Costa Rica, the Dominican Republic, Guatemala, Mexico, and Venezuela, this decline in area was compensated for by an increase in yield. However, in the majority of cases, decreased area was accompanied by a lower level of output. Food staples were generally replaced by more remunerative products; fruits and livestock frequently replaced wheat and sugarbeets in Chile; sorghum was substituted for corn in Mexico and Brazil; livestock encroached on lands formerly given over to basic crops in Costa Rica, Mexico, Brazil, Venezuela, and a number of other countries.[10] In the 1970s, the effects of the expansion of livestocking were particularly notable.[11] Between 1961/65 and 1979, cropland increased only moderately compared to the expansion of permanent pastures in Costa Rica, the Dominican Republic, Colombia, Panama, and Honduras. Cropland actually decreased in Mexico and Venezuela (see Table 5.9).

Changes in the kinds of crops produced, in addition to population growth, were clearly related to rising food import bills in almost all countries of the region in the 1970s (see Table 5.10). Between 1970 and 1980, the import of agricultural products increased an average of 8 percent a year, and represented 12 percent of the total supply in Latin America. Imports rose in current dollar value from 6.8 billion in 1969/71 to 23.1 billion in 1977/79 (López Córdovez 1982, 20). The effects of crop substitution and of declining production of basic

Table 5.9. Land Use in Latin America, 1961/65–1979 (1,000 Hectares)

Country	Arable and Permanent Cropland			Land Under Permanent Pasture		
	1961/65	1979	% Increase or Decrease	1961/65	1979	% Increase or Decrease
Argentina	28,098	35,120	25.0	146,500	143,300	−2.2
Bolivia	1,503	3,337	122.0	28,353	27,100	−4.4
Brazil	30,254	61,500	103.2	131,880	158,000	19.8
Chile	4,206	5,530	31.5	9,850	11,850	20.3
Colombia	5,051	5,600	10.8	16,682	30,000	79.8
Costa Rica	484	490	1.2	969	1,558	60.8
Dominican Republic	1,020	1,230	20.6	1,020	1,500	47.1
Ecuador	2,518	2,615	3.9	2,200	2,560	16.4
El Salvador	655	710	8.4	606	610	0.6
Guatemala	1,442	1,810	25.5	1,039	880	−15.3
Honduras	1,499	1,757	17.2	2,000	3,400	70.0
Mexico	23,613	23,220	−1.7	74,499	74,499	0.0
Nicaragua	1,335	1,511	13.2	3,384	3,400	0.5
Panama	562	570	1.4	910	1,161	27.6
Paraguay	852	1,195	40.3	13,800	15,200	10.1
Peru	2,351	3,430	45.9	27,977	27,120	−3.1
Uruguay	1,779	1,910	7.4	13,769	13,753	−0.1
Venezuela	5,218	3,705	−29.0	14,229	17,150	20.5

SOURCE: FAO, *Production Yearbook*, 1979, 1982.

crops are especially evident when the experiences of specific countries are considered. In the late 1970s, for instance, Ecuador increased its wheat imports by 38 percent and barley imports by 184 percent at the same time that its agricultural exports were increasing markedly (ECLA 1978, 224–25). In 1980, Chile imported 49 percent of its wheat, 47 percent of its corn, and 76 percent of its sugar, compared with 46, 29, and 56 percent, respectively, in the previous five years (USDA 1980, 26). Peru tripled its corn imports in 1980 and made sizable foreign purchases of rice, sugar, edible oils, and dairy products (USDA 1980, 30). By 1980, Venezuela was importing 62 percent of the grains it consumed, 52 percent of its pulses, 40 percent of its sugar, a third of its dairy products, and more than a tenth of its meat products; imports continued to rise in the early 1980s (USDA 1980, 34). In the region in general, agricultural exports increased steadily, but they did not keep pace with imported products, as Figure 5.1 demonstrates.

Agricultural exports brought high earnings in the 1960s and early 1970s, when economies in the industrialized world were expanding. After 1973, however, economic stagnation in these same countries affected export earnings in Latin American agriculture while the cost of imported food, fertilizer, oil, and capital goods rose appreciably. As seen in Table 5.11, the import value of agricultural requisites grew significantly in the 1970s. The importation of basic food items and agricultural requisites on a massive scale contributed to balance-of-trade problems and was cited by Latin American governments as clear evidence of the region's increasing dependence on countries such as the

Table 5.10. Index of Import Value of Agricultural Food and Products, Latin America, 1969–80 (1969/71 = 100)

Year	Agricultural Products		Food Products	
	Unit Value	Total Value	Unit Value	Total Value
1969	98	93	98	94
1970	99	99	98	99
1971	104	108	104	107
1972	114	125	115	127
1973	155	193	158	199
1974	213	307	218	323
1975	225	283	237	304
1976	210	288	215	303
1977	203	310	197	315
1978	214	380	211	396
1979	243	464	236	468
1980	272	663	272	709

SOURCE: FAO, *Trade Yearbook*, 1982.

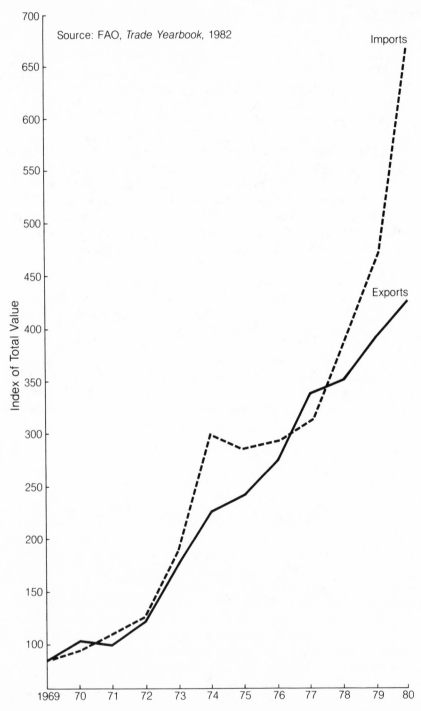

Figure 5.1. Index of Value of Exports and Imports in Latin America, 1969–80

United States, which alleviated much of the food deficit. Given the fact that agricultural exports were often an expansive foreign-exchange earner, some argued that Latin American countries should pursue their comparative advantage in such exports and resign themselves to importing the agricultural products that domestic producers could not grow efficiently (Pinto 1980). The preponderant view, however, was that the increasing import of food, particularly of staples that the countries had historically demonstrated the capacity to produce, represented an undesirable use of increasingly scarce foreign exchange and unacceptable economic and political vulnerability to food-exporting nations. Appropriate public policies, it was contended, should stimulate production for both domestic and export markets (Mexico 1980).

Unemployment and Underemployment

As we have seen, extensive mechanization accompanied the modernization of agriculture in the region. For Latin American societies, with their large labor surpluses and massive rural unemployment and underemployment, a heady expansion of mechanization often exacerbated labor and employment problems (Abercrombie 1972). In some cases, mechanization facilitated frontier expansion and this increased the potential for labor absorption (Sanders and Ruttan 1978). But in many settled agricultural areas, mechanization made it possible to expand the amount of land under cultivation on large landholdings through the utilization of areas that had formerly been consigned to sharecroppers and tenants and to expand production while reducing the amount of labor required. Abercrombie estimates that in Chile, each tractor replaced about three workers, and that in Colombia and Guatemala, four workers were similarly displaced.[12] Of course, some of this excess labor was absorbed elsewhere on commercial enterprises, such as in the labor-intensive application of green revolution inputs, or in the production of such labor-intensive crops as fruits and vegetables, but most of the excess labor was forced to migrate to urban areas or to remain in the rural areas, unemployed or underemployed. In most countries, job opportunities in the industrial sector did not expand as rapidly as agricultural employment declined; instead, the service sector absorbed the lion's share of those seeking work, often in highly insecure, informal, and low-paying jobs (see Table 5.12).

Mechanization also used up scarce capital and foreign exchange—most countries imported the bulk of the agricultural machinery used, and imports often tended to be heavy-duty, high-horsepower vehicles that did not meet the needs or financial capabilities of small producers. Since mechanization did not generally have a significant impact on yield per hectare, especially when compared to irrigation and green revolution inputs, it actually added to existing employment and foreign-trade deficits without bringing major benefits to

Table 5.11. Import Value of Agricultural Requisites, Latin America, 1973–80 (Thousands of 1975 U.S. Dollars)

Country	1973	1974	1975	1976	1977	1978	1979	1980
Argentina	32,141	55,412	52,619	25,711	67,480	57,819	91,045	102,458
Brazil	463,613	872,594	775,237	532,227	540,168	494,437	496,906	634,928
Chile	79,509	119,077	70,837	43,614	42,391	42,749	49,770	72,394
Colombia	66,434	123,442	77,093	41,042	79,484	88,170	65,183	84,433
Costa Rica	34,667	58,453	69,392	53,789	62,802	54,880	49,061	52,229
Dominican Republic	13,729	8,838	19,936	24,078	27,080	27,428	26,105	45,304
Ecuador	18,930	45,938	86,696	47,301	51,713	70,369	33,216	54,812
El Salvador	33,875	59,764	62,319	40,189	56,088	33,021	39,352	28,563
Guatemala	32,842	62,766	72,748	44,913	68,190	54,476	55,016	49,388
Honduras	19,393	23,579	28,752	28,585	41,231	34,344	42,776	37,079
Mexico	114,839	195,652	306,824	247,126	177,227	324,606	240,603	166,521
Nicaragua	25,638	52,123	39,549	24,202	46,670	45,562	13,836	46,174
Paraguay	5,338	7,445	10,590	8,321	6,863	7,338	10,598	12,324
Peru	44,033	37,656	99,837	37,167	44,595	42,097	38,166	52,065
Venezuela	39,070	87,041	178,606	153,110	220,608	205,420	88,340	130,376

SOURCE: Elaborated from FAO, *Trade Yearbook*, 1979, 1982.

NOTE: Requisites include crude fertilizers, manufactured fertilizers, pesticides, and agricultural machines.

Table 5.12. Relative Distribution of Economically Active Population by
Economic Sector in Four Latin American Countries, 1940–73 (Percentages)

Country and Year	Primary Sector	Secondary Sector	Tertiary Sector
Costa Rica			
1950	54.73	16.12	29.15
1963	49.16	18.71	32.13
1973	36.43	19.84	43.73
Chile			
1940	34.95	25.51	39.54
1952	30.07	29.36	40.57
1960	27.73	28.23	44.04
1970	21.18	25.34	53.48
Peru			
1940	62.46	23.54	14.00
1961	49.79	27.92	22.29
1970	45.06	30.80	24.14
Brazil			
1940	64.00	10.10	25.90
1950	59.90	13.70	26.40
1960	53.70	13.10	33.20
1970	44.20	17.80	37.90
1973	40.80	20.20	39.00

SOURCE: *ECIEL* 1979.

compensate for its negative impact. Mechanization did little to discourage the traditional pattern of extensive rather than intensive use of land, and in general it supported the inefficiency of land utilization on large landholdings.[13]

Land Concentration and Labor Relations

In a pattern similar to that which characterized the development of agrarian capitalism in the nineteenth and early twentieth centuries, an increase in the concentration of landholdings also accompanied the expansion of capitalist agriculture after 1940. Table 5.13 provides recent census data on landholding patterns in a number of Latin American countries. It is apparent that in Brazil, Colombia, Ecuador, Mexico, Nicaragua, and Venezuela, the medium-sized and large farms expanded both numerically and in terms of the amount of land they controlled. Moreover, this concentration of landholdings pro-

Table 5.13. Landholding Patterns in Latin America, 1960–75

Size of Holding in Hectares	Percentage of Holdings	Percentage of Area	Percentage of Holdings	Percentage of Area
		Argentina		
		1960		*1969*
0–5	15.7	0.1	18.2	0.1
5–25	24.0	0.9	23.0	0.8
25–100	27.9	4.4	26.0	3.9
100–1,000	26.7	20.1	26.6	20.6
1,000+	5.7	74.5	6.2	74.6
Total n =	475,173	h =175,142,000	n = 527,744	h =209,120,083
		Brazil		
		1970		*1975*
0–5	36.6	1.3	38.6	1.2
5–20	30.2	5.5	28.4	4.7
20–100	23.6	16.7	23.3	15.5
100–1,000	8.5	36.9	8.8	35.9
1,000+	0.7	39.6	0.9	42.7
Not reported	0.4			
Total n =	4,924,019	h =294,145,466	n = 5,007,169	h =322,621,000
		Colombia		
		1960		*1970/71*
0–5	62.6	4.5	59.5	3.7
5–20	23.4	10.0	23.6	8.6
20–100	10.5	19.5	12.6	20.2
100–1,000	3.3	35.6	4.0	37.0
1,000+	0.2	30.4	0.3	30.5
Total n =	1,209,672	h = 27,337,800	n = 1,176,811	h = 30,993,200
		Costa Rica		
		1963		*1973*
0.2–10	52.7	4.8	57.6	3.9
10–200	44.3	44.4	38.9	41.6
200+	3.0	50.8	3.5	54.4
		Ecuador		
		1954		*1974*
0–5	81.7	10.8	69.7	7.8
5–20	12.7	10.0	18.5	13.0
20–100	5.4	14.9	9.9	28.7
100–1,000+	1.2	64.4	1.9	50.7

Table 5.13—*Continued*

Size of Holding in Hectares	Percentage of Holdings	Percentage of Area	Percentage of Holdings	Percentage of Area
		Honduras		
		1952		*1974*
0–5	57	8	64	9
5–20	30	18	25	18
20–100	12	28	10	30
100–1,000	2	26	2	29
1,000+	—	28	—	22
Total n =	156,135	h = 2,507,404	n = 195,341	h = 2,629,859
		Mexico*		
		1960		*1970*
0–5	65.9	0.8	61.0	1.2
5–25	16.6	1.6	20.4	3.5
25–100	9.4	5.5	11.0	8.5
100–1,000	6.4	15.2	6.6	27.1
1,000+	1.7	78.4	1.0	59.7
Total n =	1,337,732	h = 13,490,000	n = 824,939	h = 25,662,800
		Nicaragua		
		1963		*1971*
0–7	50.8	3.4	43.8	2.2
7–35	27.4	11.3	31.7	11.2
35–350	20.3	44.1	22.6	39.9
350+	1.5	41.2	1.9	46.7
		Venezuela		
		1961		*1971*
0–5	50.1	1.4	42.9	1.0
5–20	31.0	3.5	31.9	3.1
20–100	12.5	5.9	16.4	6.9
100–1,000	5.1	17.5	7.1	22.0
1,000+	1.3	71.7	1.7	67.0
Total n =	320,094	h = 26,004,862	n = 283,616	h = 26,526,365

SOURCES: For Argentina, Brazil, Colombia, Ecuador (1974), Mexico, Nicaragua, and Venezuela, see Lott 1979. For Costa Rica, see Guess 1979, 51. For Ecuador (1954), see Farrell and da Ros 1983. For Honduras, see Ruhl 1984, 50.

* Private property only; excludes ejidos and other communal property.

foundly altered the structure of the labor force in Latin America. Throughout the region, tenants and sharecroppers were replaced by agricultural workers, and permanent workers were displaced by part-time laborers.[14] Given these changes, landowners could minimize the costs of maintaining a labor force through periods when it was not needed and expand cropping or livestocking areas by taking over lands that had been assigned to resident laborers, tenants, and sharecroppers. Labor costs were thus reduced for the entrepreneur, and the available pool of laborers, forced to provide for their own maintenance during inactive periods, was enlarged. Moreover, by replacing permanent workers with part-time ones, employers were able to avoid paying the social welfare benefits and bonuses required by law for permanent workers. In some areas where large agricultural frontiers existed, as in Brazil, displaced workers cleared and prepared land for future commercial use in exchange for temporary subsistence rights to the land.

In Costa Rica, prosperous farmers consciously reduced their demand for labor because of legal wage and benefit requirements and subsidized credit for mechanization and beef production. Similarly, use of herbicides, new varieties of coffee plants, and mechanized processing were introduced to reduce labor costs (Lassen 1980, 128). In rice and cotton production, tenant and sharecropping schemes declined all over the region. In Chile, mechanization has been credited with displacing the labor tenant on large haciendas and with introducing an agricultural proletariat. In 1935, 21 percent of the economically active rural population of that country was classified as labor tenant (*inquilino*); in 1955, the proportion was 12 percent; by 1965, it had declined to 6 percent (Kay 1977, 114–15). Between 1965 and 1976, the number of permanent wage laborers in Chile declined by 22.8 percent, while the number of temporary workers increased by 36.6 percent (Ortega 1982, 95–96). In El Salvador, 12 percent of the rural population was without land in 1961; in 1975, the proportion was reported to be 41 percent (Burbach and Flynn 1980, 147). In some cases, wages were maintained at such low levels that a labor shortage developed, thereby encouraging more mechanization. In Bolivia, for example, laborers preferred to work in neighboring Argentina or to migrate to urban areas rather than work in the commercial sugarcane areas of Santa Cruz Province (USDA 1980, 22). In Venezuela, urban migration was chosen as an alternative to agricultural labor; immigration from Colombia—often illegal—was encouraged, and employers thus avoided many legal requirements for remunerating workers.

In the four decades after 1940, then, the capitalist agricultural sector of Latin America adopted modern technology and increasingly utilized wage labor, but from the perspective of the state elites concerned with overall economic development, it did not necessarily make the best use of land, labor, or capital. In Mexico, Colombia, and Brazil, for instance, unintended consequences of agricultural modernization emerged.

CAPITALIST EXPANSION IN MEXICO, COLOMBIA, AND BRAZIL

Mexico

Mexico's agricultural entrepreneurs were among the most successful in Latin America in the period after 1940. Their success story is based on a number of impressive developments that were especially notable during the 1950s: the rising export of products such as cotton, livestock, fruits, vegetables, and coffee; rapid increases in the yield of crops such as wheat and cotton through advances in green revolution technology; greater production of corn, beans, coffee, and sugarcane on a rapidly expanding agricultural frontier; and a high rate of transfer of savings to the urban and industrial sectors.[15] Spectacular increases in the yield of a wide variety of crops and livestock were registered, especially from the 1940s to the mid1960s. During that period, wheat and bean production grew fourfold; rice, cotton, and coffee production doubled, and corn and sugar supplies increased threefold. Vegetable and livestock production also grew impressively. Overall, agricultural production grew at a rate of 6.9 percent in the decade after 1945, far outstripping growth in other Latin American countries (Hewitt de Alcántara 1976, 102). Expanding domestic demand was met adequately by these increases, and much-needed foreign exchange was channeled into the economy from rising exports. Through 1970, about 55 percent of the value of Mexico's exports was generated by agriculture, a figure that declined to about 25 percent in the late 1970s because of the rapid expansion of oil exports. From the perspective of policy makers who wished to see agricultural production expand and support the country's drive toward industrialization, this early dynamism was encouraging.

The takeoff experienced by Mexican agriculture in the 1940s and 1950s came largely as a result of the massive investments made by the state in infrastructure development and the growth in the land area under cultivation (Venezian and Gamble 1969, 58–59). The expansion to new areas was made possible by public investment, especially in transportation and irrigation. Improvements in production related to the application of green revolution inputs became important only in the latter part of the 1950s and later, when suitable new lands became scarce and public expenditures in agricultural development were cut back. In fact, lagging production of crops in the late 1950s encouraged many farmers to adopt the use of fertilizer, improved seeds, and insecticides (Hewitt de Alcántara 1976, 102). Table 5.4 indicates that major increases in the use of fertilizer occurred after 1950 and continued in the 1960s. Similarly, mechanization advanced rapidly and Mexico became one of the countries with the highest concentration of agricultural mechanization in Latin America (see Table 5.5). A million hectares of land were also brought under irrigation in the 1950s. State policies to subsidize the use of these technologies were fundamental in encouraging adoption of new methods. Thus, as Hewitt de Alcántara (1976, 309) reports with regard to wheat,

> As proof of the greater productivity of the new system of wheat cultivation became irrefutable, large farmers adopted it, but only within the framework of a federal investment programme which poured billions of pesos into irrigation works, roads, storage facilities, electricity, railroads, long term agricultural credit, and ultimately, into a guaranteed price for wheat so high that it involved a national subsidy to wheat farmers of some 250 million pesos a year. The adherence of the most progressive large landowners of the nation to the "green revolution" in wheat was thus bought with public funds at a very high price.

Thus, with credit, infrastructure, storage and marketing facilities, green revolution inputs, and mechanization concentrated in their hands, the entrepreneurs of Mexico's rural economy grew wealthy and powerful—so powerful, in fact, that they were able to challenge the hegemony of the strong presidential system in the 1970s (see Chapter 4). Their activities boosted production significantly for two decades and encouraged state elites to believe that the country's agricultural and rural problems were being solved through modernization. After this period, however, a variety of problems emerged that called attention to the gap between the private advantage of wealthy farmers and the developmental needs of the country.

First, a disparity developed in the production of crops for export and those intended for domestic consumption. Initially, the newly promoted modern agriculture was to supply urban areas with cheap food and fill government coffers with foreign exchange from export production. Until the mid1960s, production of crops such as corn and wheat grew impressively and lessened the need to import food. In 1945, 14 percent of all imports to Mexico consisted of foodstuffs; by 1955, agricultural expansion and modernization in irrigated zones had reduced this proportion to less than 4 percent (Hewitt de Alcántara 1976, 106). This rapid agricultural development was all the more impressive considering that the 1940s and 1950s witnessed extensive urbanization that increased the demand for food.

But state pricing policies discouraged the capitalist sector from producing basic crops for domestic consumption; conversely, proximity to the United States and official incentives for agricultural exports led to much-increased production of sugarcane, coffee, henequen, livestock, feed grains, fruits, and vegetables.[16] Increasingly, the ejidatarios and private smallholders, unable to compete for export markets because of the concentration of resources in the large-farm sector and the bias in credit and research and extension services, were forced to cultivate crops whose prices were controlled in the interests of urban consumers. In the absence of effective official credit and other services from the state, peasants had to rely on the services of middlemen and local-level bosses, known as caciques, who used every opportunity to exploit their

Table 5.14. Growth Rates for Harvested Area of Selected Crops, Mexico, 1950–80 (1949–51=100)

Crop	Increase (%), 1950–1978/80	Annual Growth Rate (%), 1949/51–1978/80
Corn	104.0	0.2
Beans	101.6	0.04
Wheat	110.4	0.3
Barley, oats, rice	120.0	0.6
Alfalfa	404.5	5.2
Sugarcane	249.7	3.3
Cotton	38.7	−3.4
Cacao, coffee, henequin	187.7	2.3
Eight fruits*	382.8	4.9
Sorghum†	2,621.6‡	18.8‡
Soybeans, safflower†	1,151.3‡	13.7‡

SOURCE: Yates 1981, 51.

*Apples, avocados, bananas, grapes, limes, mangoes, oranges, and peaches.

†1959/61=100.

‡1959/61–1978/80.

"clients." Increasingly, also, peasant production failed to meet domestic requirements; in fact, many small farmers ceased to produce a marketable surplus, concentrating instead on the subsistence needs of their families. These trends are reflected in Table 5.14.

In related fashion, the process of crop and livestock substitution, notable all over Latin America, was particularly evident in Mexico. For example, as the number of hectares under cultivation and irrigation increased, wheat farming migrated north to the newly irrigated lands. As a result of high official support prices and official credit, research, and extension services, impressive gains were made in wheat production, from nearly 400,000 tons in 1940 to 543,000 tons in 1950, 1,200,000 tons in 1960, and 2,100,000 tons in 1970. However, the extensive irrigation required, the increasing salinity of the water in northern Mexico, the stimulus from U.S. investors to diversify, lower support prices as the Mexican government sought to keep the price of bread low, and high international demand for other crops increasingly stimulated the substitution of fruits and vegetables—tomatoes, cantaloupe, watermelon, strawberries, onions, cucumbers, squash—for wheat. Thus, while domestic demand for wheat continued to grow, domestic supplies dwindled. After 1970, Mexico was forced to import significant quantities of wheat, reaching over one million tons by 1979. In contrast, by 1980, fruits and vegetables accounted for 30 percent of the value of the country's agricultural production (Esteva 1980, 170).

Similarly, sorghum production grew at very high rates between 1960 and

1980, and its expansion impinged on land previously sown in corn.[17] In 1970, Mexico was forced to import significant quantities of corn for the first time since the mid 1950s; by 1980, it was importing about 35 percent of its corn supply as domestic production failed to increase in spite of vigorous efforts by the state to stimulate it. Thus, a crop destined for the balanced-feed industry, one which would eventually support the middle- and upper-income taste for meat, rapidly took over areas dedicated to a crop that was directly consumed by low-income groups.

In addition to being converted to forage and luxury crops, much cropland—often on ejidos—was converted to pasture for an expanding beef industry. In Chiapas, a state particularly well suited to the production of corn, for instance, this crop stagnated while the number of cattle doubled; rural violence increased as cattlemen invaded ejido lands in the area.[18] Crop substitution led to a significant increase in the country's already large import bill. Table 5.15 indicates the rapid growth of agricultural exports and contrasts it with the rapidly rising cost of imported food.

The development of modern agricultural practices in Mexico occurred in conjunction with a greater concentration of control over land. To avoid the legal strictures that limited the amount of land that could be owned by individuals, entrepreneurs registered land in the names of relatives and close friends or rented land legally from private farmers and illegally from ejidatarios. Between the agricultural censuses of 1960 and 1970, the number of landholders with 100–1,000 hectares increased by 0.2 percent, while the number of hectares of private cropland they controlled increased from 15.2 percent to 27.1 percent of the country's total private landholdings (see Table 5.13). Because the ejido sector officially controlled 43 percent of the agricultural land in Mexico and because, until 1981, this land could not be sold or legally rented, such figures on land concentration in Mexico are highly misleading, however.[19] Hewitt de Alcántara reports that in one part of the agriculturally rich and commercialized state of Sonora in the mid 1960s, 80 percent of the ejidatarios were renting their land illegally, often hiring themselves out as workers to the large landowners and corporations that actually controlled the land.[20]

Moreover, the situation of Mexico's unemployed and underemployed rural workers became increasingly grave, and by 1979 it was estimated that 50–70 percent of the rural work force was in these categories.[21] As small private farmers sold their land, as ejidatarios rented theirs, and as both groups continued to register high rates of population growth, more and more individuals were forced to become agricultural laborers; large numbers of workers migrated to northern states each year to serve as temporary laborers for the harvest; 1–3 million migrated to the United States annually. In 1980, the Mexican government introduced a plan to create 247,000 jobs annually in agriculture, an ambitious goal, but one that would still fall far short of existing needs,

Table 5.15. Value of Agricultural Trade, Mexico, 1967–79
(Thousands of 1975 U.S. Dollars)

Year	Total Merchandise Traded		Food and Agricultural Products		Agricultural Imports as % of All Imports
	Imports	Exports	Imports	Exports	
1967	2,797,840	1,768,933	189,338	1,024,607	6.8
1970	3,384,884	1,888,524	297,492	955,303	8.8
1971	3,146,767	1,926,359	252,180	914,383	8.0
1972	3,406,617	2,097,845	337,486	1,079,338	9.9
1973	4,523,654	2,456,085	644,913	1,134,387	14.3
1974	6,604,907	3,107,929	1,189,981	1,156,744	18.0
1975	6,570,490	2,861,031	925,607	971,658	14.1
1976	5,704,436	3,088,161	532,985	1,238,863	9.3
1977	4,903,932	3,632,529	735,284	1,271,959	15.0
1978	6,290,135	4,524,043	855,472	1,393,408	13.6
1979	9,587,903	6,747,120	1,027,357	1,528,814	10.7

SOURCES: Elaborated from *SALA* 1980 (based on FAO, *Trade Yearbook*, 1973, 1976); FAO, *Trade Yearbook*, 1982.

with a backlog of approximately 5.7 million unemployed and underemployed rural workers and 300,000 new workers entering the rural job market each year (Cornelius 1980).

In addition, markets in the United States offered transnational capital attractive incentives in financing, production, processing, and distribution in Mexico. Because of the extent of land tied up in ejidos, contract farming in northern and central Mexico was widely utilized by U.S.-based transnationals. The financing and marketing of specified crops were integral parts of the contract system. The transnationals' monopolization of capital and markets therefore decreased the control Mexican producers had over their own activities. Similarly, industrial interests in Mexico exerted increasing control over the credit and markets available for crops such as rice and barley (Esteva 1980, 169). The food-processing industry—freezing fruits and vegetables for export; processing balanced feeds for the expanding production of beef, poultry, and other livestock; meat packing; and milk production—also grew rapidly in Mexico in the period under consideration, and with it, U.S. investment. In 1966, $107 million in U.S. capital was involved in food processing in Mexico; by 1978, this figure had grown steadily to $229 million (Scott 1980, 10). In the form it assumed in Mexico, agricultural expansion ultimately increased the international dependence of the country, both on foreign capital to finance and direct its expansion and in terms of the increased need to import foodstuffs. Thus, some of the gravest of Mexico's problems—unemployment, underemployment, high import bills, maldistribution of income, and economic dependency—were exacerbated.

Colombia

Capitalist expansion in Colombian agriculture was less dramatic than that which occurred in Mexico between 1940 and 1980. The overall growth of production, including that in the large but sluggish coffee sector, averaged about 4 percent between 1950 and the mid 1970s; excluding coffee, the rate reached 4.6 percent annually (Kalmanovitz 1978, 64). During the same period, the number of hectares under cultivation increased by about 2 percent a year. However, agricultural production began to expand impressively in the mid 1960s, increasing in real value by 100 percent between 1958 and 1976 (Kalmanovitz 1978, 66). And agriculture continued to be the most important sector of the national economy, generating over 23 percent of the gross domestic product in 1980 and contributing significantly to foreign-exchange earnings through the export of coffee, cotton, bananas, and sugar while still providing sufficient surpluses to respond adequately to domestic demand. Over 75 percent of Colombia's export earnings came from agriculture through the late 1970s. Moreover, food imports accounted for less than 5 percent of total imports until the 1970s. The limitations of the domestic market, however, meant that the agricultural sector was less dynamic than the overall economy, growing at an average annual rate of 3.5 percent in the 1960s compared to 5.1 percent for the economy as a whole. Then, in 1967, Colombia shifted to a regime of export promotion; tariffs were lowered and the peso was devalued to promote freer trade. Subsequently, the export of both traditional products (coffee, livestock) and nontraditional ones (cotton, flowers) was encouraged. Growth rates in agriculture improved to 5.4 percent for the period between 1970 and 1982, while the overall economy expanded at a rate of 6.0 percent annually (World Bank 1984). Commercial crops came to account for 65 percent of the value of agricultural production in the late 1970s and grew at a rate five times that of coffee and traditional crops.[22]

Much of the land expansion registered by agriculture (5.5 percent a year between 1950 and 1976) occurred through the development of cropping on rich valley land formerly given over to cattle production. The land thus freed was planted in sugarcane, rice, cotton, barley, soybeans, sorghum, sesame, and African palm. Accordingly, about 36.4 percent of the increases in production could be attributed to expanded cultivation (Kalmanovitz 1978, 70).

Increases in the levels of production of commercial crops were also accompanied by sustained growth in the utilization of machinery and green revolution technology. Advances in the dissemination of this technology were most notable during the 1960s and 1970s. In 1950, the country used 8,000 tons of fertilizer compared to 29,000 tons in 1960; in 1970, 158,000 tons were consumed, and by the late 1970s, the figure had risen to 273,000 tons (see Table 5.4). As we have seen, the utilization of improved varieties of seeds also increased significantly in the 1960s and 1970s. Mechanization increased very rapidly in the 1950s because of favorable government credit and import policies. In 1947, fewer than 3,000 tractors were in use in agriculture; a decade later, the number had risen to nearly 20,000 (see Table 5.5).[23]

In spite of this pattern of growth and modernization, however, Colombia's record does not match that of Mexico. Among the reasons for the less dynamic response of Colombia's capitalist farmers was the lack of public investment in the kind of infrastructure, research, and extension services that played such a major role in Mexican agricultural development; low international prices for many of the country's traditional exports; a high rate of inflation, which stimulated investment in land but not necessarily in its productivity; and the attempt during the 1960s to pursue an agrarian reform that increased insecurity among large landowners and discouraged them from investing in agricultural enterprises.

Nevertheless, by the late 1960s, many latifundios in Colombia had changed as landowners experimented with new crops, new technologies, and new labor relationships. Increasing numbers of entrepreneurs with management capabilities emerged from the midst of the large landowners and from urban locales; frequently they rented land from other, less dynamic landowners (Grunig 1969, 44). By the early 1970s, the top 8 percent of all landowners laid claim to 36 percent of the total income from agriculture (Kalmanovitz 1978, 218). At the same time, with the exception of the coffee sector, a sharp contrast became more apparent between capitalist farming in the valleys and subsistence and semisubsistence agriculture on the hillsides.

In spite of the agrarian reform of the 1960s, land concentration accompanied the growing influence of the entrepreneurs. Between the agricultural censuses of 1960 and 1970, farms of more than 10 hectares increased in number and size. Importantly, holdings of more than 50 hectares increased from 6.9 percent of the total number of exploitations to 8.4 percent, or 75.8 percent of Colombia's farmland in 1960, and 77.7 percent of it in 1970. Holdings of 20–50 hectares also expanded in number and size (see Table 5.13). Policies to stimulate mechanization and the reversal of the agrarian reform in the 1970s also aided the process of consolidation.[24]

The structure of Colombia's rural labor force was affected by these changes. In 1950, there were 1,855,400 agricultural workers in the countryside; in 1960, there were 2,155,600; by 1970, the number had risen to 2,457,700. It has also been estimated that by 1971 an average of 25 percent of the rural work force was unemployed.[25] The expansion of livestocking added to the unemployment problem. By the early 1970s, livestocking accounted for approximately 80 percent of the country's agricultural land but only 20 percent of its rural work force.[26] Moreover, these entrepreneurs' greater control over the land meant that they could continue to utilize extensive rather than intensive patterns of cropping and livestocking. This was particularly true of livestock production in the frontier regions, where the cost of factors of production encouraged extensive ranching.

In the period 1940–80, Colombia did not sacrifice its capacity to be self-sufficient in basic foods to the extent that Mexico did. Nevertheless, differences in the dynamics of crops grown for popular domestic consumption and for export or luxury domestic consumption were notable, especially in the 1970s. The country produced a diminishing surplus of unrefined sugar (panela, used by low-income groups), beans, plantains, yucca, corn, and wheat. Thus, while the production of rice, sorghum, sugarcane, and cattle grew rapidly, that of crops consumed by lower-income groups increased by 1 percent or less a year, except between 1965 and 1969 (Kalmanovitz 1978, 82). Frequently, the growth rate was negative. In addition, the expansion of livestocking created the need to import corn and other crops for manufacturers of animal feeds. Colombia's food import bill increased significantly between 1965 and 1979, including hefty shipments of wheat, even while exports grew much more rapidly (see Table 5.16). The costs of importing agricultural machinery, fertilizers, and pesticides also continued to mount as large landowners modernized their enterprises (Araya and Ossa 1976; Kalmanovitz 1978).

In sum, then, modernization of Colombia's agricultural sector increased

Table 5.16. Value of Agricultural Trade, Colombia, 1967–79 (Thousands of 1975 U.S. Dollars)

Year	Total Merchandise Traded		Food and Agricultural Products		Agricultural Imports as % of All Imports
	Imports	Exports	Imports	Exports	
1967	752,984	817,184	83,741	640,717	11.1
1970	1,037,964	1,011,908	111,605	821,725	10.8
1971	1,144,444	896,732	138,178	698,646	12.1
1972	1,048,246	1,085,213	113,919	787,370	10.9
1973	1,259,193	1,395,848	175,779	975,183	14.0
1974	1,741,780	1,545,134	242,722	1,037,271	13.9
1975	1,494,794	1,465,187	151,756	1,090,745	10.2
1976	1,616,007	1,651,044	199,655	1,256,457	12.4
1977	1,812,580	2,183,370	229,513	1,730,242	12.7
1978	2,359,663	2,527,700	242,814	2,028,549	10.3
1979	2,479,443	2,531,015	246,525	1,924,998	9.9

SOURCES: Elaborated from *SALA* 1980 (based on FAO, *Trade Yearbook*, 1973, 1976); FAO, *Trade Yearbook*, 1982.

the maldistribution of land in the country's rural areas, added to the influx of farm workers to the cities, where industry was unable to absorb the newly available labor, encouraged widespread unemployment, did little to stimulate more efficient use of agricultural land, and encouraged rising import bills for basic food items and agricultural inputs.

Brazil

In Brazil, output from the agricultural sector grew at an average rate of 4.7 percent between 1937 and 1979. In the late 1970s and into the 1980s, it grew at rates between 6.5 and 9 percent (Mendonça de Barros and Graham 1980, 1; IDB 1980–81). While agriculture's contribution to the country's gross domestic product dwindled steadily to about 8 percent in 1977 from 21.4 percent in 1940, the sector continued to be important for the foreign exchange it earned through rapidly expanding exports. In the late 1970s, agricultural exports accounted for about 60 percent of the value of all Brazilian exports (ECLA 1978, 71, 75; Adams 1971, 48). Production of sorghum, soybeans, coffee, palm oil, fruit, sugar, and tobacco, in addition to poultry and meat, grew at extremely high rates as entrepreneurs responded to public investment and expanding markets.[27]

The modernization of Brazil's agricultural sector, involving a small group of entrepreneurs with important financial and commercial linkages to urban and industrial interests, proceeded rapidly and with considerable technological innovation, especially in the east and south. As is apparent from Table 5.4, Brazilian farmers began using significant quantities of fertilizer in the 1950s. The 1960s and 1970s witnessed even more rapid adoption of this green revolution input. Moreover, by 1981, Brazilian farmers accounted for about 6 percent of total world sales of spray pesticides and insecticides, making Brazil the third-largest consumer of such chemicals in the world.[28] In the 1970s, Brazil overtook Argentina to become the country with the largest number of tractors in all Latin America (see Table 5.5). Irrigation of cropland also expanded rapidly during the 1960s and 1970s.

The east and south, especially the São Paulo region (where the most dramatic growth occurred), excelled in the production of export crops, and by the 1970s, domestic food crop production there could no longer keep abreast of population increases. The much less dynamic northeast showed modest gains in the production of crops for domestic use in the 1960s, but this was not maintained in the 1970s, when the production of export crops grew modestly but that of domestic food crops declined (see Table 5.17). In the country as a whole, the production of export crops grew at a rate of 5.4 percent during the 1970s, while that of crops for the domestic market increased by only 2.9 percent a year.[29]

By 1980, a fifth of all arable land in the country was planted in soybeans

Table 5.17. Increases in Agricultural Output, Brazil: Selected Crops and Regions, 1960–79

| | Annual Percentage Growth Rate | | | | | |
| | Northeast | | East | | São Paulo | |
Years	Export Crops	Domestic Food Crops	Export Crops	Domestic Food Crops	Export Crops	Domestic Food Crops
1960/69	2.6	6.9	8.4	5.2	4.4	3.5
1970/79	3.9	2.4	13.2	1.7	4.7	3.2

SOURCE: Mendonça de Barros and Graham 1980, 2.

(7,321,000 hectares in 1979, compared to only 1,314,000 hectares in 1970). Live-stocking on an extensive scale replaced coffee production in some areas and displaced considerable labor. Between 1970 and 1980, the output of many basic staples declined.[30] Rice and bean production stagnated, while the yield of an important staple, groundnuts, declined by 50 percent in the 1970s.[31] It has been estimated that the output of food crops for urban consumption declined by about 13 percent between 1970 and 1980. High prices for food were a result of this situation in the late 1970s, with costs rising much more rapidly than the general rate of inflation. By the late 1970s, Brazil was expanding over 10 percent of its import bill on agricultural products (see Table 5.18).

Expansion of production was largely the result of increases in the amount of land under cultivation. In spite of major increases in utilization of modern technologies, less than 25 percent of the increases in agricultural production could be credited to improvements in yields; the rest was the result of bringing new lands under cultivation. In the rapid development of the Amazon region into an area of extensive cattle raising, there was little incentive to save on this abundant and cheap factor of production by using more intensive techniques.[32] Official incentives for large agribusiness enterprises encouraged a situation in which farms of 10,000 hectares or more accounted for 95 percent of new development. The São Paulo region, more densely populated and with no new lands available, and with easy access to commercial channels that distributed agricultural inputs, was the only region to demonstrate important increases in yields. Moreover, yield increases tended to be concentrated in the more remunerative export crops, where most of the technological innovation was concentrated, while yields frequently declined for domestic food crops (see Table 5.19). Thus, in Brazil as elsewhere, the modernization of a sector of the agricultural economy did not mean optimizing either the use of land or the expenditure of capital.

These developments went hand in hand with the destruction of delicate

Table 5.18. Value of Agricultural Trade, Brazil, 1967–79
(Thousands of 1975 U.S. Dollars)

Year	Total Merchandise Traded		Food and Agricultural Products		Agricultural Imports as % of All Imports
	Imports	Exports	Imports	Exports	
1967	2,670,907	2,650,700	519,830	2,064,976	19.5
1970	3,919,179	3,767,431	413,505	2,713,149	10.6
1971	4,838,495	3,795,890	424,238	2,537,307	8.8
1972	5,994,076	5,001,528	484,574	3,446,241	8.1
1973	8,302,484	7,353,737	854,973	4,978,692	10.3
1974	15,450,367	8,670,661	1,236,107	5,310,013	8.0
1975	13,592,463	8,669,944	876,704	4,874,725	6.4
1976	12,985,848	9,582,122	1,052,543	5,782,800	8.1
1977	11,847,163	10,831,255	828,063	6,712,943	7.0
1978	12,524,351	10,531,567	1,286,352	5,550,773	10.3
1979	15,187,355	11,690,473	1,810,623	5,444,235	11.9

sources: Elaborated from *SALA* 1980 (based on FAO, *Trade Yearbook*, 1973, 1976); FAO, *Trade Yearbook*, 1982.

ecological zones and indigenous peoples. Between 1966 and 1975, the government directed the defoliation of nearly 4.7 million hectares of land in the Amazon region (Mahar 1979, 25). According to the regional development agency, SUDAM, approximately 5,000 square kilometers of land a year were cleared in officially approved projects. Indiscriminate deforestation, use of heavy machinery, and chemical defoliants endangered hundreds of thousands of hectares as the Amazon highway was extended in the interior. The encouragement given to cattle ranching resulted in further damage to the ecology as the forest was leveled to create grazing land and as fragile soils rapidly became leached. The opening of the Amazon region, and with it the introduction of disease and chemical defoliants, had a profound impact on indigenous groups. The Nambiquara Indians, for example, were reduced in number from around 10,000 at the turn of the century to 530 in 1980.[33] Overall, the population of indigenous groups totaled about a million in 1900, but was reduced to only about 200,000 by 1980. Not all the depredations of these groups were a result of disease and modern technology, however; many persons were simply driven from their lands by Brazilian and transnational corporations expanding lucrative cattle enterprises and supported by tax incentives from Brasília.[34]

The distribution of land in Brazil also became more unequal. As seen in Table 5.13, there was a significant increase in the percentage of land held in parcels of 1,000 hectares or more, even in the brief period between 1970 and 1975, when the amount of agricultural land available expanded rapidly. In-

Table 5.19. Average Annual Rate of Growth of Yield for Major Export and Domestic Food Crops, Brazil, 1960–77

Export Crop	%	Domestic Food Crop	%
Cotton	−1.1	Rice	−0.7
Cocoa	3.4	Beans	−1.4
Sugar	2.7	Cassava	−0.5
Soybeans	1.5	Corn	0.9

SOURCE: Mendonça de Barros and Graham 1980, 16.

creasingly, corporate agricultural interests bought up productive land in the country, especially in the Amazon region, to utilize for extensive livestocking and extractive activities (Mahar 1979; Davis 1977, chap. 8). These activities brought the large landowners into direct and often violent conflict with small-holders, squatters, and colonists in the region, many of whom flocked to the Amazon spontaneously in search of often illusory livelihoods.[35] Mechanization, especially in the south, not only displaced labor already in the region and expanded the number of landless workers by stimulating the concentration of land, but it also displaced labor in the northeast, where sugar production declined as a result of its resurgence in the south (Sanders and Ruttan 1978). In this period, half a million workers were underemployed in the northeast (Mahar 1979, 44n). The 1970s witnessed extensive expulsion of tenants, sharecroppers, and smallholders from their lands and a rise in the number of landless workers. There were approximately 8.5 million landless rural families in the late 1970s, and the number of temporary laborers rose from 3.9 million in 1967 to 6.8 million in 1972, with a corresponding drop in the ranks of permanent laborers, as indicated in Table 5.20. This trend was especially evident in the agriculturally advanced southern area of the country. In São Paulo in 1955, there were 288,000 resident agricultural laborers; in 1969, there were 32,000. Temporary laborers numbered 226,000 in 1964, 350,000 in 1970. In the coffee-producing state of Paraná, 150,000 workers were displaced when areas previously committed to coffee cultivation were changed to livestock production; 100,000 of them remained unemployed in the late 1970s (Lassen 1980; 98–100). Many of these landless workers became known as *boias frias*, so named for the cold lunches they carried with them as they sought day labor in agriculture (Saint 1980; Goodman and Redclift 1977). Thus, in Brazil as elsewhere, laborers in rural areas were increasingly subjected to unemployment and underemployment because of mechanization, land concentration, and the desire of landowners to count on a large, mobile, and independent labor force.

Foreign investment also penetrated Brazil's modern agricultural sector in the period under consideration. Large transnational enterprises, encouraged

Table 5.20. Changes in Agricultural Labor in Brazil, 1967–72

Labor Category	Percentage 1967	1972
Temporary salaried workers	54.4	81.4
Permanent salaried workers	15.8	6.6
Minifundistas	16.9	8.0
Sharecroppers and renters	10.9	2.6
Squatters	2.0	1.4

SOURCE: Sanders 1982, 4–5; based on cadastral survey undertaken by the Brazilian government.

by high international prices, were increasingly active in the financing, production, processing, and marketing of Brazilian products. In the Amazon, for example, transnational capital was heavily involved in the expansion of cattle ranching and the associated development of the meat industry. Swift-Armour, Borden, Deltec, and Volkswagon were among the names associated with the construction of facilities for meat processing and packaging in the country. These transnational firms often combined ranching with processing and marketing facilities. U.S. capital in food processing expanded from $56 million in 1966 to $285 million in 1978, accounting at the later date for 27 percent of U.S. investment in food-processing industries in Latin America (Scott 1980, 10).

In sum, Brazilian development exemplifies a pattern found elsewhere in Latin America: the increased welfare of the few and the underdevelopment of the country as a whole. The fact that this contradiction was generated and then supported by state policies makes it all the more problematic. Centrally important to an understanding of rural change in Latin America after 1940 is the fact that the modernization of agriculture brought with it deterioration in the economic, political, and social conditions of the vast majority of the rural population. Ultimately, these problems had to be addressed by state elites concerned with the political and economic ramifications of rural underdevelopment. In the following chapter, the conditions and implications of rural poverty are explored in greater detail.

6 | Poverty and Survival among the Rural Poor

Certainly the life of the rural poor in Latin America has never been an easy one. Since the period of the Spanish conquest, the mass of the agrarian population has been tied to poverty and exploitation under conditions of life that can only be described as nasty, brutish, and short. Throughout previous centuries, various means were employed by landowners and other elites to keep the peasantry dependent upon them and deprived of economic and political power. In the current century, however, traditional forms of domination have been joined or replaced by new and more ominous relationships as rural social systems have been penetrated by an expanding urban economy, agrarian capitalism, and the activities of the state. Between 1940 and 1980 the rural poor in Latin America were caught in a complex of economic, social, and political relationships that constantly encroached upon their precarious conditions of security. At the same time that policies for agricultural modernization increased the level of inequality in rural areas and capitalist farmers increasingly dominated markets and profits, peasants were driven into greater debt, squeezed from their land, forced into wage labor, and pushed to migrate in increasing numbers. In the face of these conditions, detailed in the following pages, the capacity of the rural poor for adaptation and survival was impressive, as was their continued importance to the agricultural economy. In fact, as is indicated at the end of this chapter, for the state elites who promoted the adoption of agrarian reform and rural development policies in the 1960s and 1970s, the purported contributions of the rural poor to economic growth were as critical to their arguments as were the implications of poverty for social instability.

POVERTY AND INSECURITY: THE EVIDENCE

Poverty in late twentieth century Latin America was both an urban and a rural phenomenon. There is little question, however, that it reached its most severe levels in rural areas in the region (Weisskoff and Figueroa 1976, 76–81; Altimir 1981). While there were important differences among countries, estimates made by ECLA in 1970 indicated that the income of 62 percent of rural households in the region denied them access to sufficient food to provide minimum caloric and protein requirements for the family as well as access to housing and basic public services such as health care, education, and drinking water. Fully 34 percent of rural families were considered to have an income that would not cover basic food requirements; their condition was termed "below the destitution line."[1] Moreover, the proportion of people in poverty and destitution was much higher in rural areas than in urban ones (see Table 6.1). In another study, it was estimated that 70 percent of Latin America's rural population lived at or below subsistence level in 1973 (FAO 1979).

The distribution of income in the region as a whole deteriorated between 1960 and 1975, according to World Bank figures (López Córdovez 1982, 27; World Bank 1980a, 461). Similar findings were reported in national surveys undertaken by ECLA in Argentina, Brazil, Chile, Colombia, Mexico, Peru, and Venezuela for the same period. In 1960, the poorest 20 percent of the population in these countries received 2.8 percent of the total income earned; by 1975, they received only 2.3 percent, while disposable income increased only slightly (see Table 6.2). By 1975, 10 percent of all households in the seven countries accounted for 47 percent of total income earned, while the poorest 40 percent received less than 8 percent (López Córdovez, 1982, 27). To the extent

Table 6.1. Estimates of Poverty in Latin America, ca. 1970 (Percentages)

Country	Percentage of Households below Poverty Line*			Percentage of Households below Destitution Line†		
	Urban	Rural	National	Urban	Rural	National
Argentina	5	19	8	1	1	1
Brazil	35	73	49	15	42	25
Chile	12	25	17	3	11	6
Colombia	38	54	45	14	23	18
Costa Rica	15	30	24	5	7	6
Honduras	40	75	65	15	57	45
Mexico	20	49	34	6	18	12
Peru	28	68	50	8	39	25
Venezuela	20	36	25	6	19	10
Latin America as a whole	26	62	40	10	34	19

SOURCE: Altimir 1978, 74.

* Income insufficient to satisfy need for food, housing, and basic services.

† Income insufficient to satisfy need for food.

Table 6.2. Income Distribution in Seven Latin American Countries, 1960–75

Income Strata	Share in Total Income (%)		Income per Household (1970 U.S. Dollars)	
	1960	1975	1960	1975
Poorest 20%	2.8	2.3	334	394
Next poorest 20%	5.9	5.4	707	902
Poorest 40%	8.7	7.7	520	648
30% following poorest 40%	18.6	18.1	1,483	2,023
20% preceding richest 10%	26.1	26.9	3,110	4,497
Richest 10%	46.6	47.3	11,142	15,829
Average			2,389	3,348

SOURCE: Iglesias 1982, 12; based on data from ECLA surveys for Argentina, Brazil, Chile, Colombia, Mexico, Peru, and Venezuela.

that poverty was concentrated in rural areas in these countries, the impact of the decline in levels of equity was reflected more harshly there.

Nevertheless, conditions that affect life expectancy, health, and education improved in Latin America between 1940 and 1980, and statistics on housing conditions and the availability of public services demonstrated a long-term trend toward improvement. Moreover, given high levels of population growth, the absolute number of people benefiting from improved conditions and services grew significantly, even when the proportion of the population affected remained stagnant, declined, or increased only marginally. However, urban areas were far in advance in benefiting from basic services and in few cases did the gap between rural and urban conditions narrow significantly; in many cases, the distance between city and country dwellers remained constant or actually increased, as is evident in Table 6.3. For instance, the level of illiteracy remained strikingly higher in rural areas than in urban ones, in spite of the fact that enrollment in rural primary schools in the region more than doubled between 1957 and 1975, from 8.8 million students to 19.0 million (Ortega 1982, 101). Education was much more accessible to urbanites than to those who lived in rural areas (see Tables 6.3 and 6.4). Available figures indicate that the gap between rural and urban access to running water increased in Brazil, Honduras, Nicaragua, Peru, and Venezuela, and that in Ecuador and Venezuela access to sanitation systems declined in rural areas relative to urban ones. Similarly, in many countries electricity was much more available to urban residents than to rural inhabitants (see Table 6.5). Health care, in terms of the availability of hospital beds, was concentrated in capital cities throughout the region (see Table 6.6). Clearly, then, while rural inhabitants were gaining more

Table 6.3. Illiteracy in Latin America, Urban and Rural Areas, 1950–74

Country	Year	Percentage of Total Population Illiterate	Percentage of Illiteracy in	
			Urban Areas	Rural Areas
Brazil	1950	50.5	21.1	78.9
	1970	24.1	35.2	64.8
Costa Rica	1963	15.6	13.7	86.3
	1973	11.6	19.1	80.9
Chile	1960	16.4	39.3	60.8
	1970	11.0	46.5	53.5
Ecuador	1962	32.5	13.5	86.5
	1974	25.8	16.4	83.6
El Salvador	1961	51.0	23.1	76.9
	1971	42.9	22.1	77.9
Guatemala	1964	62.0	20.2	79.8
	1974	53.8	19.1	80.9
Honduras	1961	52.7	11.9	88.1
	1974	40.5	15.7	84.3
Mexico	1960	34.6	31.9	68.1
	1970	25.8	39.2	60.8
Nicaragua	1963	50.4	17.7	82.3
	1970	42.1	23.0	77.0
Panama	1960	23.3	14.1	85.9
	1970	21.7	15.0	85.1
Peru	1961	38.9	22.3	77.7
	1972	27.2	28.2	71.8

SOURCE: OAS, *América en Cifras*, 1977.

access to many basic services, they still were not enjoying anywhere near the level found in urban settings.

The most significant change in rural areas during the post-1940 years was not the absolute level of poverty or conditions of relative deprivation, however; it was the heightened insecurity faced by rural households trying to maintain themselves at subsistence level. While it is true that rural wages generally improved, a declining proportion of rural laborers was eligible to receive them or other benefits as landowners increasingly turned from employing permanent (and eligible) laborers to temporary (and ineligible) workers, as we saw in the previous chapter. Although many temporary laborers had access to small plots of land to supplement their meager wages, the number of landless workers continued to grow. For many of these, family income was dependent on occasional and uncertain work opportunities that paid well below the minimum standards established by legislation.

Table 6.4. Percentage of Adults Who Received No Schooling, Urban and Rural Areas, Early 1970s

Country	Year	Age Group	No Schooling
Chile	1970	25+	
National average			12.4
Urban			8.3
Rural			29.8
Colombia	1973	20+	
National average			22.4
Urban			14.2
Rural			38.4
Costa Rica	1973	25+	
National average			16.1
Urban			7.2
Rural			23.6
Dominican Republic	1970	25+	
National average			40.1
Urban			22.9
Rural			52.8
Ecuador	1974	25+	
National average			31.9
Urban			13.0
Rural			45.4
Honduras	1974	25+	
National average			53.1
Urban			29.5
Rural			64.5
Paraguay	1972	25+	
National average			19.6
Urban			11.3
Rural			25.5
Peru	1972	25+	
National average			35.0
Urban			23.7
Rural			57.7

SOURCE: *SALA* 1984, 190–91.

Typical of these were the boias frias of Brazil, who migrated to urban areas when land and employment could not be found in rural zones. By 1975, they composed as much as a third of the Brazilian population in agriculture. During peak demand periods for agricultural labor, women and children joined their ranks. The boias frias were usually paid less than the minimum wage, and women and children received even less. At peak periods, wages might rise and a temporary worker might earn more than a resident laborer, but the season was short and the annual income of the boias frias was therefore lower than that of the more secure residents. When temporary agricultural labor was not available, the boias frias sought jobs in the informal sector of the urban labor market. Their precarious economic condition was reflected in frequent and chronic health problems, almost total illiteracy, and the lack of a permanent residence.[2]

Between 1940 and 1980, deteriorating conditions in the countryside encouraged much of Latin America's rural population to migrate to urban areas. Overall, annual population growth was about 2.8 percent for these four decades, but the urban population increased at a rate of 4.0 percent annually. This did not bring significant relief from population pressure in rural areas, however, for rural populations continued to grow at a rate of 1.3 percent per year and by 1980 there were approximately 15 million more rural inhabitants than there had been in 1960 (IDB 1981, 395). Poverty itself was a significant factor in generating high birth rates and extensive migration as rural households sought to utilize their one abundant resource, labor, to ensure family welfare.

For those who retained access to the land, the trend was toward ever-smaller plots to cultivate as a result of a shrinking resource base and population pressures. In the previous chapter, we saw evidence of increasing land concentration, especially in areas suited to large-scale agriculture. Capitalist expansion triggered a search for more land by the agricultural entrepreneurs who emerged in the period after 1940, especially land of good quality with adequate water resources. In areas where such land existed, its market value increased. In northwestern Mexico, for example, land values quadrupled within a few years of the completion of the irrigation districts established by the state there (Hewitt de Alcántara 1976, 313). In the São Paulo region of Brazil, the price of agricultural land increased by a factor of four between 1969 and 1976 (Saint 1981, 100–101). In a rich agricultural zone in eastern Paraguay, the situation was especially difficult for peasant producers. The area became increasingly attractive in the 1970s, especially for the production of soybeans. Land values increased from about $25 per hectare in 1973 to $300 or more per hectare in 1976. Pressed by indebtedness and poverty, peasant landholders sold much of their land, often to colonists from Brazil or to transnational agribusiness enterprises.[3] Some turned to farming on more marginal lands while others became wage laborers on the new commercial estates.[4]

Table 6.5. Basic Services in Urban and Rural Areas, 1950–75

Country	Year	Percentage of Homes with Access to Running Water*		Percentage of Homes with Access to Sanitation System		Percentage of Homes with Electricity	
		Urban	Rural	Urban	Rural	Urban	Rural
Brazil	1950	39.5	1.4	71.3	10.3	60.0	3.6
	1960	59.0	3.5	79.2	24.0	71.5	7.6
	1970	54.4	2.6	—	—	75.6	8.4
Chile	1952	73.2	4.5	—	—	—	—
	1970	91.4	32.9	—	—	—	—
Ecuador	1960	—	—	79.4	9.0	—	—
	1974	—	—	80.2	9.1	—	—
Honduras	1961	77.4	9.0	67.3	5.4	71.0	4.3
	1974	90.5	21.2	41.9	1.6	67.1	5.5
Nicaragua	1963	48.7	0.7	87.9	11.6	82.7	11.3
	1971	72.7	5.9	90.6	17.4	76.9	6.9
Panama	1950	92.6	9.7	97.7	35.2	—	—
	1960	89.5	9.6	96.5	36.8	—	—
	1970	91.6	13.3	97.1	46.7	—	—
Peru	1961	44.3	1.0	—	—	52.3	4.3
	1972	51.1	1.3	—	—	54.3	2.7
Uruguay	1963	70.4	1.8	96.9	75.0	77.1	31.9
	1975	90.8	41.2	94.7	75.5	89.2	27.8
Venezuela	1950	53.2	6.1	74.3	12.9	72.0	9.1
	1961	65.4	16.4	87.4	21.7	86.1	19.5

SOURCE: OAS, *América en Cifras*, 1963 (4), 1965 (3), 1977 (3).
*Within or close to the living quarters.

Table 6.6. Hospital Beds per 1,000 Inhabitants, Capital City and Rest of Country, 1971/77

Country	Capital City	Rest of Country
Brazil	7.1	3.0
Chile	3.4	3.0
Colombia	3.2	2.0
Costa Rica	19.4	1.9
Dominican Republic	3.9	1.0
Ecuador	5.2	1.6
El Salvador	8.6	1.0
Guatemala	4.3	0.6
Honduras	8.6	0.8
Mexico	2.4	0.6
Nicaragua	3.6	2.0
Panama	8.0	2.0
Paraguay	5.1	0.7
Peru	4.6	1.3
Uruguay	3.7	4.6
Venezuela	4.0	2.7

SOURCE: OAS, *América en Cifras*, 1977 (3:50).

For peasant smallholders in the Cauca Valley in Colombia, maintaining control over the land became increasingly difficult when a railroad penetrated the region in 1914 and as cattle and sugar production drove land values up. By 1970, four plantations and a number of other large agricultural enterprises controlled 80 percent of the cultivable land in the valley. About a third of the land controlled by smallholders in the early 1970s had passed to the control of the sugar plantations by 1976. Most of the area's minifundistas were forced to seek wage labor on the large farms and plantations; they were generally contracted by a labor boss and paid on a piece rate basis. In the 1970s, the minifundistas accounted for about a third of the labor force of the sugar plantations.[5]

All over the region, when tenants and sharecroppers were allowed to remain on the land, they had to pay higher rents for its use. Often, however, landowners wishing to modernize and expand their production terminated sharecropping or rental relationships, throwing former tenants off the land. The dispossessed in turn were unable to purchase plots in any but the most remote or unproductive regions because of higher land values. Squatting or new forms of tenancy, such as a temporary plot of land given in exchange for land clearing in frontier areas, served some as a means of gaining access to land. Agrarian reforms of the 1960s also benefited some peasants who had been residents on large estates. But most former tenants and an increasing number of smallholders were systematically excluded from the market for productive land; at the same time, population pressure on a static or declining land base under a widespread tradition of equal inheritance among offspring led to greater fragmentation of existing holdings.

As indicated in Table 5.13, in most countries for which data are available, by the mid1970s, more peasants had control of less land than was true in 1960 or 1970. Fragmentation of smallholdings was evident in Argentina, Brazil, Ecuador, Honduras, and Colombia. In Ecuador, for instance, where there were 92,387 smallholding plots of less than 1 hectare in 1954, by 1968, 206,237 minifundios controlled less than 1 hectare each (see Table 6.7). In Peru in the late 1970s, about 1.1 million families farmed plots of less than 5 hectares, compared with about 600,000 families in 1961 (Klein 1980, 116–17). In Honduras, the number of farms under 1 hectare accounted for 10 percent of all farm units in 1952, 17 percent in 1974 (Ruhl 1984, 49–50). In Argentina, Brazil, Ecuador, Guatemala, Honduras, Mexico, Nicaragua, and Venezuela, the average size of smallholdings also declined. As Durham (1979, 54) discovered in his study of resource scarcity in El Salvador,

> Land is scarce not because there is too little to go around, but rather because of a process of competitive exclusion by which the small farmers have been increasingly squeezed off the land—a process due as much to the dynamics of land concentration as to population pressure. Land use patterns show that land is not scarce for large landholders.

This suggests that the problem of the minifundios, often considered to be a consequence of precapitalist landholding arrangements, was actually exacerbated by the modernization of Latin American agriculture. Because the peasant land base increasingly incorporated only the least-productive and remote land, the incapacity of peasant smallholding families to provide minimal levels of subsistence became more stark.

OLD AND NEW CONDITIONS OF RURAL EXPLOITATION

For centuries, whether they lived on the large estates, owned minifundio, or belonged to communal Indian groupings, peasants in Latin America lived within a context of landlord and village domination and were largely unable to escape their subordinate condition.[6] The fact that traditional exploitive relationships were frequently overlaid with personal and paternalistic patron-client ties only served to increase the dependence and powerlessness of the rural poor.[7] In many countries in the nineteenth and twentieth centuries, a class of small landowners and commercial entrepreneurs also emerged that

Table 6.7. Smallholdings and Average Farm Size, 1954–75

Country	Year	Number of Holdings under 1 Hectare	Average Size of Holdings under 1 Hectare	Average Size of Holdings under 5 Hectares
Argentina	1960	—	—	2.80
	1969	—	—	2.52
Bolivia	1950	—	—	1.44
	1977	—	—	1.45
Brazil	1970	396,846	.59	2.16
	1975	463,641	.61	2.10
Chile	1965	—	—	1.05
	1972	—	—	1.67
Colombia	1960	—	—	2.60*
	1970/71	—	—	2.60*
Ecuador	1954	92,387	.49	1.72
	1968	206,273	.45	1.51
Guatemala	1964	85,083†	.39†	—
	1970	98,200†	.37†	—
Honduras	1966	27,719†	.71†	—
	1970	30,100†	.63†	—
Mexico	1960	—	—	1.48
	1970	—	—	1.45
Nicaragua	1963	2,258	.41	1.63
	1970/71	2,600	.39	1.50
Paraguay	1956	6,422	—	—
	1961	7,939	—	—
	1969	9,912	—	—
Venezuela	1961	12,666	.75	2.23
	1971	13,120	.48	2.24

SOURCE: Lott 1979.

*Under 10 hectares.

†Under 0.7 hectare.

was able to exploit the rural poor through debt, patron-client linkages, and control over access to land, water, markets, and security.[8] Thus, whether peasants were subordinated to the hacendado, the plantation management, or commercial interests in the village or regional market, or a combination of these, the end result was exploitation and powerlessness.[9] Nevertheless, patron-client relationships as well as community-level traditions and expectations of mutual help and crisis assistance ensured some stability and local self-sufficiency in a dangerous but generally locally controlled society.[10]

In the early decades of this century, and at an accelerated pace after 1940, however, monetized economies became more common in the Latin American countryside. Related to this change was the broader introduction of capitalist agriculture, following the model of modernization and discrimination discussed in the previous two chapters. Similarly and simultaneously, the state intervened, sometimes in the guise of benefactor of the rural masses, but consistently affecting the control the peasants had over productive resources, including the use of their own land and labor. These changing conditions exposed the rural poor to newer and more exigent forms of exploitation.

In the early and middle decades of the twentieth century, Latin America's rural areas were incorporated into expanding, monetized economies (Pearse 1975; Mallon 1983). Roads opened up previously isolated rural zones, market linkages and cash cropping developed to meet the greater demand for food in urban areas, and an influx of industrial goods replaced or added to those formerly provided locally. The ramifications of incorporation added up to a new and pressing need for cash, which would permit the rural poor to participate in national markets and to achieve a modicum of security in a hostile world. The process was well under way by the 1940s, when roads, radios, officials, and middlemen of all varieties were increasingly in evidence, even in remote areas (Hewitt de Alcántara 1980). Subsistence itself acquired new meaning for large numbers of people. While the rural poor had traditionally been subsistence oriented in attempting to achieve local self-sufficiency, increasingly, subsistence "needs" included the urban goods and aspirations imposed by urban values.[11] Similarly, competition from urban goods often reduced the employment and remuneration traditionally acquired through cottage industries and traditional crafts.

Obtaining cash, generally through the production of market crops and the sale of labor for cash wages, became a necessity for subsistence. For several reasons, however, the value of the crops produced and the labor sold tended to be less than the value of the goods now necessary for subsistence (Esteva 1980, 138; Hewitt de Alcántara 1980). First, when the peasant had direct access to land through ownership or rent (in kind or in cash), it was generally to land of poor quality. His yields were therefore likely to be low and extremely vulnerable to ecological disasters such as drought or excessive rainfall. Because of the low quality and limited quantity of the productive resources available to him, the smallholder or tenant was generally dependent on credit to survive from harvest to harvest; but because he was poor, because of the type of crops he produced, and often because he did not own the land he worked, institutional credit was generally not available to him. He was forced, therefore, to seek loans on highly usurious terms from local moneylenders or middlemen, and he often became systematically indebted.

If he had to buy seeds or other inputs, his purchases of these were in small amounts, sold at higher prices through intermediaries than the inputs available directly to large landowners. Moreover, rental of animal power or machinery involved proportionately higher costs for the small producer than for the large-scale farmer. Therefore, the price and risk involved in technological improvements for crops often put these inputs beyond his reach.[12] Consequently, he obtained poor yields, often lost much of his crops to natural disaster or rodents, and generally produced crops that were lower in quality than their counterparts on large farms. As a result, the prices he obtained for his crops were lower, as was the productivity of his labor. Furthermore, better prices were lost because the smallholder or tenant was forced to sell his crops as soon as they were harvested, or even before that, in order to sustain a precarious subsistence. He also generally lacked access to storage facilities that would allow him to withhold products from the market until prices improved. Already-low prices were reduced by the cost of transporting crops to market— distances were often great, conditions difficult, transportation scarce, quantities small, and the price monopolistic. Often, because of the need to repay debts, the smallholder or tenant was forced to sell the portion of a crop that was intended for family consumption; he would then have to buy this produce at higher prices at a later point in time, increasing family indebtedness in order to do so.

Debt, an ageless mechanism of peasant subordination, was thus given added impetus by the incursion of this urban, monetized economy. And through debt, the intermediary—the *cacique*, the *transportista*, or the *commerciante*—came to play a more central role in rural life. This individual, often linked to the rural community through patron-client ties, controlled access to short- and long-term noninstitutional credit and to markets. Through high interest rates and a monopoly over buying, transporting, or reselling crops, he was continuously able to extract for himself the profits from peasant productive enterprises (Pearse 1975, esp. chap. 6). In Morelos, Mexico, for instance, a rural bourgeoisie developed in the decades after 1940. This group invested in trucks to transport the crops of small farmers and ejidatarios and in machinery to rent out for cultivation and harvesting. It became active in financing the sale of fertilizer, pesticides, and seeds so that peasants could produce tomatoes and onions for large commercial agribusiness contractors. The new commercial class provided the services for weighing crops and thus was able to tamper with the scales. It also provided access to the agribusiness enterprises and managed local-level conflicts for these concerns. In all cases, the intermediaries extracted a healthy profit for their services (Warman 1980, 235–36). Similarly, in Peru, as the system of hacienda dominance declined and peasants became more integrated into the market economy, a group of small farmers, better off than the vast majority, emerged to control the credit and markets necessary for production (Deere and de Janvry 1979, 609). At times, those who thus controlled the conditions of rural life were not local middlemen but the commercial processors of agricultural products.[13] The variety and voraciousness of the intermediaries differed from place to place, but whatever their identity, the potential for the small producer to retain a profit from his labor was systematically destroyed, siphoned off by the very "patrons" who made his continued subsistence possible.

In order to manage this system of indebtedness and to acquire the cash necessary to repay loans, the peasant worked his small plot of land more intensively, but this action, too, only exacerbated his problems. Traditional farming technologies such as crop rotation and fallow periods gave way to intensive and repetitive use of the land for single crops, a process that leached and depleted the soil, adding up to increasingly poor harvests and low quality crops. This in turn necessitated greater inputs of fertilizers and improved seeds, the purchase of which led to more indebtedness.[14] And to complete the vicious cycle, the steady increase in the rural population brought even more overworking of already tiny and inadequate plots of land.

Debts sustained in order to continue a subsistence level of living, which now involved a wide variety of market relations, required much more complex personal and institutional arrangements than the debt peonage that characterized the more closed rural economy of earlier periods. Warman (1980, 238), for example, describes the expanding cycle of indebtedness that followed in the wake of "modernity" in central Mexico:

> The peasant has to combine several sources of credit, on occasion all of them, in order to bring off the miracle of continuing to produce without dying of starvation. He does it through a set of elaborate and sometimes convoluted strategies. Some people plant peanuts only in order to finance the fertilizers for the corn crop. Others use official credit to finance planting of the cornfield or for buying corn for consumption in the months of scarcity, while they resort to the local bourgeoisie or the big monopolists in order to finance a field of tomatoes or onions. Many turn to usurers to cover the costs of an illness or a fiesta. . . . Given what they produce in a year, what is left after paying the debts does not go far enough even for food during the dry season, much less for starting a crop on their own. For them, obtaining a new loan is a precondition for continuing cultivation, one that must be combined with the sale of labor if they are to hold out until the next harvest. Each year the effort necessary to maintain the precarious equilibrium increases, and it seems to be a spiral that constantly demands more work, as well as the daring and inventiveness to find it. Creating employment, inventing ways of working harder, is part of peasant leisure.[15]

In response to these new conditions, many Latin American smallholders and tenants shifted from growing crops primarily for self-sufficiency to growing those that could be marketed in exchange for cash. At the same time, the rural poor were confronted with a modernizing capitalist agricultural sector with which they had to compete for access to land, water resources, government programs, and agricultural inputs. Almost universally, they found the terms of competition stacked against them.[16] The cost of competing with the capitalist sector in the export market made this alternative infeasible for most. The cost of inputs necessary for producing quality crops rose and, as we have seen, was especially high for the small-scale producer who bought in small quantities from intermediaries and had in addition to pay for transport to remote locations. After 1973, in particular, many smallholders and tenants were forced to cut back on their use of chemical fertilizers because of world-wide increases in the price of petroleum products. Prices for commercial crops, on the other hand, were determined by the more efficient and large-scale output of the capitalist sector.[17]

Even state intervention often entrapped smallholders in market relations that caused a loss of security and control over productive decisions. In one area in Mexico, for instance, peasants began producing sorghum rather than corn in response to an official program. The credit offered by the state was accompanied by official efforts to distribute fertilizer and seed and to make machinery and market channels available, all of which was conditioned upon the use of officially approved technologies and commercial channels. The choice of sorghum was made by policy planners in response to urban, national, and international demands and needs; the need of the peasants to maintain a basic level of subsistence for the family was largely ignored, and as a result, the peasants became victims of the cycle of debt described previously (Warman 1980, 205). In Ecuador, an agrarian reform strengthened the state's capacity to dictate to reform beneficiaries. Through its control over programs for irrigation, agricultural credit, and inputs, as well as its capacity to distribute legality in the form of secure titles to land, the state limited peasant control over much farm-level decision making and simultaneously increased the vulnerability of the peasants to the national economic system.[18]

A similar process occurred in a colonization project in Mexico, where beneficiaries ostensibly came into control of land but effectively became agricultural laborers employed by the state to produce the crops determined by its priorities, utilizing the technologies dictated by its rural development agencies (Barkin 1978). Sugar production on smallholdings followed a similar path when the Mexican state began to manage sugar mills directly and to finance peasant production and labor, tasks formerly undertaken by private mill owners (Esteva 1980, 173). Often, the control over access to land and the management of productive enterprises that was achieved by state agencies for agricultural development was augmented by the political control exerted by political parties and elites who promoted factionalism and conflict among the rural poor (Schryer 1980, 18).

At times, such state-initiated development projects had devastating consequences for those involved. In the Cauca Valley in Colombia, an integrated rural development program was begun in the early 1970s, and peasants were urged by official agencies to abandon traditional crops, which required little capital or labor, for the monoculture of soybeans, corn, or beans (Taussig 1978). Much greater capital inputs were subsequently required for the seeds, fertilizers, and chemicals needed, and the new crops required more intensive labor during certain periods. This meant that outside labor had to be recruited and paid, and tractors and other machinery had to be rented. The new crops, planted after the large trees and forest cover of the traditional farms had been uprooted, were more vulnerable to flooding, and the soil was more likely to erode. The greater investment required therefore also made the peasants more vulnerable to loss.

At first, low-interest loans from the state were made available to encourage the changes, but they were terminated after two years. Loans from a nearby food processor were also advanced for a short time, but these were terminated when soybeans began to be produced in abundance. With the disappearance of these loan sources, merchants or rich peasants appeared, offering loans in exchange for the right to buy the harvested crop at rates 15 percent below the market price. When the official bank, the Caja Agraria, approved loans, it required title to the land, a certificate of rental, or a guarantor as collateral. According to Taussig (1978, 80), "In most instances, the peasants were able to persuade the local rich peasant to be the guarantor, which increases his dominance, ensures that his tractor will be used at his prices, and places him in a favored position to buy or rent the land of those peasants who fail to make a success of the new agriculture." Overall, the new form of agriculture among the minifundistas decreased the income from the plots by 40 percent and led to much higher levels of indebtedness and reliance on credit to make ends meet. As a result, wage labor on local plantations and commercial farms became more of a necessity.

Of course, some strata of rural society improved their condition over time. A small group of peasant landholders in each country benefited from official programs such as the provision of special lines of credit to riskworthy smallholders or the distribution of land through reform efforts (Klein 1980, 118–19). In some cases, these peasants became loyal clients of the state and in return were made guarantors of rural social stability and control over the rural poor (Redclift 1978, 163–64). Frequently, they strengthened their economic position by becoming intermediaries in the local or regional economy and strengthened their political position by controlling the votes and political activism of the rural underclass. Generally, this group had access to land of moderate quality and was able to produce crops for urban markets and to employ wage labor.[19]

For a small and declining sector of the landless, permanent wage labor in agriculture continued to exist, and this group actually improved its level of income and welfare, largely through minimum-wage legislation and union organization. This kind of wage labor, referred to as "[a] species of elite within the rural population," was most readily found on commercially oriented plantations, where the labor force was most easily defined as proletarian and where advances in the unionization of farm workers was most marked.[20] In areas where the state expropriated large plantations (often foreign-owned), former resident workers became such an advantaged group, often with effective political representation at the national level.[21]

For most of the rural population, however, the "modern" world that penetrated rural zones did so on terms that were profoundly disadvantageous and that threatened already minimal levels of security and productivity. Under these conditions, innovation and technological advancements, often forced upon peasant smallholders in response to new exigencies, actually exacerbated the insecurity of rural life because of the industrial inputs and capital they required (Pearse 1975, 44). Thus, for the peasant, the advance of "modernity" into rural areas could be characterized as a "bad bargain with society," entailing as it did the reinforcement of old methods of exploitation and the introduction of complex new ones (Pearse 1975, 256). The roads, radios, bicycles, tin roofs, and factory-made clothing that are often cited as evidence of rural progress and development seem to have been purchased through the increased subordination of the peasantry and its increased impoverishment.

SURVIVAL

Nevertheless, the rural poor—squeezed by a declining resource base and increasing landlessness in the countryside and limited from finding urban employment by a capital-intensive pattern of industrialization—were tenacious in adapting to the new and more hostile conditions and in searching out a wide variety of means to maintain family subsistence.[22] They were not only victims, then; they were also survivors, and their very survival calls into question easy assumptions about the ultimate disappearance or total proletarianization of the peasantry.

If in fact "creating employment, inventing ways of working harder, is part of peasant leisure," as Warman (1980, 238) suggests, rural families proved adept at finding opportunities to generate income. In Panama, Gudeman cataloged thirty-nine different occupations that peasant smallholders engaged in to supplement their income.[23] Nonagricultural occupations included weaving saddle blankets of reeds, carving kitchen utensils, thatching roofs, building bird cages, and making sandals, baskets, fishnets, thread, rope, buttons, firewood, and furniture for sale. Some rural inhabitants made clothes, food, and chicha, while others cut hair, washed clothes, raised chickens and pigs, tended animals, or worked on highway crews. Private lotteries, card games, corner "stores," religious services, and curing provided partial maintenance for others. Hunting and fishing also supplemented family subsistence. Most of these occupations required little capital outlay and utilized locally available resources, but they generally provided only a marginal increment to family income—a hat or a saddle blanket of reeds might take a day's labor to produce and result in a profit of only a few centavos when sold in a rural market. These tasks were performed sporadically as needed to ensure family livelihood.

In Latin America generally, some peasant families adapted to change by retreating from market relations, minimizing expenditures for productive inputs like fertilizer, and growing crops primarily for family subsistence, seeking the cash necessary for survival in wage employment or in the production of nonagricultural goods. In some ways, then, these peasants sought to adjust to change by becoming more traditional with regard to the use of land and technology.[24]

Permanent migration was chosen as a strategy by many. Brazilian peasants, for example, finding it increasingly difficult to retain a hold on their land or to find work in older agricultural zones, increasingly turned to the frontier regions of the country in the 1970s and 1980s.[25] The Amazon became a major route of escape from the northeast, where capricious weather conditions, a declining land base due to extreme concentration of landholdings and population pressures, and massive poverty forced peasants to become economic refugees in search of family subsistence.[26] While some northeasterners migrated to southern cities to join the ranks of the boias frias, many others, buffeted by a severe drought that affected as many as 7.5 million people and exacerbated already massive problems of poverty, illiteracy, ill health, and unemployment, looked to the Amazon. They traveled west to the states of Maranhão and Pará and then into the more southern states of Goías and Mato Grosso, which were opened up to settlement in the 1970s through infrastructure and investment programs. A very small number—15,000 by 1979—were settled in colonization projects under the direction of the Instituto Nacional de Colonização e Reforma Agraria (INCRA).[27] Most, however, sought land by squatting on unimproved land adjoining private colonization projects.

As colonists, these peasants experienced repeated hardships. Using slash-and-burn techniques, they cleared land near the new highways only to find themselves threatened by the encroachments and legal authority of the large landowners, who received government-subsidized loans and benefits as well as incentives to mechanize newly established cattle ranches. More difficult, however, was the violence they confronted as individual and unorganized families. Attempts to evict them from their new homes generally involved hiring or maintaining bands of *jagunços* (thugs), who attacked and often killed peasant squatters or colonists as the large landowners and *grileiros* (land-grabbers) attempted to extend their holdings onto the land newly cleared by the peasants. Land conflicts and extensive violence increased markedly in the region in the 1970s, and tales of atrocities committed against peasant families circulated regularly. In private land settlement areas, peasants received little aid or guidance from land companies, which charged high prices for the land they acquired on generous terms and which were quick to repossess the land and the improvements made to it by the colonists.

The most frequent form of adaptation, of course, was temporary wage labor. At times, wage labor opportunities were available in the rural community either on nearby large-scale farms, on the land of "rich" peasants, or in nearby urban areas. Often, however, wage labor opportunities implied temporary and long-distance migration. In Guatemala, for instance, the coffee, cotton, and sugar harvests involve the seasonal migration of more than 300,000 highland Indians, nearly half of the minifundia labor force that provides more than half of the labor on the coastal plantations.[28] In one rural community, necessity forced a majority of the population (not only males, but women and children as well) to migrate to the coast three times a year (Pansini 1981, 5). In Peru, a similar stream of highlanders sought temporary wage labor on coastal cotton plantations (Long and Roberts 1978, 3–4). In Bolivia, a study undertaken in 1976 indicated that 1.2 persons were involved in temporary migration for every peasant household in the altiplano (Ortega 1982, 95). In Mexico, migration took on an international character, and by the late 1970s, it was estimated that between 10 and 20 percent of the agricultural labor force emigrated annually on a temporary basis to the United States.[29]

By the 1970s, wage labor often provided the major portion of total family income for peasants who owned land. In Guatemala, temporary wage labor on the cotton plantations accounted for almost three-quarters of total family income (Burbach and Flynn 1980, 148). In São Paulo and Minas Gerais, Brazil, one study indicated that about two-fifths of the average smallholder family's income came from wage labor (Saint 1981, 96). In a study of an ejido in Mexico, DeWalt (1979) found that fully two-thirds of those who worked ejido land also sought income from other jobs—frequently engaging in several income-producing activities during the year—as a means of meeting the subsistence needs of the family. In Ecuador in the late 1970s, in both highland and coastal areas, over half of peasant household income was generated through wage labor, while in Paraguay, those who owned less than 5 hectares of land sought nearly 40 percent of their income from agricultural wage labor (Ortega 1982, 93). In some cases, wages for agricultural labor increased, but because of its seasonal nature, rural wage employment by itself could not support a family for the entire year. In general, wage laborers who had no access to land regularly demonstrated lower levels of health, nutrition, and subsistence than did those who managed to retain ownership of land, however marginal its productivity.

These characteristics of the struggle for survival have important implications for rural class relations and "peasant destinies." Because of the multiplicity of adaptive mechanisms and the diligence with which they were sought out, peasant families were often able to maintain a tenacious hold on a plot of land, even if its size and productivity were reduced over time.[30] This land was used as insurance against absolute deprivation when alternative means of obtaining family necessities were unavailable. As the need to find alternative sources of income affected all those with access to small amounts of land, the easy distinction between small private farmers, ejidatarios, colonists, sharecroppers, and tenants tended to erode, leaving a mass of ruralites who often had access to land but who were forced by the pressures of changing economic conditions to seek alternative sources of income. The precarious nature of family subsistence tended to mute the distinction between small landowners and wage laborers, for the same individuals and families often engaged in both activities.

And, although the quality and quantity of land available to the rural poor continued to decline, it is not likely that they would have been completely excluded from access to it. Many peasant holdings were located in areas of little interest to capitalist farmers—they were so remote and the quality of land, the climate, and the availability of water were so poor that they offered little to the large landowners. Thus, as those peasants with access to land were squeezed onto less desirable holdings, they marginally improved their capacity to maintain control over it. Moreover, some achieved more or less secure access to land through agrarian reform and colonization efforts pursued by the state. Even while conditions declined for the rural poor, those with access to land were unlikely to become fully proletarianized by the expansion of a pattern of agricultural modernization in which they were the victims (de Janvry 1981; Goodman and Redclift 1982; Taussig 1978).

At the same time that the struggle for survival muted distinctions among the rural poor, however, new differentiations developed as a result of the activities of the state or the incorporation of rural workers into economic and political structures. Thus, some peasants, notably those with greater resources in terms of the quantity and quality of their land and water, or those who were beneficiaries of agrarian reform initiatives, were able to solidify their position through successful production of commercial crops, protected title to the land, and access to government programs and services. Some peasants became tied to private or state-owned businesses that financed production and processed the crops and were thus dependent upon the success of the capitalist enterprises. Landless workers could be differentiated as those engaged in temporary or seasonal work and the dwindling numbers who formed a "labor aristocracy" of permanently employed, often semiskilled agricultural workers. Even within the ranks of temporary workers, a distinction could be made between those who were seasonally employed and those who were day laborers, as well as between migratory and locally based laborers. In some cases, mobilization by political parties or incorporation as clienteles of various state agencies affected specific groups of peasants. As such distinctions multiplied, so did the difficulties of mobilizing peasants around common interests other than land. In spite of this, however, the rural poor continued to hold a place on national policy agendas in the early 1980s.

THE RURAL POOR AND NATIONAL DEVELOPMENT

The rural poor, whether they had access to land or not, fulfilled important economic functions in spite of the extent to which they had been marginalized by agricultural modernization. Clearly, as the data on unemployment, wage labor, and migration indicate, they provided a large and cheap pool of labor for the capitalist agricultural sector. Perhaps more important from the perspective of state elites, they continued to account for a sizable, although declining, proportion of national agricultural production. While there was considerable variation among countries, Table 6.8 provides an estimate of the relative proportions of production accounted for by "entrepreneurial" and peasant agriculture. The importance of smallholder agriculture to the national economy is clear in our three case study countries. In 1970, Mexican smallholders and ejidatarios produced 69.6 percent of the maize; 66.7 percent of the beans; 32.7 percent of the wheat; and 48.9 percent of the fruit grown in the country. A 1973 study indicates that smallholders produced 67 percent of the staple crops in Colombia. According to a 1976 cadastral survey in Brazil, more than half of the harvest in staples, industrial crops, and fruits and vegetables was produced by 80 percent of the farm units that controlled only 17.5 percent of the country's agricultural land (Ortega 1982, 82). Of course, much of this production— an average of about 30 percent—was not marketed but was used for family subsistence. Smallholder production nevertheless remained a major source of basic food items for urban consumers. Equally important, smallholding agriculture continued to account for a significant portion of rural employment. To state elites concerned about the political and economic costs of continued rural-to-urban migration, this indicated the importance of encouraging smallholders to remain in rural areas.

In the 1960s, many state elites became concerned that smallholding agriculture should receive greater attention from the state through agrarian reform efforts in order to boost production and to enhance the contribution of the rural poor to national development. In the 1970s, as concern mounted over the production of staple crops, state elites "rediscovered" the importance of peasant production and sought to stimulate it through integrated rural development efforts. These reformist policies, the topics of the next two chapters, were

Table 6.8. Estimates of Dimensions of Entrepreneurial and
Small Producer Agriculture in Latin America, Early 1980s (Percentages)

Indicator	Entrepreneurial Agriculture	Small Producer Agriculture
Number of economic units	22	78
Total area covered by the units	82	18
Cultivable area covered by the units	63	37
Area utilized by the units	56	44
Production for domestic consumption	59	41
Production for export	68	32
Production of permanent crops	59	41
Production of short-cycle crops	68	32
Production of		
Maize	49	41
Beans	23	77
Potatoes	39	61
Rice	68	32
Coffee	59	41
Sugarcane	79	21
Number of cattle	76	24
Number of pigs	22	78

SOURCE: López Córdovez 1982, 26; estimates based on national agricultural census data.

also stimulated by concern over heightened rural poverty and insecurity. Thus, although clearly constrained in their reformism by the power of landed interests, state elites sought to redress conditions that they believed were detrimental to national development, even though the perpetuation of these conditions would have been instrumental in furthering the expansion of capitalist agriculture.

7 | Agrarian Reform: Ideology and Politics

The goals of state development policies for the rural sectors of Latin American countries between 1940 and 1980 were consistently to modernize agriculture through mechanization and technological innovation and to increase levels of production and productivity. But the rural poor, as a specific target of policy concern, were not completely ignored by state elites. In fact, the 1960s were marked by a number of efforts to redistribute land, while the 1970s were noted for the widespread adoption of integrated rural development programs. Both of these reformist efforts took as their goal increasing production and productivity among smallholding farmers and improving the quality of life of the rural population.

Nevertheless, analysis of these policy areas indicates that the primary beneficiary of policies ostensibly directed toward the rural poor was the state itself. The agrarian reforms considered in this chapter are a good example of this.[1] They coerced large-scale farmers into modernizing in accordance with official goals, gave the state greater legal authority to acquire and allocate land, increased the presence of the state in rural areas, expanded the repertory of mechanisms available for averting serious threats to social peace, and often provided the state with a dependent clientele of reform beneficiaries. With these accomplishments in hand, the Latin American states that undertook agrarian reforms during these years then disavowed the importance of land redistribution as a solution to rural underdevelopment and embraced the much less politically sensitive policy of integrated rural development, even though they kept important agrarian reform legislation on the books. How the reforms were legislated, what use was made of them, and what lessons they provided for state elites are the issues addressed in this chapter.

Much of this chapter is taken from Grindle 1980, which is based on extensive field research conducted in Colombia in 1977, and is included here by permission of the Office for Public Sector Studies, Institute of Latin American Studies, University of Texas at Austin.

THE GENERAL PATTERN

The experience with agrarian reform in Colombia, considered by many to have been a showplace of agrarian reformism in the 1960s, is indicative of the change in policy orientation that occurred in the 1970s. Writing in 1963, Albert Hirschman was encouraged by passage of the Social Agrarian Reform Law in Colombia, citing it as evidence of the "contriving of reform" or "revolution by stealth" in a society dominated by traditional social classes and conservative politics. He described Law 135 of 1961 as the culmination of a history of rural unrest dating back to the 1920s, of a series of successes and failures in experimenting with alternatives to agrarian reform, and of skillful engineering by political leaders (Hirschman 1963, chap. 2). The initial chapter of the law declared that the goals of agrarian reform were to

> reform the social agrarian structure . . . by eliminating and preventing the inequitable concentration of property . . . ; encourage the adequate economic production of uncultivated or underutilized land . . . ; increase the overall volume of agricultural and livestock production . . . ; create conditions under which renters and sharecroppers can achieve greater security . . . ; raise the standard of living of the peasant population . . . ; conserve . . . natural resources . . . ; promote, support, and coordinate organizations whose objective is the economic, social, and cultural betterment of the peasant population. (INCORA 1975, 7–8)

In order for these ideals to be achieved, Hirschman acknowledged, the reform would require strong executive support to deal effectively with those who opposed it. But he also perceived the passage of the legislation itself as heralding new possibilities for smallholders, tenants, sharecroppers, and landless laborers within the context of peaceful and evolutionary change (Hirschman 1963, 155–58).

By the mid 1970s, however, a series of laws, decrees, and agreements had brought land reform in Colombia to a standstill. In 1972, the leaders of the Conservative and Liberal parties, meeting with the Minister of Agriculture and representatives of large landholders, reached an agreement to halt expropriation of private landholdings for the purpose of agrarian reform (Bagley and Laun 1977, 68; Gómez 1975, 61). The agreement was followed by several laws giving further assurances to the landowners that the government would seek to protect and bolster the status quo. In 1976, the agrarian reform institute, INCORA, was stripped of much of its authority through the creation of a new, independent agency that was charged with responsibility for the irrigation districts formerly managed by INCORA. The laws and agreements of the 1970s brought public recognition that agrarian reform was no longer thought to be important or feasible by state elites.

The movement away from agrarian reform in the 1970s was clear in other countries as well. In Brazil and Chile, rightist military regimes quashed the hope for such change by pursuing conservative development policies. The government of Chile disbanded its agrarian reform agency in 1978, and Brazil's response to the question of land distribution continued to emphasize efforts to colonize the agricultural frontier. In Venezuela, lip service was still paid to the goal of agrarian reform, but government programs to that end in fact became paralyzed in the 1970s (Cox 1978). The military government in Honduras, in spite of a new agrarian reform law of 1975 and continued rhetoric that land reform was fundamental to economic growth, backed away from the implementation of this law in 1977 and began to use repression more extensively to halt land invasions.[2] In Ecuador, the major organization responsible for mobilizing the peasantry to make demands on the political system was disbanded in 1973 and the agrarian reform law was weakened considerably in 1974.[3] In 1979, new legislation strengthened the security of the landholdings of the large farmers and increased their privileged access to government credit and services (Farrell and da Ros 1983, 28–29). In Mexico, the problems of the agricultural sector were redefined to avoid threats to large landholders and agribusinesses.[4] In Paraguay, the agrarian reform institute consistently chose to resettle peasants on frontier land rather than expropriate large landholdings (Nickson 1981). Even in Peru, which embarked on a major agrarian reform in 1969, initiative slowed considerably after 1975, when General Morales Bermúdez ousted his more radical predecessor, General Velasco Alvarado.[5] In 1980, a new agricultural development law caused concern that the achievements of the 1969 reform might even be undone by greater emphasis on productivity and capitalist expansion in agriculture.[6]

By the late 1970s, in most Latin American countries, government institutions created and funded in the 1960s to spearhead agrarian reform programs moldered in disuse, in many cases having carried out only marginal colonization projects in frontier areas with insufficient resources, little political support, and extremely low morale. Only in Nicaragua and El Salvador was concern for agrarian reform evident in this period, and in the latter case, it was largely pursued as a means to scuttle social revolution in the countryside and was accompanied by extensive repression (Browning 1983; Deere 1982).

The record of agrarian reform was poor in terms of the numbers of families that acquired ownership of the land (see Table 7.1). The example of Colombia is again broadly relevant. Table 7.2 presents a summary of that country's land acquisition and distribution programs after 1962. Through March 1977, INCORA had acquired 814,595 hectares of private land in 3,702 parcels, or less than 3 percent of the agricultural land in Colombia.[7] Of this land, 26,548 hectares, or 118 holdings, had been acquired through expropriation; the remaining 3,584 acquisitions had been bought from or ceded by private landholders. During the same period, INCORA had benefited 26,948 smallholders through the distribution of 539,992 hectares of land. However, 47 percent of these beneficiaries received legal title to land they had already settled. An additional 159,232 beneficiaries received title to 4,381,075 hectares of virgin land

Table 7.1. Land Reform in Latin America, 1969–82

Country	Number of Rural Families Benefited through Agrarian Reform		
	1969	Most Recent Estimate	
Bolivia	208,181		
Brazil	46,457		
Chile	15,000	1973	56,159
Colombia	91,937		
Costa Rica	3,889	1981	25,000
Dominican Republic	9,717		
Ecuador	27,857	1976	63,757
El Salvador	—	1981	38,000
Guatemala	26,500		
Honduras	5,843	1979	46,890
Mexico	2,525,811		
Nicaragua	8,117	1982	75,000
Panama	2,594		
Paraguay	—		
Peru	31,600	1979	370,000
Venezuela	117,286	1976	123,960

SOURCES: *SALA* 1976, 63; McClintock 1981, 61; Seligson 1982; Handelman 1981, 73, 115; Cox 1978; Oxfam 1981; Deere 1982; Ruhl 1984, 52–53.

belonging to the state, generally in frontier areas. While over 186,000 beneficiaries received land, this was only about 6.7 percent of those considered to be economically active in the agricultural sector. Thus, although INCORA managed at various times to acquire land, improve it, and resettle beneficiaries in colonization and parcelization programs, its actual impact on the distribution of landholdings in the country was minimal. The expansion of capitalist agriculture and the abandonment of marginal holdings by peasants seeking alternative sources of income actually led to a slightly greater concentration of land in large farms in the decade 1960–70 (see Table 5.13).

As indicated in the following pages, the initiative for agrarian reform in Latin America conformed to two general patterns. In some countries, reform resulted from social revolution, in which the pressure to redistribute land came from widespread peasant mobilization and/or ideological commitment among revolutionary leaders. As we will see, however, in the majority of cases, reforms were initiated from above, by state elites, often in the absence of significant pressure from the peasant masses. The case of Colombia is representative of the forces that stimulated this second pattern and is presented in detail here along with a more general discussion of agrarian reformism and the benefits that accrued to the state in its wake.

Table 7.2. Acquisition and Distribution of Land in Colombia by INCORA; 1962–March 1977

		Number of Parcels of Land	Hectares
Land Acquisition			
Private landholdings purchased		3,375	406,669
Expropriated		118	26,548
Ceded		209	381,378
	Subtotal	3,702	814,595
Reverted to public domain		338	3,863,437
	Total	4,040	4,678,032
Land Distribution			
Definitive title granted		9,689	207,231
Provisional title granted		4,363	96,245
Legalized		12,896	236,516
	Subtotal	26,948	539,992
Title to state lands granted		159,232	4,381,075
	Total	186,180	4,921,069

SOURCE: INCORA 1977.

AGRARIAN REFORM AND SOCIAL REVOLUTION

Undoubtedly, the most extensive agrarian reforms in Latin America resulted from major social revolutions in which peasants played a significant part. In Mexico, Bolivia, Cuba, and Nicaragua, massive expropriation of landholdings followed regime changes that were characterized by violence and upheaval. In these cases, large numbers of peasants acquired land and became dependent upon the state for legal protection and development assistance. In return, the state acquired a large rural clientele whose support for the regime in power could generally be assumed, even when promised benefits were not forthcoming.

In Mexico, the multifaceted social origins of the Revolution of 1910 included a dispossessed peasantry, whose overwhelming objective was to acquire the land and livelihood that half a century of capitalist development had wrested from it. Loosely organized peasant armies under the leadership of Emiliano Zapata and a variety of local chieftains in central and southern Mexico, and diverse groups in northern areas, fought single-mindedly for access to land for themselves and their communities and bore the brunt of much of the violence in the bloody years after 1910.[8] Their claims, first recognized in a decree of 1915, were enshrined in Article 27 of the Constitution of 1917.

The Constitution recognized the right of the state to expropriate private property in the interest of equitable distribution and established the framework for a massive redistribution of landholdings based on the creation and maintenance of the communal ejido system and small private landholdings. Implementation of the reform was sluggish at best until 1935, when, under the leadership of President Lázaro Cárdenas, the agrarian spirit of the revolution was given strong support. Between 1935 and 1940, more than 20 million hectares of land were redistributed, and 770,000 peasants benefited. Between 1940 and 1979, another 1,186,800 peasants received title to private plots of land or rights to ejido properties (Esteva 1980, 231). Eventually, nearly half the nation's cropland was redistributed in the form of ejido grants. The convulsions of the revolutionary years thus fundamentally altered the structure of landholding in Mexico. At the same time, as we have already seen, the land reform itself created the conditions for incorporating the rural poor into a political regime that largely ignored or discriminated against them in the period after 1940. Nevertheless, the scope of the redistributive impulse owed much to its revolutionary origin.

Similarly, social revolution in Bolivia resulted in a massive redistribution of landholdings to peasant beneficiaries.[9] The Revolution of 1952 created 289,000 new landowners; the breakup of the large estates was rapid and effective as peasants moved, often spontaneously, to occupy the haciendas and plantations where for generations they had served as peons. Much of their activity was organized by unions of peasants (*sindicatos*) that had been formed in the 1940s and early 1950s. The revolutionary government also moved rapidly to organize the new peasant landholders into officially sponsored agrarian syndicates and, through the reform legislation of 1953, to legalize their right to the land. Various political regimes in Bolivia were subsequently able to count on the enduring political support of these beneficiaries, in spite of the extreme poverty that continued to characterize their existence.[10] Under the aegis of the reform, approximately half of all rural families acquired land by 1955 and 30 percent of the country's agricultural land changed hands in its wake.[11] However, minifundismo remained the dominant characteristic of reform areas.

Social revolution in 1958 in Cuba had a similarly profound impact on landholding in that country.[12] Ninety-five percent of the landholdings over 67 hectares in size were expropriated from private owners, primarily from the foreign corporations that dominated the sugar and cattle plantations, and were turned into state farms and cooperatives. The private sector constituted about 30 percent of the farming units, and most of these were created through the reforms. Prior to this, most smallholding beneficiaries had worked as tenants or sharecroppers or had been squatters on private and public lands. The revolutionary state created the National Association of Small Peasants to organize and control peasant political activities and reaped considerable support from it. Altogether, the agrarian reform law of 1959, among the first initiatives of the revolutionary regime, and a subsequent reform of 1963 affected owner-ship of almost all the agricultural land in the country and benefited over 470,000 rural families and nearly 40 percent of the work force. The revolution, which was fought from a rural base and which maintained an important ideo-logical commitment to the concept of "ruralism," continued to stress the im-portance of equity and welfare in rural areas, even though its goals of increased production and productivity proved elusive (Fagen 1969).

Twenty years after the Cuban Revolution, Nicaragua was shaken by a ma-jor social upheaval that also resulted in an extensive agrarian reform.[13] Like the Cuban Revolution, the Nicaraguan movement coalesced around opposi-tion to a brutal and unpopular dictatorship and was fought to a considerable extent from a rural base. Similarly, the new regime expropriated large hold-ings of good quality land from the losers of the revolutionary struggle—in this case former president Anastasio Somoza, his family, and his political asso-ciates. In the year following the July 1979 victory, approximately 23 percent of the country's cultivable land was expropriated and reorganized into state enterprises, peasant cooperatives, and private parcels. By the end of 1981, approximately 75,000 former tenants, sharecroppers, and landless workers had benefited from the land distribution efforts of the Sandinista-led gov-ernment. And, like the pattern seen in Mexico and Bolivia, conditions in Nica-ragua in the early 1980s indicated that the regime was creating a massive base of loyal support among the rural population (Deere 1982).

In each of these countries, then, a social upheaval destroyed the landhold-ing structure of the previous regime and created a new sector of peasant bene-ficiaries that served as a strong base of support for the revolutionary state. In Mexico and Bolivia, where patterns of capitalist agricultural development quickly reasserted themselves, rural support for the state endured long after national development policies had turned away from questions of equity and welfare. In the rest of Latin America, the impetus to agrarian reform came not through social pressure from below but from a combination of development ideologies held by state elites, the political entrepreneurship of particular lead-ers, elitist fears of social unrest, and the exertion of international pressures.

AGRARIAN REFORM FROM ABOVE

Prior to 1960, Latin America could count only three countries that had legis-lated major agrarian reforms; each of these countries had experienced a vio-lent social revolution. Between 1960 and 1964, fourteen major agrarian re-forms were enacted in the region (see Table 7.3). The reasons for this flowering of reformism were several. First, the influence of the structuralist economic

Table 7.3. Agrarian Reform Legislation, 1960–80

Prior to 1960	1960	1961	1962	1963	1964	1965–80
Bolivia	Venezuela	Colombia	Chile	Nicaragua	Brazil	Ecuador
Cuba		Costa Rica	Dominican	Paraguay	Ecuador	El Salvador
Mexico		El Salvador	Republic		Peru	Guatemala
			Guatemala			Nicaragua
			Honduras			Peru
			Panama			

NOTE: These dates indicate passage of major legislative reforms. In many cases, they are not dates of initial agrarian reform legislation.

analysis propounded by ECLA was felt in terms of a rationale for agrarian reform.[14] A number of influential economists and intellectuals in the 1950s and early 1960s argued that agrarian reform would have a beneficial impact on national development. Without such structural transformation, they reasoned, the agricultural sector would be unable to fulfill important economic functions, because it was based on an extreme maldistribution of land that promoted and sustained precapitalist relations of production. In their analyses, these economists and intellectuals described latifundismo and its counterpart, minifundismo, as the central problems of rural Latin America, causing agriculture to be backward and unproductive, and social and political relations to be inequitable and exploitive. The structuralist analysis indicated that both latifundios and minifundios operated at the margins of the market economy, deriving their motivation from the search for status and power on the one hand and security and subsistence on the other. Feudal and stagnant relations of production and the failure to adopt new technology were direct results of these conditions.

Logically, then, for change to occur, a redistribution of land, combined with changes in the organization of production, would be necessary. Only then would producers be forced to be efficient and to make a positive contribution to national economic development, and only then would passivity, fatalism, and dependence cease to characterize the rural poor. State elites who adopted the structuralist model considered the stagnation of the rural economy and the political power of the landlords to be principal bottlenecks to industrial development and modernization.[15] For these elites, agrarian reform promised to release the productive energies of a massive number of rural inhabitants who for centuries had been held in subservient and backward conditions by feudal social relationships. They expected that it would rid the countryside of unproductive large landholdings and the feudal lords who controlled them. In their

view, agrarian reform also promised to stimulate a more entrepreneurial atti-
tude among large and medium-sized landowners and it seemed to be an effective way of transferring resources from unproductive rural estates to the burgeoning industrial economy.[16] Finally, it promised to create a class of rural
smallholders who would not only produce efficiently but would also provide a
ready market for consumer goods produced by the nation's industries. Thus,
national development would be an inevitable outcome of ending the extreme
maldistribution of resources in the countryside.

Also important in stimulating state-led reformism in the 1960s were more
explicitly political factors. In many countries, concern among economic and
political elites about the potential for rural unrest was central. The Cuban
Revolution haunted the debates over agrarian reform in the early 1960s.
Against the backdrop of the Cuban experience, state elites expected similar
upheaval to affect rural areas in their own countries, and such fears allowed
politicians to forge a broad consensus on the need for reform legislation
among dominant elite groups. Indicative of the concern felt was a statement
made in 1960 by a Conservative Party legislator in Colombia: "If the next
Congress fails to produce an Agrarian Reform, revolution will be inevitable."[17]

An important impetus to the agrarian reform promulgated by the Peruvian
military regime in 1968 was the intense concern felt by military leaders for the
explosive character of rural conditions should land redistribution not be
pursued. Having been responsible for quashing a widespread peasant mobilization and rebellion centered in La Convención Valley in the mid 1960s, the
military leadership had firsthand experience of massive rural poverty and the
social tensions it was capable of producing. Thus, when they achieved power,
they acted on their commitment to a nationalist and radical transformation of
the structure of landholding in the society in order to stimulate national economic development, destroy the power of the dominant oligarchy, and stave
off the specter of revolution from below. Similarly, the agrarian reform promulgated in El Salvador in 1980 was clearly an attempt by concerned elites in
the Christian Democratic Party and the military to prevent the expansion of
the revolutionary confrontation and conflict then in progress. In Honduras in
the mid 1970s, concern about rural unrest also briefly stimulated greater concern for land redistribution.

Political leadership was a critical factor in bringing about legislation of the
reforms, as will become clear in the discussion of Colombia's experience. In
the years after World War II in many Latin American countries, political
parties moved into the countryside and set about mobilizing peasant affiliates.[18] These urban-based parties, responding to increased literacy, accessibility, and extensions of the franchise among peasants, saw in the rural electorate
the possibility of acquiring a stable base to aid them in their quest for national
power. Stimulated by young, reform-minded politicians and intellectuals, of

whom Betancourt in Venezuela, Belaúnde in Peru, and Frei in Chile were typical, party manifestoes of this period included commitments to achieve social justice for the rural and urban masses and indicated the appropriateness of agrarian reform to serve as a means to this end. In some cases, such as Chile and Peru, effective competition among parties encouraged the proliferation of campaign promises to carry out land reform and the organization of peasants into political action groups capable of making demands on the state and the large landowners. In other cases, such as Venezuela and Bolivia, the peasant following was committed to a single party that vowed to pursue the interests of the rural underclasses. In all cases, the commitments made by these parties encouraged them to promulgate agrarian reform legislation and to undertake to distribute both land and aid to beneficiaries. Often they did so in the absence of significant pressure from the peasants themselves and in the face of considerable opposition from landed interests.

A fourth factor critical to the movement toward agrarian reformism was the influence of the U.S. government. In the early 1960s, U.S. concern about the Cuban Revolution was clear, and the Kennedy administration expressed grave apprehension that communism would spread to other Latin American countries. As a result, the region rapidly increased in importance on the foreign policy agenda in Washington. The heightened interest in matters of hemispheric security and the infusion of ideas that accompanied the New Frontier led to the initiation of the Alliance for Progress in 1961. The Alliance, based on the premise that social, economic, and political reforms could forestall the further incursion of communist regimes in the region, made economic aid conditional on the demonstration of commitment to changes such as ending archaic landholding patterns and social relationships in the countryside, increasing the democratization of political participation, expanding educational opportunities, and adopting more equitable and efficient tax policies.[19] The 1980 agrarian reform in El Salvador received extensive technical aid and financing from the United States; the principal architects of the reform were American advisers to the Salvadoran government (Deere 1982).

In the years after the enactment of agrarian reform legislation in Latin America, the reformist commitments of ECLA ideologues and political leaders were to be tested. Ultimately, many became convinced that social revolution in the countryside was not necessarily imminent, that peasants were not important enough as a political force to court so assiduously, and that increasing levels of production and productivity on peasant holdings or cooperatives was far more complex and expensive than originally imagined. Gradually, the impetus for agrarian reform that had motivated state elites died and was replaced by disillusion and skepticism. The influences that stimulated elite reformism—development ideology, fear of social upheaval, electoral calculations, and international pressures—were in ample evidence in Colombia, as

were the factors that discouraged the successful implementation of the reformist movement.

AGRARIAN REFORM IN COLOMBIA

Colombia was not a country where significant efforts at structural changes in
rural areas would have been expected in the early 1960s. The regime instituted
in 1958, the National Front, was based on a careful portioning of power between the two traditionally oligarchic parties, the Liberals and the Conservatives. As we have seen, the state in Colombia had traditionally been weak and
deeply penetrated by specific private-sector interests. There was little sign of
the expanded power the state would assume under the National Front, nor
were the social bases of the elitist parties sufficiently distinct to anticipate major confrontations over policy issues or attempts to mobilize nonelite sectors of
the population into competitive groups, especially after the experience of La
Violencia and the military dictatorship that it ushered in. The National Front
itself institutionalized a conservative bias in policy making by requiring a two-
thirds vote of support for the approval of legislation; bipartisan support was
therefore necessary to achieve passage of any major policy initiatives.

The development of commitment to agrarian reform in Colombia in the
1960s is often accounted for by the "crisis" in the country's agricultural sector.
Land concentration was high; latifundism and minifundism were the typical
forms of landholding; title to land was frequently obscure, leading to instances
of violence in rural areas; agricultural output was low, as was the standard of
living in the countryside; and the sector acted as a brake on industrial development.[20] But such conditions were certainly not new to Colombia. Latifundism and minifundism had dominated landholding patterns since the early
colonial epoch. Rural unrest had been periodically troubling to politicians in
Bogotá and to the country's large landowners since the 1920s, reaching such
proportions in the period of La Violencia that it claimed upwards of 200,000
lives in the late 1940s and early 1950s (Dix 1967; Oquist 1980). And a marginal, subsistence standard of living was certainly not a novelty to Colombia's
minifundistas, sharecroppers, and tenants. Agricultural production, though
still low, had made considerable advances in certain crops in the late 1950s
(Hirschman 1963, 129). Such conditions were, in fact, only the broad context
in which other events stimulated passage of the agrarian reform of 1961. Primary among these were the machinations of state elites and party leaders and
international pressures to institute reform.

The first president elected under the National Front in 1958 was a Liberal,
Alberto Lleras Camargo, who had been president of Colombia from 1945 to
1946 and who had been a partisan of reformist measures in the 1930s. When he

assumed the presidency for a second time, Lleras Camargo became a more committed advocate of agrarian reform under the tutelage of his nephew, Carlos Lleras Restrepo, head of the Liberal Party and vice-president of the country. In 1960, with his uncle's presidential backing, Carlos Lleras began to maneuver a comprehensive agrarian reform law through a specially constituted National Agrarian Committee and then through the national legislature. His efforts were aided by the threat posed to the Liberal Party by the Movimiento Revolucionario Liberal (MRL), a leftist splinter of the party that had won electoral victories in the countryside in 1960. In the course of campaigning, the MRL and communist-led peasant groups had managed to raise the specter of a return to the fratricidal rural violence of La Violencia. These threats persuaded many orthodox Liberals, who considered themselves to be more representative of urban and "cosmopolitan" interests than the Conservatives, that the moment had come to expand the party's rural electoral base in order to end the incursions being made by the MRL and to counteract its potential for taking over direction of the party at the national level.[21]

The Conservative Party, its traditional base consisting of large landowning interests, also was more open to reform legislation than would normally be expected. This was largely due to its leaders' concern with changing the party's image—that of a party which had helped create the political conditions that set off La Violencia in the late 1940s and which had collaborated willingly in the unpopular Rojas Pinilla dictatorship (Dix 1967, 115–18). Certainly, while a national debate went on in the press, the Conservatives were not in a position to oppose the agrarian reform initiative strongly. Party influentials acceded to the political necessity for the legislation and spent their energies instead seeing to it that the law contained as many provisions as possible to protect large landowners and to "preserve the right to private property."[22] Further support for Carlos Lleras's position came from reaction to the Cuban Revolution, which had, in the late 1950s, swept the discredited Batista regime from power, building from a guerrilla *foco* in rural areas. By 1960, the radical course to be taken by the Cuban Revolution was becoming more clear, a development authenticated in 1961 by Fidel Castro's announcement of his commitment to Marxism-Leninism. In the wake of these events came the Act of Bogotá and then the promise of financial aid from the United States through the Alliance for Progress.[23]

Taken together, these circumstances encouraged the belief among party influentials—especially the Liberals, but also the Conservatives who supported the legislation in Congress—that passage of agrarian reform laws would be an expedient means of forestalling party strife, a method for discouraging the potential expansion of the Cuban Revolution, and a relatively easy way to acquire funds to initiate the program. It would also encourage the modernization of the agricultural sector in general, following the logic of the ECLA analysis. Direct demands for agrarian reform from the peasants were noticeably few at this point, and this gave Carlos Lleras wide scope in putting together an elite consensus within his own party and then within the national legislature.

The Colombian Social Agrarian Reform contained 19 chapters and 152 articles and covered 105 pages in the official edition. It detailed a large number of programs that were to be pursued under the rubric of agrarian reform, including colonization, infrastructure development, preparation of lands, and extension of credit and technical assistance. The law gave first priority to the distribution of government-owned lands and then provided a series of conditions under which private lands could be acquired by the government. The law enumerated the steps that had to be taken to legitimize the transfer of land from private to public hands, including the various appeals that were available to landholders. In another passage, an equally lengthy process was detailed for granting title to new landowners.[24]

Although Law 135 reflected the extreme complexity of landholding patterns and tenancy arrangements in Colombia and acknowledged that redistribution alone did not constitute an effective land reform, it also permitted landowners numerous opportunities to forestall action by the state. Clearly, it gave an advantage to those who had the time, financial resources, influential connections, and knowledge to pursue their cases through legal and administrative machinery. Moreover, many of the activities that were legalized by the reform were to rest on data and analyses derived from land surveys and accurate records of title. Since the availability of this information was negligible in Colombia, the state was frequently unable to sustain a case against private landowners who wished to retain their land or to sell it, at an advantageous price, to the state (Felstehausen 1971, 169).

The task of implementing the reform was to belong to the newly created agency, INCORA. Its first year of operation in 1962 was marked by efforts to set up appropriate administrative and financial procedures for pursuing this task. Also that year, the agency bought enough private land to distribute 128 rural property titles and it granted 1,133 titles to public lands (INCORA n.d.). The choice of which lands to acquire and who would benefit from their distribution was made on the basis of settling long-standing disputes over titles that were thought to endanger public order. INCORA's initial budget to carry out these activities, however, amounted to only 100,000 pesos, approximately 1 percent of the national budget, hardly a sufficient sum to allow the agency to pursue effectively the large number of tasks assigned to it.

Although the Conservatives had acquiesced to the 1961 legislation after negotiation and compromise, and most had supported it in Congress, they considered agrarian reform to be a Liberal Party issue (Bailey 1975, 37). When the Conservatives took their turn at the helm in 1962 under the National Front agreement, it was clear that they were more concerned with maintaining the loyalty of the landowners than with benefiting the peasants. Moreover, the

Conservatives were not concerned, as the Liberals had been, with internal factionalism that might result in a loss of power by the top-level party regulars. Indicative of the greater reserve with which agrarian reform was treated during the administration of Guillermo León Valencia was a decree establishing criteria to determine the measures of "adequate use" that would exempt private landholdings from expropriation (Bagley and Botero 1977, 42; Gómez 1975, 51). The criteria were generous to landholders and complicated the task of acquiring land. During this administration, from mid 1962 to mid 1966, only 1,711 beneficiaries received title to private land acquired by INCORA. At the same time, however, INCORA's efforts to distribute state lands continued, and approximately 24,000 families were given provisional title to such property, much of it of marginal fertility or located in remote or even inaccessible regions. The institute also continued to acquire land that it integrated into irrigation regions and improved but did not distribute. From 1963 onward, INCORA invested close to 40 percent of its total annual expenditures in infrastructure development. An additional 20–25 percent was used for a program of supervised credit, and approximately 11 percent was spent on administrative costs (INCORA 1975). These expenditures, which INCORA justified as necessary to the accomplishment of its tasks, nevertheless diminished the funds available for acquiring and distributing land.

Thus, while something was being done in the name of agrarian reform between 1962 and 1966, it was evident that a full-scale attack on the structure of land tenure in the country was not proceeding apace, nor were reform monies being spent in the rapid accomplishment of such a goal. State and party elites reached an agreement that permitted the legislation of an apparently reformist solution but not one that allowed for its vigorous implementation. The agrarian reform institute, in the meantime, set about responding to its mandate through the acquisition of state property and only secondarily through expropriation or purchase of private landholdings. In this, they were carrying out both the letter and the spirit of the law.

The Liberal Party, in accordance with the National Front agreement, assumed the presidency in mid 1966. Carlos Lleras, erstwhile champion of agrarian reform, became president and used his period in office to infuse life into the reform effort and to mobilize peasant organizations to support his initiative. In terms of agricultural policy, Lleras pledged his administration to increasing productivity and to transforming Colombia's peasants into productive small farmers through the distribution of land, credit, and technical assistance. The commitment to ameliorating social inequities in the countryside, which set him apart from most other Colombian politicians, is partly explained by a deep and personal concern for rural conditions.[25] In addition to his moral commitment, however, Lleras was anticipating the end of the National Front agreement in 1974, when he hoped to be launched again as the Liberal candidate for president. To this end, he and the Llerista faction of the party calculated that widespread electoral support in the countryside could be mobilized through agrarian reform.

But in 1966 there were strong impediments to the vigorous pursuit of such a strategy. The pressures that encouraged the legislation in 1961 had lessened considerably. In addition, the complex and vague legislation had itself become a tool allowing the landowners to forestall action. Finally, there was little organized pressure from the peasant population, which might have served as a counterpoint to the powerful landowning interests in the country. Lleras, if he wished to pursue a more vigorous agrarian reform, was therefore in a position of having to stimulate a more supportive environment for his initiative. He attempted to do this in two ways: first, through the mobilization of a peasant organization to offset the pressures brought by landowners; and second, through the promulgation of clarifying and facilitating legislation.

In May 1967, in response to the recommendations of a special study committee, Lleras spearheaded the creation of what was to become the National Association of Peasant Beneficiaries (ANUC), which, through state sponsorship, quickly enrolled a membership of a million peasants in about 500 affiliates (Affonso 1973; Bagley 1982, 22–29; Bagley and Botero 1977, 45–46). The organization was given the task of providing vocal support to the agrarian policy and providing part of the administrative infrastructure through which the reform would be implemented. The following year, Lleras succeeded in ushering through Congress Law 1 of 1968, which was designed to facilitate agrarian reform by specifying the conditions under which tenants and share-croppers could become owners of the land they worked (Felstehausen 1971, 175; Gómez 1975; Moncayo 1975, 36). It called on tenants and sharecroppers to register their claims with local officials in order to become eligible to benefit from INCORA programs.

INCORA's activities in the next two years indicate the changes that occurred under Lleras. In terms of constant 1972 prices, the agency's budget increased from 564 million pesos in 1967 to 1,082.7 million by 1970 (INCORA n.d.). From 1961 through 1967 the agency had distributed 2,243 titles to land purchased by the agency; between 1968 and the end of 1970, it distributed 5,003 titles to land it had acquired. In the latter period, the agency also distributed over a million hectares of state land, twice the annual average of the previous six years. Nevertheless, private land still amounted to only about 6 percent of the total distributed.

Ultimately, the fate of agrarian reform in Colombia was sealed by the unintended consequences of Lleras's initiatives. To begin with, although the 1968 law strengthened INCORA and stimulated land acquisition and distribution, it also precipitated a massive expulsion of sharecroppers and tenants from private estates (Gómez 1975, 59). The law, by requiring registration of those sharecroppers and tenants who wished to become eligible to purchase land, made it possible for landowners to identify "troublemakers" and to take measures to drive them off the land. Also during this period, a new word found its way into the Colombian vocabulary and was used frequently by disgruntled landowners to describe the effect of the agency on their agricultural holdings. To be "incorada" meant to have one's land become the subject of an investigation by INCORA to determine if it was being utilized productively and if its legal status was clear. While being investigated, the land could not be sold, and many landowners complained that the procedure made it inadvisable for them to invest in crops or improvements (Emiliani Roman 1971).

The Lleras reform initiative not only stimulated the activities of the landlords, it also set in motion a process of peasant mobilization that quickly eluded the control of the state. In 1969, peasant invasions of private and public lands began to accelerate rapidly. In 1970, invasions in various areas of the country were reported to number in the thousands, in spite of Lleras's advice to the peasant organizations that they "must not associate for purposes of violating the law."[26] When the Conservatives assumed the presidency in 1970, ANUC took on a life of its own. Moreover, the distance between the government and the peasant organizations increased, since much of the mobilization effort had been carried out under the thinly veiled initiative of the Liberal Party (Bagley and Laun 1977, 53). In 1971, in a manifesto adopted at ANUC's national directors' meeting, the organization demanded a rapid acceleration of the reform that was certain to strike terror in the hearts of large landowners, party leaders, and state elites. The manifesto called for an end to tenancy and sharecropping, the free distribution of land, a total restructuring of economic, social, and political relations in the countryside, and a recognition of the legal right of squatters to acquire title to the land they had recently invaded (ANUC 1971; Zuleta 1973). In response to the loss of control of the radicalized ANUC, the government of Conservative president Misael Pastrana attempted to consolidate some peasant acquiescence to its policies through the support of a rival wing of the organization, which it viewed as the "official" ANUC. Nevertheless, the more radical wing of the movement continued to encourage and support land invasions, public protests, and marches throughout 1971 and 1972 (Bagley 1982, 29–42; Soles 1974).

These instances of rural pressure and unrest from an organized and more independent peasantry forced a reluctant Conservative government to continue the redistributive effort of the Lleras years while at the same time attempting to quash the radical wing of ANUC. During 1971 and 1972, the Pastrana administration distributed 7,066 permanent and provisional titles to land acquired by the state, amounting to over 125,000 hectares, and INCORA's budget reached 1,143.9 million pesos in 1972 (see Fig. 7.1).

But the land distribution, the threat of further state action, and the radicalization of the peasant movement also set up a fierce reaction among the landowners and their sympathizers in national politics. The years 1970–72 were punctuated by a national debate that centered on the agrarian question

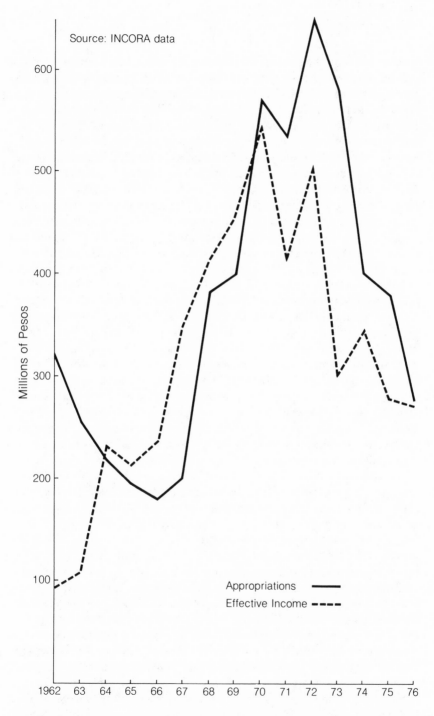

Figure 7.1. Appropriations and Effective Income of INCORA (Colombia), 1962–76

149

(DANE 1971). In the process, INCORA, the Lleras administration, and the peasant organizations all came under severe attack. Reports issued by official investigators criticized INCORA for its inefficiency and its support of the radicalization of the peasant movement. INCORA officials were said to be encouraging illegal takeovers of private property and openly collaborating with communists in the countryside (DANE 1971; Emiliani Roman 1971; Samper 1971). The Colombian Agricultural Society (SAC), representing the large landowners, mobilized an extensive public and private campaign to force the state to clarify its policies and halt the redistributive effort (Pardo Buelvas 1972). Conservatives railed against the lack of incentives to invest in agricultural enterprises occasioned by rural unrest and unclear policies, while the Liberal Party, in its own rejection of Lleras's policy, argued that more impetus should be given to an agrarian reform based on colonization efforts in frontier areas (Gómez 1975).

Then, with the announcement of its development plans in 1971 and 1972, the Pastrana administration, little committed to reform in any event, made redistribution secondary to the necessity of increasing agricultural output (Fedesarrollo 1975, 11–12). In a subsequent meeting between representatives of the Pastrana administration, the political parties, and SAC in Chicorral, Tolima, an agreement was reached to set extremely low standards for determining whether or not a plot of land was adequately exploited, thus qualifying or disqualifying it for expropriation. Moreover, the agreement permitted landowners to use both social and economic criteria to avoid the actions of IN-CORA. This meant that if landowners could offer proof that they had made even minimal efforts to provide social benefits for the peasants associated with their land—contributions to schooling or the community chest, for instance—expropriation would not be deemed justifiable (Gómez 1975, 61). In addition, new credits were to be made available for large- and medium-scale agriculture, and land taxes were to be eased. Importantly, although Liberal Party representatives participated in the meeting, none of the Llerista faction was invited.

The Chicorral Agreement formally ended the period of "progressive" agrarian reform in Colombia. The period left its mark on party leaders and on the policy makers staffing official ministries and agencies, but it was hardly the kind that would encourage a return to a redistributive policy in the future. Landowners indicated their reluctance to invest in increased production until the social situation in rural areas became calmer. Land invasions were stimulated by the government's decision to pursue a more vigorous reform, and though it never recognized the vailidity of invasions as a means to acquire land, the Liberal administration found it difficult to inhibit them, given its own support of peasant organizational activities and the desire to win friends among the peasants. Lleras himself lost the leadership of the Liberal Party. Ultimately, the peasant support he tried to mobilize was ineffective in a situation in which major political decisions, such as who would be the party's candidate for the presidency, were made through deals reached within high-level councils of the country's oligarchic parties. Without access to such discussions, the peasants could not really help Lleras. Moreover, in the 1970 election, a newly organized populist party, ANAPO, supporting former military dictator Rojas Pinilla, made a significant showing in urban areas, emphasizing the need of the traditional parties to shore up their support there (Campos and McCamant 1972; Solaún 1980).

After these events, one looked largely in vain among state and party elites for those with the temerity to support agrarian reform. Even Carlos Lleras stated publicly that he accepted the Chicorral Agreement as being necessary to the coalition politics required by the National Front (Gómez 1975, 62). No national politicians repeated his "error" in later years; Lleras had clearly stepped outside the boundaries of oligarchic politics and had stimulated a situation that was difficult for the state and the parties to cope with. By the end of the Pastrana administration in 1974, the minister of agriculture was arguing that an effective agrarian reform could never be consummated, because it would be impossible to dedicate enough resources to accomplish it. Moreover, he stated, rural incomes would increase as more peasants became wage laborers engaged on the large commercial agricultural enterprises (Gómez 1975, 54).

Parallel to these events came laws that impeded any expansion of agrarian reform. Law 4 of 1973 further specified the conditions for expropriation, lightened the burden of land taxation, and emphasized cooperative enterprises among peasants rather than small family farms (Fedesarrollo 1975, 112–13). Law 5 of 1973 sanctioned the capitalization of agriculture as a means of increasing production and established provisions for securing a salaried work force in the countryside (Moncayo 1975, 42). Law 6 of 1974 stabilized and legitimized tenancy agreements with the purpose of normalizing social relationships in the countryside, which were considered to have been upset by Law 1 of 1968 (Fedesarrollo 1975, 114). These laws were accompanied by actions to cut back on INCORA's programs. The budget of the agency diminished sharply, declining to 860.6 million pesos in 1973 and then to 743.8 million in 1974 (constant 1972 prices). Distribution of titles and land declined by more than one-third from 1973 to 1974.

In the 1970s, policy makers became more explicit in differentiating between landowners and "agricultural entrepreneurs." The latter were to receive extensive government protection and support, while the former would be encouraged to enter the ranks of the entrepreneurs. In a broader sense, *traditional agriculture* became a term of disapprobation and referred to both latifundism and minifundism. *Commercial agriculture*, on the other hand, was used as a catchword for capitalist agricultural enterprises that used advanced technologies and wage labor.[27] Thus, when Alfonso López Michelsen won the presidential election of 1974, he followed the Pastrana administration in encouraging large-scale agriculture, stating the necessity of achieving a 5 percent growth rate per year in agricultural output (Fedesarrollo 1975, 13). The administration's most complete statement of policies to be pursued, "To Close the Gap," indicated that the agricultural sector had gained in importance in national development plans (DNP n.d.). Large-scale commercial agriculture was cited for its contributions to export earnings, a recognition of the impact of the coffee "bonanza" of the mid 1970s and developments in the production of crops such as flowers, cotton, rice, and sugar, as well as in livestocking. Moreover, this sector was credited as a major source of labor absorption and as thus worthy of increased support from the state. The López Michelsen administration was more explicit than previous ones in stating that "social conditions will be the criteria for deciding whether or not land reform should apply, and not the search for greater efficiency through land improvement."[28]

The administration declared a moratorium on the further acquisition of land by INCORA and championed the creation of an agency that would assume control over the institute's irrigation and drainage projects. Then López Michelsen gave the reform agency the tasks of distributing title to the land it already owned, legalizing outstanding claims, and ameliorating social tensions in rural areas (when they became threatening) through the implementation of marginal reform activities. The budget of INCORA continued to be sharply reduced each year, and it was allotted only 541.1 million pesos, in 1972 prices, in 1976. The perspectives of this administration on rural development and agrarian reform were then accepted by the government of Julio César Turbay Ayala (1978–82). During Turbay Ayala's term in office, the rejection of agrarian reform was manifested in the return of some land acquired by INCORA to original owners; a number of large-scale evictions of peasants from estates and private lands were officially sanctioned through police and military operations and a tough national security law. National development plans of the late 1970s and early 1980s called for strengthening the commercial agricultural sector and weakening the role of the state in agriculture (DNP 1980).

The peasant mobilization that had provided an impulse to redistribution in the late 1960s and early 1970s was increasingly subjected to repression and co-optation under Pastrana, López Michelsen, and Turbay Ayala. The radical wing of ANUC alienated its only ally in the national government, INCORA, through what many officials considered "irresponsible and ridiculous" demands for free distribution of land. It also became factionalized and encountered difficulties forming effective coalitions with students and workers. At the local level, many of its leaders were imprisoned, and others joined guerrilla bands. The "official" wing of ANUC was a creature of the state and thus was incapable of making effective demands on it. Moreover, the state was successful in confining much peasant activity to local areas, where it could be dealt with most easily by piecemeal concessions and co-optive devices (Bagley 1982; Bagley and Botero 1977). Then, under the Turbay Ayala government, rural areas were heavily militarized and peasant organizational activities were more firmly repressed.

The two decades of Colombia's experience with agrarian reform can be summarized briefly. First, the initial phase of the reform indicated the political capital that elites could accumulate on the national and international levels through the apparent commitment to social and economic reform; the commitment to legislate and the commitment to implement could be usefully separated by states that were more interested in forestalling radical changes than in spearheading them. Second, the "radical" phase of agrarian reform in the late 1960s left party leaders and state elites aware that mobilizing the countryside could be a difficult process to control. The careers of individuals and institutions could in fact be damaged by the zealous championing of reforms that threatened powerful interests. With the winding down of the agrarian reform that occurred in the 1970s, the rejection of agrarian reform was justified on technical grounds and the expansion of large-scale capitalist agriculture was championed as a rational means to achieve national development.

THE DEMISE OF AGRARIAN REFORM

The process of policy change in Colombia was echoed in most other Latin American countries. Even in Mexico and Bolivia, where social revolution spurred massive land redistributions, disillusion with or distaste for agrarian reform became as marked as it was in countries where the land reform process had been dominated primarily by elites. Extensive agrarian reform in general came to be seen by state elites as a risky, expensive, and politically volatile policy, difficult to implement and often unrewarding in terms of increases in production or political support.

To begin with, as we have seen in the case of Colombia, the support for agrarian reform as a development ideology by state elites and some politicians in the early 1960s gradually evaporated as the reforms proved difficult and expensive to effect and as opposition to them mounted. Proponents of agrarian reform had stressed that it could serve as a means to increase agricultural productivity and as a solution to social inequities (Dorner and Kanel 1971; Griffin 1976). Citing evidence that yields per unit of land were at times higher on smallholdings than on latifundios due to the intensive nature of cultivation, they contended that the redistribution of landholdings would redound at the national level in terms of greater agricultural output. However, they also acknowledged that for the expected increases to occur, redistribution had to be accompanied by major commitments in terms of organization, infrastructure, technical assistance, credit, and green revolution technology—a costly investment for states pinched for money, appropriate administrative structures, communication channels, and time.

The experience of Venezuela is instructive of the expense and production problems involved in pursuing a redistributive path. Venezuela's agrarian reform, spearheaded by an urban reformist party in search of a rural support base and aided by an economy flush with oil revenues and industrial development potential, was more extensive than most reforms that were carried out without social revolution. Nevertheless, it left a number of unmet needs in its wake. Table 7.4, cataloging the accomplishments of seventeen years, provides data on the achievements and shortcomings of the 1960 reform. It attests to the small size of the plots distributed, the large number of peasants unaffected, and the extent of the needs yet to be met with official aid for schools, housing, credit, and infrastructure. Moreover, as we saw in Chapter 5, the productivity of Venezuela's agricultural sector declined, especially in terms of the provision of basic foodstuffs, to the point that the country was importing massive amounts of food by the mid1970s.

Similarly in Chile, two administrations—one reformist and one revolutionary—made major attempts to redistribute land and channel public resources to the new beneficiaries. Between 1965 and 1973, approximately ten million hectares of land were distributed to about 60,000 families, or approximately 10 percent of the economically active population in agriculture (Klein 1980, 101–4). But during these years, political upheaval discouraged private investment in the sector, and peasants adapted to their new status by consuming much of the food they had formerly been denied. Administrative bottlenecks and extensive rural conflict and disorganization further impeded productive gains from the land distribution effort. Production of basic crops also fell in these years. Ultimately, of course, the Allende administration was overthrown in a violent coup organized on the basis of opposition to his redistributive efforts in both rural and urban areas.

The reform carried out by the military government in Peru also was fraught with difficulty, in spite of major expenditures of public funds and commitments of personnel. Most of the 8 million hectares expropriated were organized into agrarian cooperatives. Approximately 400,000 families benefited from the reform, but by 1980, the number of peasant families eking out a living from plots of less than 5 hectares had almost doubled the number for 1961 (Klein 1980, 116–17). Temporary workers, who provided the cooperatives with seasonal labor, were excluded from the reform and frequently ended up being exploited by its beneficiaries. They, along with minifundistas and members of indigenous communities who did not benefit from the reform, became active claimants for redistributive policies and were involved in numerous invasions of the newly formed cooperatives in the 1970s. In one region, 80,000 hectares of land were taken over from reform beneficiaries by surrounding rural communities that received neither land nor technical or finan-

Table 7.4. Accomplishments and Needs after Seventeen Years
of Agrarian Reform, Venezuela

Accomplishments	Needs
8,300,000 acres of land distributed	47 percent of beneficiaries received plots of only 3–12 acres
160,000 families settled	190,000 beneficiaries are waiting for land
1,910 new schools built	51 percent of beneficiaries are illiterate
57,750 new housing units constructed	59 percent of beneficiaries live in shacks
$186,000,000 in credit granted	55 percent of beneficiaries have never received credit of any kind
34,500 miles of new roads built	53 percent of the roads are impassible during the rainy season
238,300 acres irrigated	90 percent of the settlements are without irrigation and 83 percent are without wells

SOURCE: Reproduced, with minor changes, from Schuyler 1980, 189–90, by permission of the Schenkman Publishing Company, Inc., Cambridge, Mass.

cial aid from the state.[29] Those who did not benefit from the reform, about a third of the economically active population in rural areas, increasingly asked for the breakup of the cooperatives into individual holdings. Moreover, in the 1970s, production of staple crops became a problem of concern for the state. Disillusion with agrarian reform was subsequently reflected in public policy. Through an agricultural development law of 1980, it became possible to offer land as collateral for credit, a process prohibited in the 1969 reform in order to help beneficiaries retain control over their holdings. Private investment from national and foreign sources was encouraged on the agricultural frontier in the Amazon region, and the acquisition of extensive estates was made possible through a more open land market.

These experiences do not mean that agrarian reform is not an effective means to raise levels of production and productivity in Latin America, but that it is a policy that requires far more than mere distribution of land if goals are to be achieved over the long term. In practice, the short-term problems of implementing the reforms and of providing basic services to peasant beneficiaries in terms of credit, extension, organization and marketing aid, health, education, sanitation, infrastructure, and technology, as well as the political upheaval implicit in redistributive measures, caused sufficient disillusion among state elites to make them skeptical of the long-term advantages of reform. Indeed, the provision of a complex package of programs to peasant beneficiaries was a major problem faced in Peru, Bolivia, and Chile, where a sincere commitment to reform did exist.[30] Thus, although it was possible to demonstrate that, given certain conditions, smallholdings, peasant cooperatives, or collective farms can be very productive, the provision of such conditions turned out to be both politically explosive and economically onerous in most Latin American countries.

Moreover, the threat of social upheaval that was sparked by the Cuban Revolution diminished during the late 1960s and 1970s, until events in Nicaragua in 1979 renewed some apprehensions among state elites in other countries.[31] The reduced threat was apparent in terms of diminished pressure from the United States to undertake reforms by the mid to late 1960s. The reduction in pressure to pursue structural changes was followed by the withdrawal of economic incentives for such actions.[32] While U.S. foreign policy failed to sustain concern with reform in the region, international lending agencies developed new priorities and solutions to the problems of the agricultural sector that minimized the importance of land reform. In particular, the World Bank and the Interamerican Development Bank offered rationales for alternative approaches to the improvement of subsistence-sector agriculture that largely avoided addressing questions of land tenure and distribution, as will be discussed in Chapter 8.

The political importance of the peasant population also diminished during this period. In some cases, as in Venezuela, Bolivia, and Mexico, the rural poor were incorporated as more or less quiescent elements in national party organizations. In other cases, as in Peru, Chile, and Colombia, rural followings that had been mobilized on the basis of redistributive promises proved to be difficult to control and to be a source of headache for the party in power once they learned to make effective demands on the government.[33] Moreover, the expanding urban electorate failed to support redistribution in the countryside for fear it would bring higher food prices. Thus, for party leaders, the electoral incentives of promising agrarian reform lost considerable impact through experience.

More important in terms of the political influence that was at stake for the peasant masses, many openly competitive regimes, in which the creation and maintenance of a base of electoral support required some concern for redistributive policies, were replaced by military regimes ideologically opposed to such undertakings. Events in Brazil, Argentina, Uruguay, and Chile are the most notable examples of authoritarian and repressive solutions to economic and political problems that diminished the importance of numbers in national politics. Elections themselves were postponed indefinitely in most of these regimes or were carefully controlled as a means of legitimizing the government and leaders in power. In Chile, the move away from agrarian reform after the 1973 coup was rapid; in the first five years of the military government, 4,000 out of a total of 6,000 expropriated estates were returned to their original owners or sold at auction. This and other modifications of the agrarian reforms of the

Frei and Allende administrations meant that 21,000 families (of a total of 60,000) were excluded from the reformed sector (Klein 1980, 105–7). Even in Peru, the lack of competition in the electoral arena made it easier for the military junta to move away from the reformist policies of the 1968 coup. Similarly, in Mexico, Ecuador, Paraguay, and Nicaragua before 1979, although authoritarian regimes felt the need to cultivate some popular support, there was little need to outpromise the opposition when the opposition was banned, repressed, or effectively controlled. Thus, although the rural masses may once have seemed to be an attractive constituency to national political leaders, regime changes clearly eroded their importance.

At the same time, because of increased national concern about the agricultural sector and the economic resources controlled by large landowners, the political influence of those groups rose. Their support became vital to the continued strength and economic progress of the regimes in power, as we saw earlier in the cases of Mexico, Brazil, and Colombia (Chapter 4). The political opposition of elite interests was able effectively to block delivery of promised reforms to the peasants. In northeast Brazil, for instance, the regional development agency, SUDENE, was stymied by the political power of large landowners and was effectively unable to distribute land to needy peasants. Instead, in a pattern similar to the experience of INCORA in Colombia, about 40 percent of the agency's funds for land reform were spent on road-building projects.[34]

From many perspectives, the agrarian reforms failed in the sense that they did not result in increased production or in notable improvements in the conditions of rural life. Moreover, redistributive efforts created considerable tension in the countryside—from threatened or dispossessed landowners, from peasants seeking to become beneficiaries, from those who were already benefiting but who wanted more extensive state aid, and from those who were excluded from the reforms altogether. Nevertheless, from the perspective of the Latin American states themselves, the reforms had some positive ramifications.

THE STATE AS BENEFICIARY OF AGRARIAN REFORM

Even after the heyday of agrarian reformism ended and state elites had rejected a redistributive path toward rural development, the reform legislation was not annulled. This was not an oversight on the part of state elites. Rather, it reflected their recognition of the benefits that could accrue from having established and maintained the right to appropriate and distribute landholdings when this was considered to be of "social value" or economic necessity. Indeed, the experience in many Latin American countries during the 1960s and 1970s indicated that the threat of expropriation was an effective tool in encouraging the modernization and increased efficiency of agricultural estates by forcing landlords to make their holdings more productive or sell off their land to the more entrepreneurially inclined. This was the case, as we have seen, in Venezuela, Ecuador, Colombia, Chile, and Peru.

In addition, distribution of land to hard-pressed peasants on a piecemeal basis offered significant opportunities for curtailing mobilization among land-hungry peasants. As a co-optive mechanism, as a means to help keep the lid on the aggregation of rural protest and violence, agrarian reform proved to be useful.[35] In a related fashion, to the extent that the agrarian reforms were implemented, they created new social divisions in the countryside that increased impediments to class-based rural protest. A more fragmented peasantry was an obvious outcome of reform in Peru, for example, where nonbeneficiaries frequently directed their protest activities not toward the large landowners but toward other peasants, those who had benefited from the reform efforts. In effect, state elites were able to use agrarian reform to manipulate the tensions created by the expansion of capitalist agriculture without fundamentally altering the conditions that gave rise to such tensions.

Moreover, in many countries, those who benefited from the reforms became dependent upon continued state services and benefits. Thus, in Ecuador, Redclift (1978, 116–17) reports:

> Although some organizations . . . emphasize their independence of the government, active participation in the process through which land is transferred and agricultural credit obtained, has served to neutralize the more politically radical peasant organizations. Their relations with government are not so much "bargaining relations" in which the peasantry exerts pressure on the government as an unequal exchange under which peasants take their place in a queue.

In Mexico, where a major agrarian reform occurred, the continued viability of the ejido sector was fundamentally tied to support and services provided by the state. And in Peru, Colombia, and elsewhere the economic weakness of reform beneficiaries left them little alternative but to continue to rely on and petition for support from the state. Thus, while agrarian reforms in Latin America failed in many respects, it provided the individual states with an increased capacity to fragment and control the political behavior of sectors of the rural poor.

In a related fashion, the state also gained greater control over the rural economy. In appropriating land, generally from inefficient landowners, it gained immediate control over productive resources. In Nicaragua, for instance, where a social revolution placed control of about 23 percent of the agricultural land in the hands of the agrarian reform agency (INRA), the state gained control over 18 percent of the land planted in cotton, 15 percent of that producing coffee, 40 percent of the sugarcane areas, 31 percent of the rice land,

21 percent of the area planted in sorghum, and 9 percent of the land growing sesame, as well as a considerable amount of the land given over to tobacco and bananas, the commercial and export crops that were essential to the national economy (USDA 1980, 19). Elsewhere, of course, gains were much more modest, but new territories brought into production through colonization efforts in frontier areas also expanded the role of the state in the economy. Furthermore, the state's credit policies for reform projects, its extension work, and its marking and input services generally came with strings attached, strings that required the recipients of its services to sow certain crops, utilize certain inputs, and follow certain agricultural practices. Technical and financial assistance to the reformed sector therefore had the potential to help the state meet national development goals such as increases in the production of certain crops. In fact, as Redclift reports, the more economically successful the peasant beneficiaries were, the more dependent they became on the state for continued support and supply of resources.[36] In this regard, the state often used its power over the peasant beneficiaries to incorporate them more fully into market relationships involving both the production and the consumption of goods.

Finally, the experience with agrarian reform, the increased familiarity with its difficulties, and the development of agencies responsible for problems of production and welfare in rural areas made the states' move toward alternative approaches to the problems of rural development easier to accomplish. As in the case of Colombia, the 1970s witnessed a regionwide shift toward the concept of integrated rural development. These schemes and the experience of putting them into practice are the subject of the following chapter.

8 | Integrated Rural Development: The "New Dualism"

Agrarian reform was widely touted as a solution to national development problems and agricultural stagnation in Latin America in the 1960s. As we have seen, reform experiments had a number of beneficial results for the state. They successfully goaded many of the region's large landowners to modernize their estates or to sell their holdings to the more entrepreneurially minded. In addition, the reforms benefited a modest number of peasant families, who became stable, dependent, and supportive clienteles of the agrarian reform agencies, specific political parties, and the state itself. Related to this was the increased presence of the state in rural areas in terms of development projects, resource allocation, and conflict management. Importantly, the state reaped these benefits without significantly altering dominant landholding structures, an outcome found only in countries where major social revolutions had occurred. Thus, the agrarian reforms were useful to state elites even when they were not vigorously pursued and therefore remained as part of the legal and institutional apparatus of the state long after they were repudiated as viable policies.

By the mid 1970s, further efforts to redistribute land had become unlikely, given the greater capacity of the state to respond to rural conflict and the growth in the economic and political importance of the capitalist agricultural sector that had taken place (see Chapter 4). At the same time, the 1970s were marked by a new consensus among state elites that agriculture had become an impediment to national economic development and rapid industrialization. Increasing concern was voiced over the national and international ramifications of lagging domestic food output, high rates of unemployment and underemployment, massive rural-to-urban migration, and a constricted internal market for domestic manufactures (see Chapter 5).

Interestingly, the urban and industrial bias that characterized development policy after the 1930s and 1940s was important in encouraging state elites to direct major infusions of capital, goods, and services into rural areas in the

1970s. The provision of cheap food for the urban work force had been undermined by the failure of domestic producers to increase output; increasingly large food import bills accounted for precious foreign exchange that might otherwise be used to stimulate further industrialization. Both added to inflationary pressures that state elites linked to the potential for urban political unrest and the lack of capital for further industrialization efforts. Moreover, in an increasingly constrained international economy of rising oil prices and declining prices for many traditional primary exports, Latin American governments were concerned about the alarming growth of foreign debts and debt-servicing responsibilities. Thus, increased production of food became a major development priority during the 1970s, and as a consequence, rural development figured prominently in national plans.[1]

Within the realm of development policy making, many critiques of the agricultural sector argued that increases in the production of domestic foodstuffs would follow upon the infusion of credit, infrastructure, technology, health care, education, and other amenities in poor rural areas. With the World Bank in the lead, this perspective was strongly supported by international lending agencies, especially after 1973, when Robert McNamara, president of the World Bank, indicated the priority that would be assigned to rural development by the Bank.[2] "New style" projects were encouraged and development planners reached the broad agreement that not only would they improve the standard of living of the "poorest 40 percent" but they would also stimulate national development. In the 1970s, the World Bank added considerable international capital along with technical and rhetorical justifications for a nonredistributional approach to rural poverty. In fact, by 1980, rural development had become the largest loan category of the Bank.[3] Much of this money was directed toward integrated rural development programs.

The integrated approach to rural development called for extensive infusions of development aid in rural areas in order to raise productivity among peasant farmers and address some of the more visible aspects of poverty and underdevelopment.[4] The programs adopted during the 1970s asserted that peasants would not be able to escape from centuries of poverty and exploitation unless they were supplied with access to credit, extension services, green revolution technology, water, roads, markets, health facilities, education for their children, and nonfarm sources of rural employment.[5] The approach was oriented toward providing locally appropriate packages of these goods and services to rural communities; fundamental to it was the idea that peasant beneficiaries must be active participants in the planning and implementation of integrated projects for their communities.

Generally, programs were designed with three components: (1) direct inputs to improve production (usually given the largest portion of program funds); (2) infrastructure to encourage and support increased production; and (3) social infrastructure such as health and educational facilities and peasant organizations (usually given the smallest portion of program funds). The approach largely avoided the issue of redistribution of land, indicating that goods and services could be provided that would enable the peasant to produce more at a greater profit; these could be applied without altering the structure of landholding and would still have a significant impact on the standard of living in rural areas.

Throughout Latin America, discussions about the new approach to rural development took place within national and international bureaucracies with little input from legislators, party officials, representatives of large-scale farmers, or the peasants who were to benefit from the programs. The decisions to pursue integrated rural development were made largely in response to the fact that it offered planners a well-reasoned argument about the causes of rural poverty and underproductivity and provided coherent ideas about how public policies could be designed to respond to these questions. These programs were not undertaken primarily in response to the pressures or influence of specific societal interests. In contrast to the agrarian reform initiatives, the integrated rural development programs, which threatened few interests, were therefore generally planned and initiated without the need for strong political leadership to put together supportive coalitions or to maneuver around political opposition. It was only during the implementation of the programs that state elites encountered serious impediments to the pursuit of their plans.

Integrated rural development programs recommended themselves to state elites for a variety of reasons. They were based on a dualistic perception of the agricultural economy, a "new dualism" which asserted that peasants and large farmers faced distinct environments that presented them with distinct incentives and disincentives to produce particular kinds of crops and to adopt particular kinds of innovations. According to this perspective, the rationale for productive activities differed between the two types of agriculture. Capitalist farmers produced for a market and were interested in maximizing their long-range and absolute level of profits; peasant producers sought to maximize short-range security needs and to provide for family subsistence. Both large-scale farmers and peasants were judged to act rationally, given the constraints they faced in achieving their basic priorities. Further, the new approach argued that peasants had been profoundly discriminated against by previous development policies and by their inability to compete effectively in the market for goods and services or to receive adequate remuneration for their productive labor.

Thus, compared with the dualistic analysis that underlay earlier efforts to modernize agriculture in the region, the new dualism did not assume that all farm enterprises would eventually benefit from the same policy instruments in a gradual transformation from traditional to modern practices (see Chapter 3). The new analysis affirmed that the old dualistic "trickle down" approach would not work and was inappropriate to resolve the problems of the rural poor. Therefore, programs to develop agricultural potential and to improve conditions in rural areas had to be designed specifically to affect each sector of the agricultural economy. At the same time, the two sectors were seen as operating in relative isolation from each other. This meant that distinct public policies could be directed toward each and the state could continue to provide aid and subsidies to large-scale operations while a panoply of new programs targeted for the rural poor was added. In addition, the rural development approach affirmed the experience of colonization and agrarian reform efforts that extensive inputs of capital and resources were required if production and productivity were to increase. Politically, the new programs offered a method of diminishing rural poverty without requiring a redistribution of land and the political confrontations that such a course would signify.[6] They envisioned a larger role for the state in rural areas and they also promised considerable tangible resources with which to reward state and local politicians and with which to deal with unrest. Thus, the integrated approach to rural development was attractive to state elites because it appeared to make sense both technically and politically.

In practice, however, the integrated rural development programs encountered great difficulties.[7] Problems at the program level were endemic. From the most general perspective, the plans developed by state elites in the relative isolation of national bureaucratic headquarters became subject to administrative shortcomings and political patronage. For example, the administrative complexity of the programs mushroomed as the implications of the term *integrated* became apparent. A large number of agencies at all levels of government were assigned responsibilities and were expected to coordinate their activities with a variety of related organizations. At times, fifteen or twenty organizations were involved in a plan for a specific community. Problems of bureaucratic competition, personal animosities and ambitions, differing philosophies and clientele groups, as well as issues of compliance, scheduling, funding, and corruption, were extensive. Most pervasive was the problem of trying to ensure control over personnel and resource allocation while allowing for flexibility to meet local conditions. Moreover, program resources were often allocated according to political criteria, with little concern for maintaining the integrity of integrated solutions to local economic constraints. These issues loomed large as the programs moved from the formulation of neat "packages" to the implementation of real projects.

Pursuit of the administratively and rhetorically ambitious integrated rural development programs was bound to involve serious obstacles. Beyond the problems of management and administration, and regardless of the capacity to implement successfully, integrated rural development as an approach to rural development failed to address the limitation placed on peasant-based agriculture by the given distribution of land and water resources and failed to take seriously the question of increasing landlessness. The limitations and outcomes of such programs were clearly evident in initiatives undertaken in Mexico, Colombia, and Brazil.

INTEGRATED RURAL DEVELOPMENT IN MEXICO, COLOMBIA, AND BRAZIL

In the early 1970s, government planners in Mexico, Colombia, and Brazil began to call for a new approach to the problem of rural areas, orienting separate policies toward what they had come to define as the modern and traditional sectors. Concern with the inability to provide sufficient food for internal consumption figured prominently in the justification for an integrated approach to rural development in Mexico and Colombia. As we have seen, by the early 1970s, Mexico was importing large amounts of corn, wheat, and other grains each year and Colombia also faced a growing need to import food. In Brazil, policy makers' concern for rural development initially tended to center on the northeast and to focus on the potential volatility of the region's population if its intense level of poverty were not lessened. Concern mounted in the late 1970s also because of growing food import bills and inflationary prices for food in urban areas. Similarly, some officials, especially those in Mexico and Brazil, voiced concern over high rates of rural-to-urban migration and the desirability of increasing the size of the domestic consumer market by raising rural incomes. A further stimulus, most noticeable in Colombia and Brazil, was the availability of loans from international lending institutions for programs directed toward the "poorest 40 percent." In all three cases, the initiative to address these problems emanated from public officials, and policy development was largely confined to planners in national agencies. A variety of programs were initiated in response to the problems perceived by state elites; among the largest and most well planned and publicized of the programs were PIDER in Mexico, DRI in Colombia and POLONORDESTE in Brazil.[8]

The Programs: PIDER, DRI, and POLONORDESTE

In Mexico, planning for the PIDER program began in 1972 and 1973, within the administration of Luís Echeverría (1970–76); the first projects under the program were initiated in 1973. The Colombian DRI program was first considered by planners in 1973 under the Misael Pastrana administration (1970–74), but no action was taken until the López Michelsen administration (1974–78) committed itself to the plan in 1975. The POLONORDESTE program, which included both colonization and integrated rural development projects, was initiated in 1974 under the Ernesto Geisel administration (1974–79). The first projects were undertaken in 1975.

PIDER and DRI were designed to be national in scope. The Mexican program was based on the identification of microregions—131 by 1980—selected for characteristics of rural poverty and development potential.[9] The microregions were located throughout the country, with some concentration in the most heavily populated areas of central Mexico. About 50 percent of the rural poor lived in PIDER regions. The Colombian program was carried out in five regions, also selected on the basis of poverty indicators and development potential.[10] These microregions were found in the southwestern, central, and northwestern parts of the country and represented nine departments. In the early 1980s, plans were approved to add eight more departments to the DRI. In contrast, the POLONORDESTE program was limited to northeast Brazil, even though it covered an area of approximately 300,000 square miles (44.6 percent of the northeast) and was planned to benefit directly or indirectly 13 million inhabitants by 1980, nearly 9 million of whom lived in rural areas (Brazil, 1979b, 84; POLONORDESTE 1980). It included four colonization projects and 42 integrated rural development areas by 1980. The POLONORDESTE rural development projects were undertaken in priority areas; these areas were chosen for their agricultural potential and represented five major climatic zones.[11] Surveys of the selected regions were carried out, after which detailed programs for development aid were designed to meet region-specific needs. All these programs were multisectoral, involving projects for agriculture, physical infrastructure, health care, sanitation, and education. In each case, between 45 and 70 percent of program funds were allocated to directly productive activities (credit, product development, irrigation, conservation, rural industries), while another 20–35 percent were allocated for production support activities (extension, roads, rural electrification, marketing, and storage). From 10 to 20 percent of the funds were allocated for social infrastructures (educational facilities, rural health services, water supply, self-help materials).

The Mexican program, which cost $1.8 billion between 1973 and 1980, was expected to affect over six million people, or 22 percent of the rural population, by 1980 (PIDER 1980). Plans called for the program to be implemented through fourteen federal agencies coordinated by a staff office in the Ministry of Planning and Budgeting and by a committee at the state level. National, state, and microregional committees were expected to be involved in planning and monitoring investments in specific regions. In early 1981, PIDER was decentralized to the state level, and governors and state development committees assumed a central role in site selection, programming, and resource allocation. Program beneficiaries were expected to be actively involved in investments for their areas and to provide approximately 7 percent of the costs.

The Colombian program was in part modeled on the PIDER idea and was designed with some knowledge of the difficulties encountered in implementing the Mexician program. Comparatively, the Colombian plan was based on much larger regions and placed much greater emphasis on the dissemination of green revolution technology and on training than did the Mexican program; in DRI, no investment was planned for rural industries. [12] In addition, the experience of other Colombian rural development programs was incorporated into the program design (Swanberg 1981). The first-phase, five-year program was to cost $270 million, $129 million of which would be financed by the World Bank, the Interamerican Development Bank, and the Canadian International Development Agency. Project beneficiaries, about 1.5 million poor people, each of whom owned, rented, or sharecropped 20 hectares of land or less, were expected to finance approximately 10 percent of the program costs. Program planning, coordination, and evaluation were the responsibility of the National Planning Department; management, implementation, and monitoring were the responsibility of the Caja de Crédito Agrario, an agricultural credit institution attached to the Ministry of Agriculture. Thirteen government agencies were involved; organized hierarchically, planning and coordination activities involved community, municipal, departmental, and national committees composed of agency and community representatives (DRI 1980).

The Brazilian program, which cost 20.7 billion cruzeiros (constant 1979 prices) between 1975 and 1980, resulted from two years of discussions in the planning apparatus and fifty years of frustrating experience with various approaches to the problems of the northeast. By 1980 the World Bank had agreed to loan Brazil more than $150 million for six areas in the program, and the Interamerican Development Bank had advanced an additional $14 million for the program. POLONORDESTE (1980) emphasized credit for production and farm-level improvements and included credit for land purchases. It relied strongly on the state-level Secretariat of Planning for planning and implementation, while financial control, planning assistance, and policy guidelines remained in the hands of the Interior Ministry, the Secretariat of Planning, and the Ministry of Agriculture, in Brasília. Coordination of the programs at the regional level was to be carried out by the regional development agency, SUDENE, but the relatively strong and more enthusiastic planning and administrative structure at the state level resulted in direct state-national relationships that by-passed SUDENE, with coordination actually occurring at the state level. Often as many as thirty separate entities were involved in coordinating the individual projects (Finan and Fox 1980). Less emphasis was placed on local participation in POLONORDESTE than was the case in the Colombian and Mexican programs. The small farmer was the principal target of the Brazilian program, although only holdings of 200 hectares or more were officially excluded.

After the initial years of operation, planners generally continued to be optimistic about all three programs, stressing the relatively strong institutional development of the countries, their relatively high levels of national wealth, the technical preparation of program officials, and the generally nonconflictual nature of public programs that distribute resources without threatening the power of economic elites in the countryside. In Mexico and Brazil in particular, observers were encouraged by the apparent enthusiasm and dedication of field-level personnel and by the technical competence of program officials. Evaluators often referred to the three programs as valuable learning experiences for national and regional bureaucracies, as models that acquainted officials fully with integrated programs directed toward the alleviation of rural poverty. Moreover, each of the programs was credited with receiving considerable political support at the national and regional levels. Despite these positive evaluations, however, PIDER, DRI, and POLONORDESTE were inherently difficult to implement. In addition, the impact of greatly increased resources was minimal in terms of raising productivity or increasing rural welfare; this suggests that these integrated rural development programs and the assumptions of the new dualism on which they were based did not address the fundamental dynamics of rural poverty and underproductivity.

The Problems of Program Implementation

Perhaps the most persistent criticisms of PIDER, DRI, and POLONOR-DESTE related to organizational matters—planning, coordination, and monitoring—as would be expected from these multisectoral and multiagency approaches. Among the complaints made about PIDER, for example, was the failure of program agencies to work together at the national, state, or microregional level. In a 1978 evaluation, it was reported that over 50 percent of the problems involved in implementing the program related to issues of coordination and design (Cernea 1979, 25). State- and local-level action was especially deficient, due largely to the strong Mexican tradition of centralized decision making. In a renewed effort to achieve state-level coordination, the program was placed in the hands of state governors in January 1981 and state development committees and subcommittees for rural development were given the responsibility of programming and approving investments. Similarly, in Colombia, coordination of the DRI program proved difficult to achieve because of what one observer described as "excess bureaucratization and jealousies among agencies."[13] The two-headed management of the National Planning Department and the Caja de Crédito Agrario increased tension and confusion within the program. Delays in approval and funding of specific projects often amounted to a year or more. Bureaucratic and other problems created numerous conditions of overproduction and falling prices for staple items.[14] In Brazil, planning and organizational tensions were unavoidable given the large number of agencies involved in POLONORDESTE. In an analysis of one program area considered to be very successful by public officials and international lenders, the relationship among participating organizations was termed one of "coexistence" rather than coordination. Each agency continued to define its own priorities and determine the activities of its field agents.[15] Moreover, although the World Bank supported only six of the project areas, these ultimately consumed as much as half of all program funds; the attention given to Bank-financed projects, and the need to meet Bank criteria, caused serious shortages of funds and personnel for the others.[16] In a problem similar to that experienced by DRI in Colombia, disbursement of funds from Brasília and international lenders was slow and erratic, causing uncertainty and frustration for project implementers. In all three countries, the programs were criticized for being overly ambitious for the existing organizational and monitoring systems.

Another persistent problem was that of the "shopping list" mentality ("We want this, this, and this . . ."), in which case little thought was given to an integrated strategy, even though this was the central organizing concept of the programs. In Mexico, the extensive personnel turnover that occurred with each new administration minimized the emphasis given to long-term planning and maximized that given to expanding programs and expending resources as rapidly as possible in order to enhance the importance of political and bureaucratic officials. In this regard, filling orders on shopping lists became a positive benefit of the PIDER program, politically speaking, and the emphasis on integration became secondary to officials who in all likelihood would not be involved in the program in the next administration. One evaluator of PIDER complained that "instead of being concentrated to form a more coherent local development program, investments were scattered, aiming at providing something for everyone, which reduced their impact" (Cernea 1979, 32).

PIDER was also affected by changes in political administrations. It was widely regarded as an "Echeverría program" because it was initiated under his administration and was the most important and largest effort in rural development at the time. The administration of José López Portillo developed other poverty-oriented rural programs, notably those for rain-fed areas, deprived zones, and forestry and fishery development, and PIDER became "just another government program."[17] Salaries for PIDER officials were reduced under the new administration, exacerbating recruitment and personnel problems.[18] While formerly PIDER was credited with having the most aggressive, dedicated, and technically and politically astute leadership available, under López Portillo these characteristics were ascribed to individuals spearheading the programs to develop rain-fed areas and deprived zones. By the mid 1980s, PIDER had been subsumed in an organizational integration of several programs directed toward rain-fed agriculture.

In Colombia, although full requirements of Liberal and Conservative Party parity in all elected and appointed offices were phased out in the elections of 1974 and 1978, political realities continued to dictate the wisdom of carefully apportioning government ministries between partisans of the traditional parties, which encouraged the institutionalization of rivalry and suspicion among them. Additionally, ministries were often identified with important interests in the country—the Ministry of Agriculture with organizations representing large landholders, for example—a pattern that became an impediment to full commitment to the poverty-oriented approach taken by DRI. In this context, coordination was elusive. Nevertheless, while individual agencies differed in their commitment to DRI, it was an attractive program to political leaders, who were interested in the constituency-related payoffs promised by the distribution of state-sponsored goods and services in local areas. Here again, a shopping-list approach to resource allocation was as useful to politicians as a more integrated one, and had the advantage of being more easily and quickly accomplished.[19]

In Brazil, the program so carefully planned in Brasília was appropriated for political use during implementation. Local officials became involved in selecting sites for facilities, routes for roads, locations of other infrastructure, and recipients of jobs. Their participation in the distribution of program benefits was important for maintaining support for the military regime (Finan and Fox 1980). But official commitment to POLONORDESTE waned by the late 1970s and program funds diminished by more than half in real terms from 1978 to 1979. As crises and other priorities arose, program funds were siphoned off to meet more pressing needs, such as emergency drought assistance in the northeast. In this case, most of the funds were directed toward public works projects to employ 700,000 peasants made landless by the drought. Generally, the large landowners controlled the "work fronts" and distributed jobs on the basis of political criteria.

In addition, beneficiary participation was an especially weak link in the implementation of PIDER, DRI, and POLONORDESTE. The programs resulted from discussions and studies carried out in Mexico City, Bogotá, and Brasília, or in state-level capitals; they were not stimulated by demands from below and therefore did not have a developed infrastructure of beneficiary organizations to build on. In Mexico and Colombia, extensive hierarchies of committees were formed at the community, municipal, state/department, and national levels and numerous meetings were held, but the planning and monitoring of programs continued to be done at national headquarters or by field personnel of the planning agency, with the added involvement of state/departmental governors. In Mexico, participation generally meant the increased involvement of state-level officials in planning and coordination, not beneficiary mobilization. In Brazil, from the outset of POLONORDESTE, participation at the local level was given very low priority and almost no attention. Planners at the state level, with assistance from the World Bank, followed guidelines established in Brasília and gave little thought to the concerns of the local community. Program benefits reached the local level in the guise of patronage or government largess, not as goods and services claimed by the rural poor (Finan and Fox 1980, 15). Lack of experience with encouraging participation, as well as long traditions of top-down planning and implementation, were clearly important in explaining these failures. In addition, however, political regimes in each country had a vital interest in limiting the extent of participation and controlling its impact.

The state elites who spearheaded the integrated rural development programs were wary of the political problems that would result from mobilizing the rural poor. When they argued for participation, they meant organizing peasants to benefit effectively from the goods and services offered and to monitor the delivery and use of resources. They did not intend for the scope of participation to go beyond the local level and demonstrate to the state and society more generally that peasants should be taken into consideration as important actors in national development. This broader form of beneficiary participation was recognized by state elites to have serious implications for those who wielded economic and political power. As stated by one PIDER official in Mexico, echoing the experience of agrarian reform in Colombia under Carlos Lleras,

> If participation is stimulated too much it gets out of PIDER's control and brings political problems. It becomes a political problem for PIDER when it begins to break up or threaten commercial interests or interests outside the specific ejido or community. If they want to collectivize the ejido, that's fine and it creates no problems. But if they make other decisions that threaten particular interests, then PIDER is in hot water.[20]

The devolution of power, especially to the masses of the population, was seen as a direct threat to the carefully maintained and much touted stability of the Mexican regime. Colombia's political regime in the 1970s was more openly competitive than Mexico's, but its dynamics remained confined to the "politics of compromise" among the elite and urban populations (Dix 1980; Solaún 1980). In rural areas, local bosses (*gamonales*), clientele linkages, traditional party loyalties, state-sponsored co-optation, and extensive rural repression discouraged independent organization and demand making (Bagley and Edel 1980). Memories of La Violencia and peasant mobilization in the late 1960s as well as guerrilla activity in rural areas in the 1970s reinforced government awareness of the importance of maintaining social control in the countryside. Given these experiences, it is not surprising that the participation encouraged in DRI was more formal than authentic.

The authoritarian and technocratic nature of the Brazilian regime after 1964 was evident in POLONORDESTE's lack of concern for beneficiary participation. Official documents indicate that peasant participation was a nonissue for those who planned and implemented the program. For this reason, one official complained, "peasants don't know why things are being done, they see no reason for working together or unifying in the program. "[21] Participation of local elites, on the other hand, helped perpetuate a highly inequitable pattern of resource distribution. Effective rural organization and participation implied a redistribution of political and economic power; the political history of each of the countries strongly suggests that such an alteration was not likely to come about as a result of officially sponsored activities in programs like PIDER, DRI, and POLONORDESTE.

PIDER, DRI, and POLONORDESTE were effective in delivering some public goods and services to needy rural areas in spite of the implementation problems they encountered.[22] The problems of implementation they suffered involved understandable failures to provide sufficient resources and pointed to the need for improved methodologies to encourage beneficiary participation. They also indicate that state elites often have more autonomy to plan policies than to implement programs. Evaluation of these programs must also be linked to an assessment of them as part of a larger political economy of agricultural development. Only in this way can the long-term effect of the programs on the distribution of wealth and power in the society be considered.

Solutions to Which Problems?

The integrated rural development programs in Mexico, Colombia, and Brazil were developed by state elites to address the problems of rural poverty in isolation from the expansion of large-scale agriculture. The "new dualism" was evident in terms of overall agricultural development policies. Within the agricultural sector, at the same time that PIDER, DRI, and POLONORDESTE evolved, extensive efforts to stimulate modernization of large-scale enterprises continued apace. Regimes in all three countries revitalized efforts begun in the 1970s to ensure the economic attractiveness of large-scale farming by increasing the security of landownership and increasing the amount of credit and support activities available, as we saw in Chapters 4 and 7.

In 1980, for example, Mexico promulgated a new agricultural development law, which, among other things, recognized the previously tacit practice of renting ejido land and labor to private farmers, an alteration in the basic agrarian code of 1917 which was expected to encourage greater de facto concentration of landholdings. Extensive efforts were also made in the 1970s to increase the security of tenure for large landholders and to stimulate investment of private capital in agriculture, including transnational expansion. The Sistema Alimentario Mexicano, or SAM, strategy was announced in 1980. It incorporated a large number of programs to encourage the production of basic foodstuffs and was expected to stimulate smallholders and ejidatarios to grow traditional crops for the market—especially corn, beans, rice, wheat, and oleaginous crops through increased price supports, a variety of subsidies for seeds, fertilizer, credit, and other inputs, and an attractive crop insurance program. Through the generous use of subsidies, totaling $3 billion between 1980 and 1982, the SAM strategy attempted to affect not only production but also commercialization, processing, distribution, and consumption. Although ostensibly directed toward peasant producers, the benefits of the subsidies for production were not restricted and were widely allocated to large-scale farmers in the harvests from 1980 to 1982.[23] While budget allocations to agriculture increased in the late 1970s and early 1980s, plans for 1982 called for only 15–20 percent of the agricultural budget to be spent in regions where peasant producers predominated. The remainder would continue to be spent in the irrigated and highly productive zones that had traditionally received the lion's share of public investment.[24]

The Mexican state also repudiated distribution of land to landless peasants, tenants, sharecroppers, or others as a solution to the country's grave problems of rural poverty and unemployment. President López Portillo frequently insisted that agrarian reform, a centerpiece of the Revolution of 1910 and formerly an important aspect of the revolutionary ideology, was no longer a feasible solution to agrarian problems. This perspective became the "official line" of his administration, although organized peasant groups—including even the politically obedient National Confederation of Peasants (CNC)—argued that land was still available for distribution.[25]

In Colombia, agreements of the 1970s to increase the security of landholders and to concentrate development resources on commercial farming, such as the 1972 Pact of Chicorral and new tenancy laws, continued to be honored by the administrations in power. Evictions of peasants and repression through official action marked the Turbay Ayala administration's response to peasant protest and organization. Moreover, expanding sources of credit were assured after 1973 to assist large and medium-sized farmers responsible for Colombia's important exports (coffee, cotton, fruit, beef, etc.).[26] As we have seen, landholding in the countryside became more concentrated after 1960, and the administrations of the 1970s rejected agrarian reform as anything more than a palliative for localized rural unrest.[27] Interestingly, DRI initially excluded participation by INCORA, the agrarian reform agency and the institution with perhaps the most experience in integrated approaches to rural development.[28] Given the importance of INCORA as a symbol of the redistributive approach to rural problems, its exclusion was a clear signal to large and medium-sized farmers that such a policy was not contemplated within the DRI.

In Brazil, the state's primary concern was stimulating the growth of the large commercial farming sector and expanding the agricultural frontier in the Amazon region to make this possible. In particular, the state looked to the large farmers to produce both domestic and export crops, with an eye to halting inflationary trends in urban food prices, reducing the food import bill (which reached $1.5 billion in 1979), increasing the export of certain crops, and stimulating the production of sugar and other crops for its alcohol program.

As we saw in Chapter 4, state policies favored large private agribusiness concerns and were oriented to facilitating private-sector investment. In the late 1970s, inflation and austerity measures decreased government investment and subsidies for the sector, but those most hurt by the cutbacks were the small farmers, who had only recently become beneficiaries of expanded sources of credit.[29]

The issue of landlessness and land concentration continued to be especially acute in northeast Brazil. In one state the distribution of land was so skewed, and redistribution of it was so evidently fundamental to any kind of rural development, that the World Bank refused to become involved in financing a program there unless agrarian reform were central to it.[30] While the Bank generally avoided meaningful commitment to land redistribution and was instrumental in defining rural development as primarily a technical and organizational issue, not a redistributional one, in the case of northeast Brazil it took the extraordinary step of publicly recognizing the importance of changing the structure of landholding in ways that would permit rural development to occur. A line of credit for land purchases was in fact included in POLONORDESTE, but the number of participants in this aspect of the program was minimal. Colonization continued to be promoted as an alternative to redistribution, a policy that had been explicit since 1970 (Cehelsky 1979, 218-19). Moreover, repression was frequently the response to peasant land invasions, and little official concern emerged over the growing crisis of landlessness in the country. Programs such as POLONORDESTE were actually seen as a means of alleviating, not solving, the problems of rural poverty in Brazil.[31]

PIDER, DRI, POLONORDESTE, and similar programs in other countries were politically attractive because they did not entail touchy issues such as the structure of landownership or the distribution of water resources in rural areas. But as we have seen, since the 1940s, national development policies have in fact stimulated the concentration of land and water in the hands of entrepreneurial farmers and agribusinesses, whose mode of operation is capital intensive and export oriented. The "new dualism" that characterized agricultural policy in the 1970s ignored the consequences of the distribution of land and water resources in the sector. The integrated rural development programs were technocratic in orientation; they predicted that through targeting, research, credit, and inputs, the green revolution that had been so successful for large-scale producers could be re-created in a fashion that would permit peasant agriculturalists to take advantage of them. As we saw in Chapter 6, however, peasants were increasingly squeezed off irrigated and productive land and marginalized onto extremely small plots of undesirable land. Often located on dry, rocky hillsides, this land was extremely vulnerable to erosion and declining soil quality and was generally available in areas where rainfall was sporadic and either too scarce or too abundant for any but the most risky and rudimentary production. Thus, while land was becoming less available to peasants, population growth was placing further pressure on the size and security of peasant landholdings. Peasants who were condemned to produce crops on half a hectare of dry, stony, and mountainous ground were not likely to be able to improve their level of production or standard of living significantly, regardless of the goods and services directed toward them by the state. From this perspective, the integrated rural development programs were much more a politically attractive palliative than a solution to the problems of rural poverty.

Although the integrated rural development programs failed to address the basic causes of underdevelopment in rural Latin America, they did increase the level of resources managed by the state. They added to the state's presence in rural areas by providing the extension agents, credit officials, engineers, economists, agronomists, sociologists, and managers needed to pursue such programs. They expanded the arsenal of development projects that were available for a variety of purposes, including the amelioration of local-level conflict or dissent and the co-optation of potentially troublesome elements. They increased the capacity of the state to manage demand-making by peasants and to keep it disaggregated. And they created clientele groups of the more secure peasants, who in their political activities were unlikely to favor actions that would cause them to be cut off from the new sources of largess. As in the case of the agrarian reforms, these programs and projects linked the rural poor directly to the state. Thus, the state itself benefited significantly from the integrated rural development programs, as it had from the agrarian reform initiatives. As we will see in the next chapter, the new resources of power and policy available to the state were frequently used to deal with the threat of rural protest.

9 | Conclusion: Agrarian Protest and the State

In spite of agrarian reform and rural development initiatives, by the early 1980s, there was increasing evidence of conflict in rural Latin America. Peasant-based organizations were proliferating, reports of land invasions were becoming more frequent, guerrilla activities in the countryside were on the rise, and the number and variety of peasant demands was escalating.[1] Prior to 1940, most of the conflict in rural areas involved a direct confrontation between those who controlled resources—land and water in the case of the hacienda-based economy; jobs, wages, and working conditions in the case of the plantations—and those who desired access to them—smallholders, tenants, sharecroppers, landless laborers, and indigenous communities. When the state became involved in conflicts over the distribution of resources, it did so largely in the role of a repressive force enlisted to aid dominant rural elites. Military, police, and judicial institutions were those most likely to be involved. After 1940, however, with the tremendous expansion of its presence in the economy, the state began to play a more prominent and multifaceted role in situations of rural conflict. By the 1960s and 1970s, demand-making by the rural poor was no longer directed primarily toward landowners or other elites at the local level but was instead addressed to the state.

In the previous two chapters we have seen that the state's repertory of responses to rural protest and demand-making mirrored its increased responsibilities in rural areas. While the state remained in command of its traditional weapon, repression, it also utilized agrarian reform measures, infrastructure projects, colonization, organizational initiatives, and access to credit, social services, and technological innovations to respond to or counter specific peasant demands. Frequently, these responses were sufficient to disaggregate, co-opt, diffuse, or relocate potentially threatening peasant protest, as was the case in Mexico. In other cases—Colombia and Brazil, for instance—the level of conflict, coupled with effective peasant organization and linkages to other groups in society, made it more difficult for the state to limit the degree of demand-making by the rural poor. Even in these countries, however, state elites avoided regime-threatening commitments to a fundamental restructuring of access to productive resources in rural areas and sought to maintain the dominant model of development. Thus, the state's response to rural protest and demand-making was for the most part shaped by the characteristics of the regime in power. In addition, state elites in all three countries responded to peasant-based political activity as a situation to be managed rather than as a potential base of support for altering the course of national development policy.

PATTERNS OF AGRARIAN PROTEST AND REGIME RESPONSE

Mexico

Historically, rural conflict in Mexico has centered on the land, and since the Revolution of 1910 the state has been a primary participant in this conflict. The Constitution of 1917 and the subsequent editions of the Agrarian Code gave the state virtually unlimited legal power to allocate land and water resources and to determine the identity and organization of those who had rights to them. Moreover, the extensive growth of development agencies, programs, and projects increased the state's influence in rural areas and its control over the organization of peasant groups. Important to the continued dominance of the state in the pursuit of development policy for rural areas was the incorporation of the peasantry into the regime through the dominant-party structure.

The guarantee of agrarian reform that was incorporated into the Constitution of 1917 laid the groundwork for the massive distribution of land to peasant beneficiaries that took place in the 1930s under President Lázaro Cárdenas. As we saw in Chapter 7, rural lands—often marginal in quality—were distributed to 770,000 beneficiaries between 1935 and 1940. Most beneficiaries were organized onto ejidos, their access to land and other resources was made conditional on their membership in the group, and their control over the land itself in terms of rental, purchase, or sale was sharply curtailed. Ejidatarios who benefited from the Cárdenas distribution, and those who received land prior to or after his presidency, became a dependent clientele of the state. In order to prosper on the land, they required the credit, markets, extension services, infrastructure, and inputs the state could provide. Without these resources, most were barely able to subsist.[2] Among small private farmers and minifundistas, who had more open access to the market in land and who frequently had greater access to state-controlled inputs, recourse to the state as an arbiter of rural conflict also was of primary importance. Thus, throughout the period after the revolution, the state was at the center of the creation, control, and resolution of rural conflict.

In the 1930s, the organization of Mexican peasants stimulated by the Cárdenas reform was generally an expression of independent rural mobilization under authentic agrarian leadership. With the guidance of a supportive state apparatus, the National Confederation of Peasants (CNC) was created to aggregate local- and state-level agrarian leagues to give peasants increased leverage in national politics. Subsequently, the CNC was incorporated as one of the three corporate pillars of the dominant political party, the PRI. After 1940, however, when the development model favored by the state was emphatically geared toward rapid industrialization, the inclusive organization of the CNC and the dependence of ejidatarios on the state became the primary means for co-opting and controlling political demand-making and protest in the countryside. Through this process, the leadership of the ejidos and peasant organizations was denatured and the organizations themselves became primary vehicles for mobilizing regime support rather than for representing peasant interests to the corporatist regime. Thus, the agrarian leaders, through the awarding of jobs, prestige, land, credit, and other benefits, were transformed into political and economic *caciques* whose primary interests lay in controlling their rural followership in the interests of the state (Esteva 1980). The CNC— whose informal structure was based on a multitude of patron-client relationships stretching from the local level to the highest peaks of national politics— was effective in maintaining control of the demand-making and protest activities of the ejido sector and in forestalling the emergence of leaders dedicated primarily to the interests of the peasants.

The state in Mexico, especially after the Cardenista reforms, was not able to inhibit all rural protest activities, but it did manage to control these activities so that they would not escalate into a threat to the stability of the regime itself. Rural protest was isolated at the local level, co-opted to limit the extent of demands made, and channeled into loyal petitioning of state agencies for recognition and favors (Anderson and Cockroft 1970; Hellman 1983). These tactics were also employed when the organization of peasants proceeded outside the formal control of the regime and the CNC.

A good example of this is the process by which the Independent Confederation of Peasants (CCI) emerged and became incorporated as a clientele group within the official political apparatus (Anderson and Cockroft 1970). The CCI emerged in 1963 in Baja California, organized by dissident members of the CNC and concerning itself centrally with agrarian issues of land, water, and state policies. Gaining adherents rapidly in 1963 and 1964 and expanding its organization nationally, the CCI directed its activities toward public protest demonstrations and support for "unofficial" candidates for public office. The response of the Mexican state was not long in coming. Through the CNC, the PRI began to pressure CCI leaders to moderate their protest activities and support "official" candidates. By 1965, two CCI factions had emerged, one interested in making peace with the CNC, and the other, a group with close ties to the Communist Party, remaining committed to radical protest. Moreover, some of the demands of the CCI were met; for instance, public efforts were made to rehabilitate damaged farm lands, and an agreement was reached with the United States to halt salination of the Colorado River. Then, the more radical faction of the organization became subject to official repression when its leaders were imprisoned and its protest activities suppressed. Gradually, the CCI was incorporated into the PRI, and in the early 1970s, along with other "independent" peasant organizations, it became part of the officially sponsored Pact of Ocampo.

Similar actions were taken against the General Union of Mexican Workers and Peasants (UGOCM), which had been organized by the Popular Socialist Party (PPS) in the late 1940s (Sanderson 1981, 156–57). The organization's early years were marked by radical agrarian protest but in later years it also joined in support for the official party, the PRI. In 1957, under the leadership of Jacinto López, the UGOCM and the PPS prepared their members in a rich agricultural region of the state of Sinaloa to invade large landed estates unless the government moved quickly to break up the estates and distribute the land among the peasants. When the invasions occurred, federal troops were used to dislodge the peasants and Jacinto López was arrested. These actions stimulated resistance from the peasants, who subsequently engaged in more invasions. In 1959, the government moved to resolve the issue by distributing land in the state and releasing López from jail. However, few of those who had participated in the UGOCM invasions received land; instead, local adherents of the CNC were the primary beneficiaries. More land invasions, once again organized by Jacinto López, followed in Sonora in 1959 and 1960. The local branches of the CNC were used effectively to resist UGOCM activities and the ranks of the peasants were divided. The message was driven home to many potential supporters of UGOCM: few benefits would accrue to those who organized political action outside official structures. Jacinto López subsequently became a federal deputy representing the Popular Socialist Party, an "opposition" party that regularly followed the lead of the PRI. The UGOCM joined the Pact of Ocampo along with the CNC and CCI in the early 1970s (Collier 1982).

In 1975 and 1976, agrarian protest activities did reach a level that might have threatened political stability. This was largely because of the activities of the incumbent president, Luís Echeverría. In the rich agricultural states of Sinaloa and Sonora, land conflicts among a variety of rural inhabitants emerged—conflicts among ejidatarios, between ejido members and small farmers, and among landless peasants, ejidatarios, and large commercial farmers (Sanderson 1981, 186–202). After repeated instances of violence and increased peasant mobilization, the national government promised land to some of those involved, and a portion of it that was subsequently distributed was irrigated, a fact that stimulated more peasant action, now by groups that had not been involved in the original rash of invasions. Echeverría, who had become a firmer partisan of the renewed push for agrarian reform, attempted to use the mobilization and land invasions to support his view.

Landowners were quick to rally to the defense of their property; public demonstrations, work stoppages, threats to curtail the production and marketing of produce, and capital flight were the weapons used by the powerful farmers to make their case with the state. By early 1976, the three-way confrontation had reached a crisis point with the formation of the Independent Peasant Front (FCI), which organized land invasions in Sonora. Negotiations with invaders and the threat of military action followed. Echeverría backed away from support of the invasions as they increased in number, and military force was used more frequently, leading to the loss of many lives. Simultaneously, concessions to some peasant demands—a limit on the amount of irrigated land that could be acquired by individuals, for example—were made in an attempt to manage the situation. Land distribution activities increased and FCI members were excluded from organizing efforts to claim land; the latter were to be the responsibility of the captive Pact of Ocampo groups, the CNC, the CCI, and the UGOCM. The state worked diligently to divide the peasant groups through competition for followers and to bring them firmly into the fold of official organizations.

Ultimately, however, official support for many of the land takeovers led to an outbreak of invasions in other parts of the country and helped precipitate a major crisis for the regime. When José López Portillo assumed the presidency in December 1976, he faced a mobilization of peasant demand-makers and threatened landowners. The response of his administration was to return to conventional means to quell rural protest movements: land distribution was brought to a stop; land conflicts were referred to the courts and mediated in time-consuming bureaucratic procedures; laws against invaders were strengthened; owners of invaded and expropriated properties were handsomely compensated by the state; credit and other benefits were extended to peasants in areas of unrest; those who had organized independently found it difficult to claim land in newly created ejidos; and eventually the president declared that the agrarian reform of 1917 had come to an end because there were no lands left to distribute in the country. In 1980, the commitment to rural development was strengthened with massive new resources, but access to land was not one of the benefits extended through the wide variety of new programs.

Rural protest continued and it continued to focus on access to land—as many as 40,000 peasants were involved in land invasions in various parts of the country in 1980—but the variety of co-optive and repressive measures available to the state also increased, often undermining the effectiveness of peasant organizations, especially their ability to spread widely.[3]

Colombia

Like Mexico, a long history of violence and conflict characterizes rural Colombia. And once again, the issue central to most conflicts has been land. But unlike Mexico, regimes in Colombia have not been as successful in mediating and controlling conflict. In the 1920s and 1930s, rural violence resulted from the expansion of the coffee economy when landowners attempted, with the help of local authorities, to evict tenants, sharecroppers, and squatters from potentially valuable land (Hirschman 1963, 96–106). In some areas, the Communist Party was active in organizing peasant cooperatives and resistance to landlord exploitation. Perhaps the most well known of the rural conflicts in the period after 1940 was La Violencia, which erupted in 1948 and was still causing 3,000–4,000 casualties a year in 1957 and 1958 (Oquist 1976). While much of La Violencia was a result of the mobilization of partisan clientele linkages by political elites and their rural supporters, and much was centered on personal vendettas and banditry, another important dimension of the conflict was access to land. Once again, the Communist Party was active in defining the conflict in terms of agrarian issues and in mobilizing peasant support groups around the question of land distribution. Many landlords took advantage of the unsettled conditions to drive smallholders and Indian groups, as well as tenants and sharecroppers, from the land. Oquist (1976, 364–78) reports that nearly 400,000 parcels of land were lost or changed hands as a result of La Violencia. Most of the losses affected small landholders.

Ultimately, 200,000 persons, most of them from the ranks of the rural poor, lost their lives; a military dictatorship was initiated in 1953 largely on the basis of a commitment to end the violence and guerrilla warfare. The state, which had expanded its presence in rural areas from the 1920s through the 1940s, primarily in order to promote the modernization of the coffee economy, was weakened to the extent that in many areas it was simply nonexistent as an authoritative mediator of the conflict among partisans of the political parties, the various guerrilla groups, and the landlords. The attempt by the Rojas Pinilla military regime to bring an end to the violence was largely limited to repressive actions. By the 1950s, the level of conflict had become so great and the administrative infrastructure of the state so weak that few other alternatives were available to it.

This was less true of rural conflicts that occurred after 1960. As we saw in Chapter 7, in order to achieve passage of agrarian reform legislation in 1961, party leaders had to compromise on a cumbersome law that gave considerable protection to the landowners and to agree implicitly that efforts to implement the reform would be mild and unsystematic. These agreements were faithfully observed until 1968. Efforts to mobilize peasant organizations to demand an expansion of the reform were short-lived, however, and the radical phase of the reform was quickly halted through repression, co-optation, and piecemeal distribution of land. Nevertheless, an alternative that promised some response to the deteriorating conditions of the rural poor and migration to urban areas was needed. Integrated rural development programs introduced in the 1970s increased the presence of the state in rural areas and provided a plethora of projects and services that could be used to ameliorate conditions that threatened the social peace in rural areas, as was suggested in Chapter 8. The DRI program called for the identification of smallholders who, although they had little land, could be encouraged to be more productive with a series of inputs and services amounting to a green revolution. In 1981, the program was expanded to new areas of the country; new locations coincided with areas of widespread rural tension. The state also initiated a nutrition and basic-needs program known as PAN (Plan de Alimentación y Nutrición), which was directed toward the rural poor who would not necessarily benefit from the DRI. A major rural electrification program also was initiated in the early 1980s (Bagley 1981, 80–81).

Neither the half-hearted agrarian reform initiative of 1961 nor the integrated rural development efforts of the 1970s succeeded in putting an end to rural conflict, however. The issue of control over land remained on the agenda of the rural masses, if not on that of the state. By the 1970s, it appeared that the state had a greater repertory of responses for dealing with rural violence, but did not have the capacity to end it. Indeed, as conditions of life for many of Colombia's rural poor deteriorated in the 1970s, and as drug- and smuggling-related violence added to their insecurity, rural protest and conflict became endemic and the state increasingly resorted to the use of force to control it. Thus, in addition to the expansion of the DRI program, the 1970s witnessed the greater militarization of the countryside in order to deal with widespread guerrilla warfare, which was often linked to the question of control over land. The Colombian regime—lacking the ability of the Mexican regime to manage peasant political activities or its strong statist orientation, which provided some autonomy from the landowners—was less effective than Mexico in using co-optation and piecemeal reform to discourage the activities of independent organizations in the countryside and was compelled to use repression more frequently.

By the mid and late 1970s, 4,000–5,000 guerrillas, organized into four well-established organizations, were reported to be operating in the country (Bagley 1982, 63–74). A security statute promulgated by the Turbay Ayala administration in 1978 increased the legal capacity of the state to move against the organizations, especially the largest of them, the Revolutionary Armed Forces of Colombia (FARC). It also provided the means to break up rural organizations of peasants and Indians. In the 1970s, FARC emerged as a major challenger to the state and even influenced the outcome of disputes over land in some areas. Because of the long-term presence of the Communist Party in rural areas and the consequent support for it among peasant groups, FARC managed to prosper as a guerrilla organization while other armed groups, such as the National Liberation Army (ELN), were largely destroyed by military actions against them and by internecine conflicts among their leaders.[4] The continued existence of FARC, however, enabled the military to move actively against rural protesters.[5] These military actions were justified as necessary in the face of communist subversion of the countryside.

The army helped evict squatters from disputed lands and apprehended rural leaders, whose subsequent imprisonment was facilitated by the 1978 security statute. Indian groups, which became more organized and militant in the 1970s because of encroachment on their traditional lands, were singled out for repressive action and the ranks of their leadership were decimated. The strongest of the indigenous groups, the CRIC (Regional Council of Cauca Indians), had encouraged the creation of cooperatives and had supported a number of land invasions. Subsequently, the organization was specifically targeted by the military, and units moved onto Indian reserves under the guise of carrying out exercises against guerrilla groups. Landowners also hired armed gangs (*pájaros*) to subdue the mobilization efforts of the CRIC.[6] Elsewhere, squatters were the targets of evictions and repression, and even land reform beneficiaries suffered. Tenancy laws of the 1970s made it easier for landowners to ask for these evictions and call on the military for assistance in carrying them out.[7]

Brazil

Rural violence and peasant organizational activity also confronted the Brazilian state. The late 1950s witnessed the emergence of the now famous peasant leagues of Brazil.[8] Prior to this, uprisings against monopolistic landowners, massive population movements of *flagelados* resulting from drought and land concentration, messianic movements, and protests over conditions of work on plantations had been frequent, especially in the poverty-stricken northeast. The peasant leagues and rural organizations formed in the 1950s and early 1960s were markedly different. These organizations were widespread, they were interconnected, they were promoted and supported by urban-based political parties, and they challenged the political control of the countryside maintained by landowners.[9] Most important, the leagues developed at a time of rising political tension, mobilization, and demand-making in the country as a whole and were interpreted by state elites to be a threat to political and economic order. Thus, in contrast to the Mexican regime,

In Brazil, when militant peasant organizations appeared in the second half of the 1950s, the government had no loyal organization which it could use as an instrument for co-optation of the new, independent groups. Rather, these groups appeared in a vacuum, posing a threat both to the major political leaders, who had no control over them, and to the landowning elite, whose power rested on their political control of the rural areas in a country which had never had an agrarian reform. (Collier 1982, 91).

The peasant leagues, which eventually built a large organizational network on the base of a practically unmobilized population, emerged in the northeast when peasants of the Galiléia sugar plantation created the Agricultural Society of Planters and Cattle Ranchers of Pernambuco (SAPPP), and sought the protection of local political figures against plantation owners (Cehelsky 1979). Among those they sought out was Francisco Julião de Paula, a member of the Brazilian Socialist Party, who soon became honorary president of the organization. In 1959, the Galiléia peasants were successful in achieving distribution of the land of the plantation and their success stimulated further organization of peasant groups. As the organizational effort grew in network fashion, a reformist governor, Cid Sampaio, was elected in the state of Pernambuco. Sampaio subsequently legalized the land invasions that had been carried out under the banner of the leagues.[10] The actions of the leagues in the northeast as well as those of Governor Sampaio were important in stimulating concern about agrarian reform nationally. The organizational efforts of the leagues were primarily directed toward those tenants, sharecroppers, and minifundistas who were thought to have sufficient resources to become involved in a prolonged struggle with landowners and the state (Moraes 1970).

In addition, other organizations became active in mobilizing the rural poor. The Union of Agricultural Laborers and Workers of Brazil, supported by the Communist Party, and the Movement of Landless Associations had links to important political parties and personalities, and activists of both liberal and conservative tendencies in the Catholic Church also helped organize leagues in the countryside of the northeast and Rio Grande do Sul (Cehelsky 1979, 49). According to some estimates, by the early 1960s, as many as half a million peasants had been organized into rural unions and leagues.[11]

In spite of differences in organizational form and leadership style, their demands were clear and consistent: access to land and the legislation of a redistributive land reform; regulation of tenancy arrangements; labor legislation; elimination of intermediaries in the peasant economy; and government support for smallholders. Access to land was foremost among their demands. Even the sugar workers on the plantations insisted that they needed land, not just better working conditions. Julião, the symbolic leader of the leagues in the northeast, began to call more forcefully for radical agrarian reform and suggested the need for revolution in order to bring it about (Page 1972, chap. 3). And it was to the national government that the peasants directed their actions and statements. Because of the competitive nature of the regime in power between 1945 and 1964, their demands sparked some response from the state.

First, the state created a massive regional development plan to industrialize the northeast, provide better infrastructure (especially irrigation), create opportunities for permanent migration to colonization projects outside the region, and rationalize land use in the area. These goals were to be achieved under the guidance of SUDENE, the regional development agency created in 1959 to address the problems of the northeast.[12] Then, in response to rising mobilization and social unrest in both rural and urban areas, the administration of João Goulart legalized rural unions, a move that gave greater impetus to organizational efforts, especially those spearheaded by urban-based politicians and parties eager to enlist a newly enfranchised and available support base.[13] Rural syndicates emerged rapidly as the state attempted to bring rural labor under the same control that characterized urban unions. An extensive effort was made to control most of the rural organizations by incorporating them into an umbrella organization, the state-sponsored Confederation of Rural Workers. The peasant leagues were excluded from this organization, however, and were beset by internal divisions over leaders and strategies. This marked the beginning of the disintegration of the northeastern leagues.[14] The other organizations quickly became clientele support groups for the national political leadership, and their autonomous demand-making activity was curtailed.

The state's effort to control rural unionization was followed by legislation that gave it the right to expropriate underutilized land surrounding important infrastructure developments such as roads, railroads, and dams. This was to be the initial step toward a more comprehensive and redistributive agrarian reform. However, João Goulart was overthrown soon after the promulgation of this March 1964 law, and the military regime that succeeded his government was far more concerned with curtailing rural and urban political activity than with pursuing an agrarian reform that it considered to be counterproductive for agricultural modernization.

The authoritarian military regime issued a series of laws and decrees that emphasized the importance of productivity and taxation in addition to land distribution in rural areas, and that prohibited expropriation except with full and immediate payment to landowners (Cehelsky 1979). It set up new official agencies and programs to stimulate colonization and the development of agroindustry. In addition, the military regime's response to rural mobilization efforts such as the peasant leagues was swift and harsh. In rural areas, those who had been active as leaders of peasant organizations were arrested and imprisoned. The peasant leagues were abolished and political activity was sharply curtailed and monitored. In this context, landlords were quick to reclaim land that had been invaded by organized groups of peasants. The military's presence in rural areas increased, and its actions included the suppression of a communist guerrilla movement in the Amazon region in 1972 and 1973.[15] Public funds and programs continued to be channeled to rural areas, but aside from increased colonization efforts, little attempt was made to respond to the peasants' most persistent demand, that for land.

Twenty years after the formation of the peasant leagues and other rural organizations, rural protest continued to focus on the issue of land.[16] In the early 1980s, the influential National Council of Brazilian Bishops, through its Pastoral Land Commission, which had been created to support the rural poor in their quest, announced the following results of a survey: 916 land conflicts and the murder of 47 rural leaders between 1979 and 1981, involving 260,000 families and over 37 million hectares of land. It claimed that the state was doing little to resolve the conflicts or prosecute the murderers. In another announcement, it claimed that 78 major conflicts remained unresolved and that 4,500 families were involved.[17] The National Confederation of Rural Workers claimed that 75,000 people were involved in land disputes between 1976 and 1979 in the states of Mato Grosso, Maranhão, Bahía, and Rio de Janeiro. According to another survey, 113 deaths occurred as a result of land conflicts between 1971 and 1976 in Ceará, Pernambuco, Minas Gerais, Paraná, and Maranhão.[18]

Invasions by land-hungry peasants, armed confrontations, organizational efforts, and demands for protection and action by the state punctuated the movement of people to the Amazon and southern frontier regions. Involved in the conflicts were large landowners—among them large transnational corporations—and peasants who wanted access to the land. The landowners frequently hired thugs (*jagunços*) to drive squatters from the land through murder and terrorism. Also involved were land-grabbers (*grileiros*), who murdered and intimidated smallholders and squatters in order to acquire their land.[19] The peasants in turn called upon the state to alleviate their situation and on the Catholic Church, which did much to publicize the plight of the rural poor. Brazil's Indians, who had witnessed the invasion of their lands by migrating peasants, colonists, and agribusiness efforts, also mobilized. They added to the climate of violence when efforts to engage the state on their behalf failed and they attacked the invaders.[20]

By 1980, the extent of rural conflict and violence over access to land had become serious enough for the military regime to begin to take some action to control the unrest. It responded to the demands of some peasant groups by expropriating 44,000 hectares to distribute to squatters in seven states.[21] In a region of Pará where the level of violence was especially high, the Executive Group for Lands of Araguaia-Tocantins (GETAT) was established to mediate land conflicts that reached proportions thought to be a threat to national security. Subsequently, the relatively well-funded GETAT built roads, began to provide some social service infrastructure such as health care facilities, and distributed land to peasants in the jungle area.[22] In 1980, the regime entitled 10,000 peasants to land and promised to benefit 120,000 in 1981. Its activity was aimed at quelling the unrest and spurring migration to western Amazon states (Mato Grosso and Rondônia).[23] In 1981, the state legislated a "preagrarian reform" that gave greater protection to squatters who wished to claim title to the land, but that at the same time limited the amount of land that could be claimed.[24] Numerous efforts were undertaken to clarify and legalize outstanding land claims, and a large number of land titles were distributed.

These actions were spurred not only by concern over the level of rural violence and its threat to national security but also by the linkages of peasant protesters to the Catholic Church, whose National Council of Bishops emerged as the strongest and best-organized defender of peasant and Indian interests in the 1970s. In the absence of other legitimate channels for registering protest or organizing, the church became increasingly important to the incidence and mediation of conflict. Indeed, the preagrarian reform measure was credited as being an effort to alleviate tensions between state and church over the land issue.[25] By opening up the Amazon region, the state increased its presence in rural areas and the amount of land available to it for mediating rural land conflicts. Such was the pressure for land from peasants, Indian groups, land companies, and individual landowners, however, that efforts to exclude the rural poor from political participation under the authoritarian regime had begun to lose their effectiveness by the early 1980s. The level of rural violence and conflict continued to rise.

STATE INTERESTS, DEVELOPMENT POLICY, AND AGRARIAN PROTEST

Elsewhere in Latin America, the characteristics of rural protest were similar, indicating the increased level of conflict and a greater role for the state as a focus of demand-making and conflict resolution. Throughout the region, invigorated organizational efforts by indigenous groups in the 1970s were directed against state actions and in demand of more supportive government policies.[26] Protest activities that focused on demands for higher wages and better working conditions also involved the state, often as the target of these demands.[27] And in the case of more immediate confrontations among social groups in the countryside, the state frequently emerged as a principal mediator of the conflicts.[28]

Between 1940 and 1980, the list of demands made of the state lengthened considerably. The state was expected to provide access to land, divide resources among various rural social strata, raise minimum wages, curb exploitation by middlemen, improve working conditions, and provide infrastructure and services. But increased demands did not necessarily imply a generalized confrontation between the state, primarily concerned with modernizing its agricultural sector, and the ranks of the rural poor. The expansion of the state in pursuit of modernization after 1940, as well as its reformist policies after 1960, also created for it a greater capacity to manage peasant demand-making and protest, as has been argued in previous chapters.

In Chapter 3, it was suggested that between 1940 and 1980, state elites in Latin America sought to use policy and the legal, bureaucratic, and coercive apparatus of the state to achieve specific goals of national development. In the case of the agricultural sector, considered in this book, the initial impetus to state policy generally was an effort to gain greater control over the national economy. In pursuit of this goal, state elites were influenced by specific development ideologies that guided them in the analysis, planning, and implementation of public policies. Within the ideologies adopted after 1940, industrialization was considered the measure of economic development; agriculture was viewed in terms of its capacity to promote or hinder efforts toward rapid industrialization. Thus, from the 1940s to 1980, development policy makers consistently sought the modernization of agriculture and the promotion of capitalist modes of production and labor relations.

In the 1940s and 1950s, the most influential view among those who wished to see the agricultural sector modernized was that the long history of inefficiency and stagnation of Latin America's agricultural sector reflected the absence of incentives for investment and technological innovation by entrepreneurially inclined farmers. Adopting this view, state elites considered the sector as a whole to be backward and tradition-oriented, characterized by feudal relations between landowners and peasants. If change were to occur, they believed, the structure of incentives would have to be altered. Infrastructure would have to be widely provided, credit extended to those who demonstrated the capacity to modernize and expand production, and research and extension services made available to potential entrepreneurs.

The pursuit of such policies, however, led to different outcomes than those expected by policy elites. Rural poverty and underproductivity were not overcome but in fact became more widespread; rural-to-urban migration far exceeded the needs of industrial expansion and came to be viewed as politically and economically dysfunctional; international dependence grew noticeably in terms of food imports; and higher levels of unemployment and underemployment had grave social and political implications. The policies adopted in the name of agricultural modernization in fact resulted in conditions that state elites came to perceive as inimical to both economic growth and social control. Thus, subsequent policies were viewed not only from the perspective of their purported contribution to economic development but also from the perspective of what they meant for the maintenance of social peace.

In the 1960s, a structuralist perspective, indicating the importance of agrarian reform to the modernization of agriculture, was widely adopted. According to this view, dominant forms of land tenure, and the dependent social and political relationships they engendered, were principal constraints on agricultural development because they impeded the efficient utilization of resources. The latifundios and minifundios were uneconomical, inhibited the adoption of new technology, dampened productivity and industrial development, and promoted feudal relationships between landowners and the rural poor. Accordingly, it was argued that agriculture would become productive and farmers would become market- and profit-oriented only when the region's archaic landholding system was made more equitable and both land and labor relations were modernized.

In the 1970s, a perspective amounting to a "new dualism" characterized policy making in the agricultural sector, and a two-pronged approach to agricultural development was adopted. On the one hand, it was argued that integrated rural development should introduce extension services, infrastructure, and green revolution technology to small farmers in order to transform them into modern entrepreneurial producers; at the same time, other policies continued to provide alternative forms of production aid, credit, and extension to large commercial farmers, who were now considered to be part of the modern sector. By this period, then, the agricultural economy had come to be differentiated into modern and traditional sectors that were assumed to be operating in relative isolation from each other.

The reformist policies of both the 1960s and the 1970s were directed toward the rural poor, or specific subsectors within this broad category. The timing of their adoption suggests that state elites had considerable choice and room for maneuver in the selection of appropriate policies. They were constrained in terms of how far their reformist efforts could proceed by the opposition of important interests, but they were frequently motivated more by the content of the development models they adopted and by their own perception of impending social unrest than by actual pressure from peasant organizations or by the influence of dominant economic classes or alliances. Particularly important in the case of the adoption of integrated rural development policies in the 1970s was the widespread view among state elites that previous agricultural development policies had directly aided the large capitalist farmers but had also created a series of conditions that were hindering national economic growth and the maintenance of social control. Such views were adopted even as the dominant social classes were benefiting from the very conditions that caused grave concern to policy makers.

And indeed, as we saw in Chapters 7 and 8, an important beneficiary of the reformist initiatives in both decades was the state itself. The agrarian reforms of the 1960s aided some peasants but markedly increased the role of the state in keeping the lid on social unrest: they helped divide peasants as a social class; they made piecemeal land distribution a viable means of responding to agrarian protest; and they incorporated peasant beneficiaries into a variety of state agencies and political organizations. Likewise, the rural development programs of the 1970s benefited some rural inhabitants but they did so at the cost of more penetration of the countryside by the state; indeed, they increased the capacity of the state to co-opt and diffuse the demand-making of the rural poor. Moreover, they avoided the issue of land distribution, an issue that continued to be central to peasant livelihood and concerns.

During the period in question, the state expanded noticeably in terms of the number of persons staffing executive and administrative agencies. Among its new personnel, a commitment to statist approaches to economic development was often notable. In addition, a virtual explosion of new entities within the state apparatus—new ministries, agencies, bureaus, semiautonomous institutions, and parastatal corporations—significantly expanded the presence of the state in the economy and in social life. Moreover, through its activist role and its expanding administrative infrastructure, laws, decrees, and regulations gave it greater authority and potential to intervene widely to bargain with various groups, and to claim the protection of legitimacy for its actions. In addition, political parties, ideology, and organized interests were often created or incorporated as support structures for state activism in general and specific state policies in particular. Often, leaders such as Cárdenas in Mexico and Carlos Lleras in Colombia acted as vigorous and skilled entrepreneurs in the expansion of the state.

However, while the state grew in size, complexity, and capacity to influence economic and political behavior in the countryside, it did not necessarily increase its capacity for autonomous decision making. In fact, as was argued in Chapter 4, through its policies to modernize agriculture, the state helped create the very economic elites that subsequently became central to the maintenance of certain kinds of agricultural policies. Thus, state expansion was paralleled by the increasing influence of agrarian capitalism. In many cases what emerged from this was an implicit or explicit bargain between the agricultural entrepreneurs and state elites to continue and even invigorate past support for capitalist expansion, but also to introduce new sets of policies to diminish dependency, increase production of certain crops, limit rural-to-urban migration, and maintain the rural peace. Thus, as was suggested in Chapters 7 and 8, successful state policies did much to create a structure of power and influence that eventually limited the range of options available to the state for changing conditions in rural areas.

REFORMIST INITIATIVES AND REVOLUTION

The picture that has emerged in this book is not a happy one. The changes that occurred in agriculture between 1940 and 1980 created profound problems for national development. Change, and the problems of underdevelopment that came in its wake, was stimulated by policies whose purpose was to modernize the agricultural sector. Concomitantly, the state developed new potential for intervening in rural areas to affect political, social, and economic relations; the impact of its activities was often to limit the effectiveness of peasant-based demand-making and protest. Given the increased economic and political power of capitalist agriculture, incumbent state elites cannot be expected to reorient the trajectory of national development radically, thereby enabling the rural poor to capture and retain control over land, other agricultural resources, and employment opportunities. Reformism in the future is likely to be constrained, as it was in the 1960s and 1970s.

In the future, reformists will continue to seek solutions to problems of social welfare, employment, and security for landless workers and marginalized smallholders. In the early 1980s, education, health care facilities, sanitation, housing, roads, electricity, and transportation channels continued to be needed in massive quantities throughout rural Latin America. However, in spite of the obvious need for these services and despite their nondisruptive political effects, all are costly and most would have only minimal or long-term payoffs in terms of increased production and productivity, which remain the central goals of state development policy. Thus, with the exception of countries where considerable economic surpluses exist—and there were fewer of these in 1980 than in 1970—state elites that are committed to broad reforms will be pressed to utilize their limited resources to address only the most socially threatening rural conditions. Social welfare measures, particularly, can be expected to be strongly affected by economic limitations on the state, and perhaps especially by the availability of international development loans.

Employment opportunities had clearly become a central need in Latin America by the early 1980s; indeed, in some countries, more than half the rural work force was unemployed or underemployed. Urban industrial expansion continued to absorb few workers, and policy makers were increasingly concerned to halt the flow of rural-to-urban migrants, which they viewed as clearly detrimental to national development. Ruralization or decentralization of employment opportunities had become a major reformist priority by the early 1980s and efforts were undertaken in a number of countries to explore its potential. However, labor-intensive industrial technologies were often elusive; political and economic centralization constrained industrial decentralization; and growth poles were almost universally constrained by infrastructure bottlenecks and lack of private investment. Everywhere, the demand for jobs continued to far outstrip the states' capacity to create gainful employment opportunities. And in many cases, states that were experimenting with job creation in rural areas were also simultaneously encouraging further mechanization on large farms and doing little to discourage the conversion of cropland to land-extensive cattle ranching.

By 1980, attempts were also being made to expand minimum-wage legislation, social security, and employment contracts to rural areas—rights long ago achieved by organized urban workers in most countries. In rural areas, these efforts faced formidable barriers in terms of enforcement in an extensive and sparsely populated geographic setting where most of the labor force was temporary and migratory, where there was a large surplus of labor, and where there were extensive political and social impediments to the creation of effective labor organization. Most centrally, a direct assault on labor relations in the countryside would be strongly opposed by the large-scale farmers, who depend upon cheap and mobile labor.

Secure entitlement to the land is another central need of smallholders throughout the region. By 1980, demoralized agrarian reform institutes were often kept busy formalizing title to the land of reform beneficiaries, long-term squatters, or colonists on selected parcels of land. Such efforts, which increased the dependence of these groups on the state, were not likely to be widely applied, however, for two general reasons. First, the large landholders would oppose any but the most limited efforts to secure entitlement, and second, extensive legalization programs would spark higher levels of rural demand-making once peasants became aware that such programs existed. In fact, in many countries in the 1970s—Mexico, Chile, Peru, and Brazil, among others—agricultural development laws actually made peasant smallholdings more vulnerable to the capitalist sector, which has the greatest ability to acquire land.

Finally, reformist efforts will continue to emphasize the need to supply rural smallholdings with technological innovations, credit, and infrastructure. It is important to note, however, that such efforts to improve the productivity of the rural poor were double-edged in the period 1940–1980, often entrapping peasants in spiraling levels of debt or binding them to inappropriate or expensive technologies as they increased their productive potential. In the past, these outcomes often increased the rationality of subsistence production for rural smallholders, thereby causing domestic food supplies to diminish. Ultimately, innovations and increased production on many rural smallholdings, even with appropriate forms of technological innovation, will be severely limited by the small size of most plots and their generalized low physical quality. Moreover, in the 1970s in some countries, as governments discovered that they could use subsidies, credit, and other incentives to entice the large-farm sector into producing domestic food crops, policy commitment to the productive potential of peasants was curtailed. If the capitalist entrepreneurs help solve the domestic food problem, as seemed to be feasible in Colombia, Mexico, and Brazil by the early 1980s, peasant production will be reclassified as residual for supplying domestic needs and will enjoy even less official attention.

Applying these reformist measures, even in the limited forms that seem politically feasible, might do much to make life more tolerable and more secure for some rural inhabitants. But because of resource constraints, lack of administrative capacity, and political opposition if they were massively implemented, it is unlikely that such policies could address the problems of the

vast majority. Widespread and well-organized rural mobilization might stimulate more concern among state elites to pursue such policies, but there are
formidable obstacles to this kind of mobilization. In particular, the rural poor
would have to contend with major impediments to widespread and aggregate
organization: their ranks had been divided during four decades of modernization, agrarian reform efforts, rural development, and political incorporation;
they were vulnerable to the often sophisticated response of the state to threats
to the social peace; and they continued to suffer from dispersion, infrequently
effective leadership, and other problems for sustained organization.

Revolution also is a difficult path toward the solution of Latin America's
rural underdevelopment and as uncertain in its outcome as reformist initiatives. Obviously, most revolutions by their very nature extract enormous costs
in terms of the destruction of human lives and property. The violence and
brutality attendant upon the Mexican, Cuban, and Nicaraguan revolutions
will not soon be forgotten by those who suffered from them. The fact that most
of the violence was visited upon the rural population in the name of the forces
of order and officialdom only underscores the risk to life and limb faced by the
peasant who takes up arms against centuries of exploitation and powerlessness. But the problems associated with revolutions only begin with efforts to
take over control of the state. Importantly, revolutions in contemporary Latin
America face technical, administrative, organizational, economic, and time
constraints that influence efforts to improve rural welfare and productivity.
And ultimately, those who see in revolution the salvation of the masses must
address the problem of the power of the state and the impetus given to centralization, coerciveness, and authoritarianism by attempts to restructure society.

Unlike reformist efforts, however, revolutions do address the central issue of
land distribution and offer much hope for improving levels of rural welfare
and security. In some cases, they make available the best land in the country
for redistribution or organization into peasant cooperatives and state farms.
They may also encourage the rapid extension of health care and education
facilities to deprived rural zones. Cuba and Nicaragua are the best examples of
these results of a revolution. Immediately, however, the revolutionary state
faces major organizational and technical problems. It must be concerned not
only with rural welfare but also with production and productivity; it must
create productive organizations—cooperatives, communes, state farms—and
disseminate education, extension services, marketing aids, credit, technology,
infrastructure, and managerial expertise so that urban areas can be fed, foreign
exchange accumulated, and primary products for industry supplied. It must
address the fact that peasants may be more eager to increase personal consumption than to provide the state with agricultural surpluses, more interested
in farming individual smallholdings than in cooperating effectively with others, more inclined to resist the direction of state bureaucrats than to welcome

it, and more willing to use tried and trustworthy old technologies than to adopt risky new ones.

Above all, successful reorganization of rural areas through the activities of a revolutionary state requires firm commitment to the interests of the rural poor, substantial reserves of money and personnel, and time to experiment and compensate for the disruptions caused by revolutionary upheaval and structural change. However, under pressure to rebuild an economy, the revolutionary state is inclined to consider the interests of the state above the interests of the rural poor (Colburn 1984). Production must be encouraged as a high priority because of the economy's (likely) reliance on the export of primary products. Foreign governments, investors, and marketing channels are likely to be hostile to these efforts, as was clearly the experience of Cuba and Nicaragua in their relations with the United States, its investors, and its markets. Resources and time are therefore precisely what revolutionary state elites feel they do not have in developing viable solutions to rural social and economic conditions.

These problems exacerbate others faced by revolutionary states in attempts to consolidate power—domestic and international opposition, recalcitrant social sectors, economic constraints, administrative inefficiency, and lack of organizational control. The response of such states to these constraints in the past has been to increase efforts to centralize power and control in order to impose revolutionary priorities on the population in general, urban and rural. Even though the reasons for such efforts are often well-intentioned and even understandable, given the obstacles to achieving revolutionary goals, the end results are authoritarianism and an accumulation of coercive power under the aegis of the state. Thus, while there are many indications that the revolutions in Cuba and Nicaragua did indeed improve the welfare and security of the rural poor, in neither case did the rural poor acquire much greater capacity to control the conditions of their production or to determine their political behavior (Colburn 1984).

In revolutionary states as well as reformist ones, then, effective power to limit the expanded control of the state must, of necessity, come from the grass roots. Additionally, the rural poor must be broadly organized beyond the local level so that their capacity to interact effectively with the revolutionary state will increase. Such organizations may prove to be particularly difficult to create, however, given the sensitivity of a centralizing revolutionary elite to competing sources of power. Moreover, having fought a revolution in the name of the people, this elite is likely to attempt to deny legitimacy to organizations and leaders representing "class fractions" or "unrevolutionary interests."

Rural poverty is, and will continue to be, a frustrating reality in Latin America. Revolution offers the potential to improve the conditions of more rural inhabitants than is the case with reformist measures, but the costs in terms of disrupted lives, conditions of production, and control can be great. Without achieving the difficult goal of independent and sustained rural mobilization, both the reformist and the revolutionary path toward increased rural welfare and peasant-oriented production units will almost inevitably benefit the state first, and only then the rural masses.

Notes

CHAPTER 1. Introduction: Development Policies and Politics in Latin America

1. This argument is based on a different conceptualization of the state than that used by de Janvry, as discussed in Chapter 2. De Janvry adopts a wide definition of reformist policies, one that includes virtually all policy interventions in agriculture since 1940. Here reformist initiatives refer only to efforts by the state to address problems of rural poverty, exploitation, and inequality. General policies for agricultural modernization are thus not considered reformist.

2. These claims are fully explored in Chapter 6. Useful analyses are found in Gomes and Peréz 1979; ILO 1977; Klein 1978; and Pearse 1975.

CHAPTER 2. The State and Agrarian Change

1. This literature expanded rapidly in the 1970s and 1980s. See, in particular, Skocpol 1979; see also Nordlinger 1981. On the state in Latin America, see Cardoso and Faleto 1979; Collier 1979; Evans 1979; Hamilton 1982; Stepan 1978.

2. See, in particular, Engels 1968. On Marx and Engels and their views on the state, see Tucker 1969.

3. See Miliband 1969; Poulantzas 1973. For a discussion, see Hamilton 1982.

4. Cardoso 1980, 38. For O'Donnell (1979, 286), "The state is fundamentally a social relationship of domination or, more precisely, one aspect—as such, comprehensible only analytically—of the social relations of domination." For Foweraker (1981, 12), "The authoritarian capitalist State . . . reposes upon and guarantees the reproduction of social relations which are far from being homogeneously capitalist." For Cardoso and Faletto (1979, 215), the expanding role of the state in economic development is a result of its dependence on the economic elite: "The state is the expression of the dynamism of business enterprises and of the classes that control them as they operate in a context in which bureaucracies and the regulative and organizational capacities of the state are expanding."

5. The case of agrarian reform in Colombia that is discussed in Chapter 7 reviews the role of Carlos Lleras Restrepo in bringing about the reform law. See especially

Hirschman 1973. Massive land distribution in Mexico in the 1930s demonstrated considerable political entrepreneurship by President Lázaro Cárdenas. See Cornelius 1973.

6. Weber (1946, 78, 82) argues that the state can be defined only in terms of its means, not in terms of its ends.

7. Stepan 1978, xii. Nordlinger (1981, 11), arguing that individuals rather than institutions make policy, nevertheless centers his definition on the formal decision-making process. For him, the state is narrowly construed to be "all those individuals who occupy offices that authorize them, and them alone, to make and apply decisions that are binding on any and all segments of society." Although Hamilton (1982, 23) claims a Marxist perspective, she nevertheless defines the state "not in terms of its class nature and functions but as a set of institutions (the civil and military bureaucracy—the state apparatus) and those who formally control them (the government)." For Bennett and Sharpe (1982, 203), the state is "an amalgam of bureaus, agencies, commissions, and the like, each with its own resources and distinctive orientations, and all liable to compete and conflict with one another."

8. Anderson 1967. This perspective is often adopted in textbooks about the political systems of Latin America. See, for example, Adie and Poitras 1974; Fagen and Cornelius 1970; Wynia 1978.

9. Baer, Newfarmer, and Trebar 1976; Bennett and Sharpe 1980; Canak 1984; Purcell 1981; Redclift 1978; Spaulding 1981.

10. Baer, Newfarmer, and Trebat 1976, 84–85. See also Canak 1984, 11.

11. In some cases, state interests may clearly diverge from those of the dominant class, as in the state's efforts to incorporate nonelite groups into the political and economic system. "For example, although both the state and the dominant class(es) share a broad interest in keeping the subordinate classes in place in society and at work in the existing economy, the state's own fundamental interest in maintaining sheer physical order and political peace may lead it—especially in periods of crisis—to enforce concessions to subordinate class demands. These concessions may be at the expense of the dominant class, but not contrary to the state's own interests in controlling the population and collecting taxes and military recruits" (Skocpol 1979, 30).

12. These are often identified as the neoclassical and structuralist arguments. For a brief analysis of each, see Gomes and Pérez 1979. The schools conform to the views ascribed to the "Technocrats" and the "Reformers" considered by Feder (1971). Much of the neoclassical analysis was based on the dualist perspectives identified with W. A. Lewis. See Lewis 1954. See also Schultz 1964, 1968; Fei and Ranis 1964. For an analysis of Brazilian agriculture based on the neoclassical perspective, see Schuh 1970. The structuralist argument was adopted by the Economic Commission for Latin America, especially in the 1950s and 1960s. See CEPAL 1965 and Dorner 1971. Maldistribution of land as a structural constraint on rural modernization is a dominant explanation found in textbooks and general analyses of development in Latin America. See, for example, Adie and Poitras 1974; Hunter and Foley 1975; Chonchol 1965. For general discussions of landholding and income distribution, see Griffin 1976. In addition, see Barraclough 1973; Feder 1971; Lindqvist 1979.

13. This argument is particularly identified with Frank 1967. See also Dos Santos 1970; Cardoso and Faletto 1979; Stavenhagen 1975.

14. On this debate, see Laclau 1971. See also de Janvry 1981, chap. 1; Amin 1976; Wallerstein 1974; Goodman and Redclift 1982, chap. 2.

15. From this perspective, relations of production in the agricultural sector of peripheral states were established to provide cheap foodstuffs and raw materials for central economies. In most of the period prior to 1940, this was achieved through the traditional hacienda and plantation systems, which, by monopolizing land, were able to establish and maintain institutional control over labor and to keep wages depressed. In this way, the system directly fueled the accumulation of capital in the center and locked the agricultural sector firmly into the international capitalist system in a subordinate role, a dynamic that was particularly evident in the period between 1850 and 1930. See de Janvry 1981, chap. 1, for an elaboration of the interdependence of traditional and capitalist forms of production and for an overview of the debates relevant to this general perspective.

16. Some of the more advantaged peasants were able to continue to produce a surplus to feed urban low-wage consumers, but only through the "hyperexploitation" of family labor or by assuming the role of "peasant capitalists," who monopolized local resources and extralocal networks to establish themselves as a class of rich peasants and middlemen.

17. See Chayanov 1966; de Janvry 1981; Gudeman 1978; Pearse 1975; Mallon 1983. For a useful analysis, see Klein 1980.

18. The rural proletarians are described as those who derive all their income from wage labor, however temporary or insecure. Semiproletarians continued to have access to land, but of insufficient quantity or quality to provide for subsistence; they therefore had to seek out wage labor to meet subsistence needs. Analysts from a variety of disciplines and ideological persuasions are increasingly agreed that rational (even wise) risk-minimizing thought underlies peasant decision making. See the seminal works by Chayanov (1966) and Geertz (1963), and the useful discussion by Lipton (1968). Scott (1976) and Popkin (1979) disagree over the nature of peasant rationality. They are at odds over whether peasant rationality is primarily oriented to risk aversion or will allow for risk-taking in order to improve living conditions. Seligson (1980) and Forman (1975) also deal with this question, from the perspective of anthropological studies in Latin America. Bauer (1979) argues that considerable historical evidence supports the belief in peasant rationality. In addition, considerable research suggests strongly that the unit of response is the peasant household, not the individual peasant or the peasant community. See Bourque and Warren 1981; Pearse 1975. Scott (1976) and Popkin (1979) are inexact on this issue, using *family* and *individual* (Popkin) or *family* and *village* (Scott) interchangeably.

19. See Bartra 1974 and Pearse 1975 for development of this perspective. For a discussion, see Heynig 1982.

20. On this process in Chile, see Kay 1978. On Mexico, see Bartra 1974.

21. Those taking this perspective on Mexico are Paré (1977) and Warman (1972). For discussions, see Goodman and Redclift 1982; Saint 1981. See also Heynig 1982.

22. See Paré 1977; Surj 1980. For a discussion, see Feder 1977.

23. See de Janvry 1981; de Janvry and Ground 1978; Mallon 1978; Paré 1977; Taussig 1978; Winson 1978. Dillon Soares (1977) relates peasant agriculture to capitalist expansion in urban areas.

24. For dependency theorists taking this perspective, the cost of production in capitalist enterprises continued to be internationally competitive and encouraged a new international division of labor.

25. Paré (1977) argues that because of their insecure nature, wages are clearly secondary to peasant households that maintain some access to land; more secure and permanent conditions of wage labor are not necessarily desirable, because they would make it difficult to continue to exploit agricultural property. See Harris 1978 for a discussion.

26. Gustavo Esteva (1978) argues that the issue of land increasingly coalesced peasant behavior, resulting in extensive land invasions in Mexico in the 1970s. He argues for a vital "peasantization" process as both landed and landless peasants seek to acquire secure access to the land to improve their conditions.

27. Deere and de Janvry (1979) argue that peasant households as producers of marketable surpluses will disappear, although they will continue to meet some subsistence needs. See Chayanov 1966; Esteva 1978; Paré 1977; Scott 1976.

CHAPTER 3. Legacies of the Past

1. The *encomienda* is well described in Keith 1977, 6–8. The Chilean adaptation of the institution is discussed in Bauer 1975, 5–6, and Loveman 1976, xxv–xxvi. On Mexico, see Chevalier 1963; Taylor 1972; Warman 1980, 26–27. On Peru, see Keith 1976. On Central America, see MacLeod 1973.

2. "This is why the *encomienda* was successful only where a tribute system of some kind had existed before the conquest, that is, where a surplus was already being produced and concentrated in the hands of a non-productive class. It did not work with poorer and more nomadic peoples like the Caribs of the West Indies, the Chichimecas of northern Mexico, or the Araucanians of southern Chile" (Keith 1977, 7).

3. For various estimates, see Keith 1977, 7–8; Haring 1947, chap. 13; Stein and Stein 1970, 37–38. Brading (1981) estimates that the indigenous population of Mexico in 1620 was only 3 percent of what it had been at the time of the conquest a century earlier. See also Warman 1980, 24–25.

4. The richest of the Mexican mines, those of Zacatecas and Guanajuato, were discovered in 1548. The Potosí deposits of Peru (now Bolivia) were discovered in 1545.

5. See Chevalier 1963 for an extensive study of how the encomienda was replaced by the hacienda and how the large estates were consolidated in Mexico. Chevalier also provides extensive evidence of the efforts of the crown to limit the power of the encomenderos and landowners and its attempts to regulate the treatment of the Indian population. See also Brading 1977, 28–29. On Peru, see Keith 1976; on Central America, see MacLeod 1973. In the sixteenth and seventeenth centuries, a system of forced labor known as the *repartimiento* was widely used in mining and agricultural zones to extract labor from indigenous communities.

6. "The irregularity and scarcity of the supply of indigenous labor was perhaps the most important motivation for the last and definitive territorial expansion of the Morelos *oriente* haciendas, which expropriated enormous areas that they could not and did not intend to work. With this, they met many goals, all aimed at guaranteeing a regular, sure supply of labor for cultivating sugar cane. First, they squeezed the *comuneros* into a territory incapable of producing sufficiently for the subsistence of its possessors, who worked it with extensive systems and had no possibility of replacing them with intensive ones. The compression required the villagers to make up their subsistence with the sale of their labor power for the benefit of the hacienda. Those who did not obtain space on

the communal lands had to take hacienda lands for sharecropping or emigrate without a clear destination. Tying down the sharecroppers [was] fundamentally . . . [an effort] to ensure the supply of seasonal labor. As part of payment for renting the land, the Indian was required to work for the hacienda without payment one or two weeks a year; more important than the free labor was the fact that the landholder could establish the calendar for its delivery. Sharecropping secured a work force that inevitably depressed the cost of salaries. As if this were not enough, the estate obtained an income in the form of corn and fodder as another part of the payment for the rental of land that it could not work and that was not in its interest to work directly" (Warman 1980, 40–41).

7. "In early colonial Peru there was nothing particularly aristocratic about owning land; most chacras and haciendas were established for the thoroughly practical purpose of supplying their owners with income" (Keith 1976, 132). On Mexico, see Warman 1980, 33–41.

8. On these developments, see Bauer 1975; Keith 1977, 9; Stein and Stein 1970, 31–39; Warman 1980, chap. 1.

9. Eventually, three million African slaves were transported to the Spanish colonies and between four and five million to Brazil. See Burns 1977, 20; Forman 1975, 22–23; Furtado 1963, esp. 1–42; Mörner 1967, 16–19.

10. On these developments, see Furtado 1963, 6–7, 58–66; Forman 1975; Hall 1978, 2–3.

11. On different types of haciendas in Peru, see Keith 1976. On Mexico, see Brading 1977.

12. The economic viability of agricultural enterprises and their need for proximity to markets varied by crop. "In the case of wheat it was narrow, but for sugar, livestock, and especially for wine, it was much wider" (Keith 1976, 31).

13. "This high cost of labor was on the whole the most serious obstacle to the development of commercial agriculture in the New World, and the effort to overcome it led to the adoption of four main patterns of agricultural exploitation in Latin America: (1) a pattern based on migrant labor which was most closely associated with the plantation; (2) a pattern of extensive exploitation and low labor utilization which was most characteristic of the ranch; (3) a pattern based on wage labor, tenant farming, or both, which was most commonly found in the fundo regions; (4) a pattern of enserfment which was particularly associated with the manorial hacienda" (Keith 1977, 24–25).

14. Using data from the nineteenth century, Grieshaber (1980) asserts that Indian communities survived in much of the altiplano because of Spanish disinterest in the region, with its low agricultural potential, and because of the ease with which Spain could extract tribute through the traditional chieftaincies.

15. On Mexico, see Brading 1977, 36. Greater labor mobility seems to have existed in Chile; see Bauer 1975 and Loveman 1976, xxvii. On labor mobility generally, see Martínez-Alier 1977.

16. See Harris 1975 for an example of an entrepreneurial *hacendado* family.

17. For a contrary view, see Chevalier 1963, 311–12. On the limitations of the expansion of commercial agriculture in highland Peru, see Long and Roberts 1978, 13.

18. See Burns 1977, 38. On Colombia, see Hirschman 1963, 96. On Mexico, see Chevalier 1963.

19. These restrictions were of fundamental importance in stimulating the movements for independence of the late eighteenth and early nineteenth centuries.

20. Bauer (1975, 49–50), commenting on agriculture in Chile in the mid nineteenth century.

21. On Costa Rica, which participated early in the export boom, see Seligson 1980, 14–22. For Latin America generally during the early nineteenth century, see Burns 1977, 111–12.

22. Useful discussions of these developments are found in Cortés Conde 1974; Bauer 1975; Scobie 1964; Duncan and Rutledge 1977; Warman 1980, 47–49.

23. The steamship first appeared in Latin America in Brazil in 1819, but it was of commercial importance only in later decades. See Burns 1977, 112.

24. See Bauer 1975, 68 for the role of the telegraph in Chile.

25. The sources of these data are Burns 1977, 129; Kay 1977, 109; Eisenberg 1977, 352; Seligson 1980, 19; Klarén 1977, 238; Scobie 1971, 108.

26. On the role of the state in Argentina, see Cortés Conde 1974, 133–38.

27. For an interesting discussion of the liberal reforms of the nineteenth century, see Veliz 1980.

28. Wolf 1969, 38–39. See also Paige 1975, 141; Klarén 1977, 233.

29. Klarén 1973, 26–28; 1977, 244. On methods of recruitment, see González 1980. He argues that between 1880 and 1905, highland labor was recruited through the use of violence and coercion as well as monetary incentives. Demographic pressure and economic hardship in the highlands made migration attractive; debts often kept Indians on the lowland sugar plantations.

30. Hansen 1971, 27; Warman 1980, 62–67. Useful studies of Portfirian and revolutionary Mexico that deal with the question of land are Cosío Villegas 1965; Simpson 1937; Whetten 1948; Wolf 1969; and Womack 1968.

31. Hirschman 1963, 98–100. However, see Martínez-Alier 1977 on how the existence of Indian communities limited the growth of the haciendas.

32. Cardoso 1977, 192–96. A smaller elite gained control over credit, processing, and marketing facilities and thus emerged in a position to dominate the coffee producers.

33. Taussig 1977. In other areas of Colombia, large coffee estates predominated. See Deas 1977, 269.

34. Bauer 1975, 70, 193. For Brazil, see Furtado 1963, 179.

35. An exception to this was irrigation, "an investment that required few new techniques and was in keeping with the general Chilean response of more land and labor" (Bauer 1975, 105). Interestingly, most of the investment in irrigation came from private rather than public sources, a pattern that changed considerably in the twentieth century.

36. In countries where plantation agriculture developed as a result of the export boom, as in the development of coastal Peru and Ecuador, power shifted from the hacienda landlords to the new export elites. See Redclift 1978, chap. 3. Where the export economy was based primarily on mining, as in Bolivia, the mining elite dominated politics and the landed elite was largely peripheral. See Malloy 1970, 18.

37. In 1855, the Chilean government established the first long-term credit institution, the Caja de Crédito Hipotecario, whose loans were limited to large estates in close proximity to the capital city. See Bauer 1975, 90–91, 118–19. For Central America, see

Woodward 1976, 150–51. Burns (1977, 157) indicates the nature of the political dominance of agricultural interests in Brazil: "The alliance of the coffee planters and the federal government in 1894 superseded all previous political arrangements. Thereafter, the political dominance of the coffee interests characterized the First Republic (1889–1930). The new oligarchy, principally from São Paulo but secondarily from Minas Gerais and Rio de Janeiro, ruled Brazil for its own benefit for thirty-six years. The coffee interests arranged the elections of presidents friendly to their needs and dictated at will the policies of the governments. Sound finances, political stability, and decentralization were the goals pursued by the coffee presidents." See also Eisenberg 1977, 350; Topik 1982.

38. An unusual exception to this pattern was Costa Rica, which used piecemeal agrarian reform to respond to instances of rural conflict. See Edelman 1982.

39. This was the case in Colombia and El Salvador. In El Salvador, an estimated 30,000 peasants were killed by the army in response to a rural rebellion in 1932. See Durham 1979, 43–44.

40. On Chile, see Bauer 1975, 68. On cotton and coffee booms in El Salvador, see Durham 1979, 30–36.

41. Brazil, Argentina, and Mexico are particularly good examples of this kind of political incorporation.

CHAPTER 4. The State and the Ideology of Modernization

1. See Stepan 1979, chap. 3, for a useful discussion of the state-building efforts of political leaders Getulio Vargas, Juan Perón, and Lázaro Cárdenas. Populist movements such as those led by Perón and Vargas, the APRA in Peru, MNR in Bolivia, and Acción Democrática in Venezuela are discussed in Malloy 1977. See also Collier 1982.

2. To conserve dwindling supplies of foreign exchange, governments imposed protective tariffs, import quotas, overvalued exchange rates, and exchange controls to discourage importation of foreign manufactures, especially light consumer goods. Frequently, the continued importation of heavy industrial goods was permitted or encouraged by these same instruments. In this protected environment, and often with the aid of state-financed development loans, domestic entrepreneurs were encouraged to invest in industries to produce previously imported goods. In addition, governments encouraged inflation through fiscal and credit policies to expand the domestic market for new industrial goods and they sought to divert capital from the export sector to manufacturing. During World War II, with imports of industrial goods largely cut off by the war economies of the United States and Europe, opportunities for indigenous industrial development expanded. For an overview of Latin American efforts to promote import substitution, see Baer 1962; see also Kaufman 1979.

In Chile, informal import substitution began in the early 1930s, and with the creation of the Chilean Development Corporation (CORFO) late in the same decade, it became a more conscious state development policy. Similarly, in Venezuela, import substitution became explicit government policy after 1944 with the creation of the Corporación Venezolana de Fomento. Uruguay used multiple exchange rates and import restrictions and taxes between the 1930s and early 1950s, and similar instruments were applied in Ecuador to protect domestic manufacturing. In Peru, in spite of a strong export sector, the state managed to impose government-determined priorities on the use of foreign exchange between 1945 and 1948. In the late 1950s, tax incentives and tariff protection were strengthened through an industrial promotion law, reflecting the emergence of a private industrial sector linked to official policy making. Argentina's first Five-Year Plan, announced by Juan Perón in 1947, explicitly favored further industrialization and the growth of consumer-goods industries. Import substitution measures were introduced in Bolivia after the 1952 revolution and remained a model of development for the country through the 1970s.

3. Prebisch 1950, 1951. For an overview of the ECLA perspective, see Baer 1962. Some have viewed this period as important for the emergence of a technocratic elite in Latin American bureaucracies. See, for example, Skidmore 1967.

4. On the development of planning in Latin American bureaucracies, see Mattos 1969. For an interesting critique of the emphasis on planning, see Hirschman 1979.

5. For a discussion of dominant sectors and economic planning and policy, see Mamalakis 1969.

6. See the important statement of these functions in Johnston and Mellor 1961. For a discussion of early perspectives on agricultural development policy, see Fei and Ranis 1975.

7. See, for example, Schuh 1970, for perspectives on Brazilian agricultural development.

8. For example, major infrastructure developments, especially in road building, accounted for a significant proportion of government and foreign-aid expenditures in promising agricultural zones in Bolivia from the mid 1950s through the early 1960s. In Chile, credit, tax incentives, and the maintenance of favorable prices were intended to spur modernization in agriculture through the mid 1950s. In Mexico, between the 1930s and 1960s, heavy investments were made in irrigation as well as in road building and other infrastructure programs to encourage a modern and technically advanced agricultural sector; this period also witnessed significant research efforts to bring the green revolution to the country. Agricultural research stations were widely established in Brazil after World War II, and extension services were expanded after the mid 1950s. A similar pattern was followed in Venezuela in the promotion of extension and research activities; large investments in irrigation followed in the 1960s.

9. Deere and de Janvry 1979. For a discussion of the impact of state policies on Colombian agriculture, see García García 1981.

10. For data on urbanization in Latin America, see *SALA* 1983, 86–96. See also Portes and Walton 1976; Butterworth and Chance 1981.

11. See Pinto 1980 for an overview of the rationale behind this policy reorientation.

12. In alliance with domestic capitalists and foreign investors, the state would continue to treat the industrial sector as dominant in the national economy and would pursue a variety of policies to stimulate its further growth, emphasizing external markets and international competitiveness.

13. Similarly, various governments in Latin America began to take a firmer hand in promoting direct taxation to pay for public services and to introduce increases in the prices of basic public services. Important exceptions to the growth of state intervention during the 1970s occurred in Chile and Uruguay after 1973 and in Argentina after 1976. In Chile, the state was especially concerned to reduce its involvement in the agricultural sector by deregulating the sale of land and removing much public financing.

14. Critiques of the early emphasis on import substitution focused on the lagging productivity of agriculture that resulted from the negative impact of many policies, the lack of attention to the agricultural sector in terms of public investment, the failure to encourage a substantial increase in the exportation of primary commodities, and the increasing need to import food for domestic consumption, which was adding to already severe balance-of-payments deficits.

15. See FAO, *The State of Food and Agriculture*, 1978, 2/36. Crops such as soybeans and the sources of other edible oils, fruits and vegetables, livestock, wheat, sugar, and cotton were singled out for special attention and incentives. Through increased availability of credit, improved prices, extension, marketing, and infrastructure investments, state elites attempted to encourage expanded production and productivity for export markets. In addition, they liberalized trade regulations and tax incentives in an effort to remove some of the traditional disincentives to the export of agricultural commodities. Thus, by the 1970s, development planners in a number of countries were partially or totally rejecting the ECLA argument that terms of trade were biased against primary-product exports.

16. Consumer food prices rose about 30 percent in 1974 and an additional 20 percent in 1975. At the same time, income growth did not keep pace with price increases (FAO, *The State of Food and Agriculture*, 1978, 2/30). By discouraging production of basic crops, cheap-food policies added to food scarcities, which drove up the price of food for the urban population. At various times during the 1970s, self-sufficiency in basic food crops was adopted as a goal in Mexico, Brazil, Colombia, Guatemala, Argentina, Ecuador, and Venezuela; prices for farm products were raised to increase compensation to farmers; consumers in turn benefited from subsidized food prices in many countries. In some cases, constraints on the export of particular crops were imposed. In country after country in the 1970s, rural development policies that were aimed specifically at the peasant population, the major producers of domestic food crops, were elaborated with the purpose of increasing production and encouraging modernization (see Chapter 8).

17. In other cases, state aid for agricultural development was targeted for specific crops or regions that promised high returns on investments in terms of increases in production.

18. In one region in Brazil, from five to seven visits to the urban-based loan institution were needed in order to complete the application process. See Adams and Nehman 1979, 169.

19. *LAWR*, WR-81-12 (March 20, 1981), 9–10.

20. In the early 1960s, there was one field extension agent for every 12,500 adult males engaged in agriculture in Paraguay; and one for every 10,000 in Colombia, 9,000 in Ecuador, 8,000 in Chile, 3,500 in Argentina, and 1,000 in Venezuela. See FAO, *The State of Food and Agriculture*, 1965, 144.

21. Ejido land, closely regulated by the state, cannot be sold, and, until 1981, could not be rented legally. Most ejidos are divided into plots that ejidatarios farm individually. Ejido committees and officials are charged with assigning plots and managing ejido interests in concert with the state.

22. On the process of agricultural development in Mexico, see Barkin 1978; CDIA 1974; Eckstein 1966; Esteva 1980; Freebairn 1983; Hewitt de Alcántara 1976; Sanderson 1981; Stavenhagen 1970; Yates 1981.

23. Between 1917 and 1935, 10.5 million hectares of land were distributed to 6,250 ejidos.

24. In the years after 1940, the organization of the peasants into the Confederación Nacional de Campesinos (CNC), and the confederation's incorporation into the Partido Nacional Revolucionario (later the Partido Revolucionario Institucional—PRI), became fundamental means of co-opting and controlling the peasantry.

25. For a discussion of this policy shift, see Solís 1971, 17–25; Hansen 1971.

26. In 1940, holdings of this size accounted for 42 percent of the cultivable land of Mexico. Another 10 percent was in the hands of private farmers owning 5 hectares or less.

27. President Avila Camacho (1940–46), quoted in Hewitt de Alcántara 1976, 6. Investment for industrial promotion reached 20 percent of total federal investments by the early 1950s and 30 percent by 1960, compared to 5 percent under Cárdenas. See Hansen 1971, 45.

28. The Agrarian Code of 1942 emphasizes the importance of private property in rural areas and scores the "ejidalist" policies of the past. President López Mateos (1958–64) briefly revived the agrarian emphasis of the Cárdenas years in terms of land distribution, but not in terms of the collective ejido. On the political threat of collective ejidos, see Eckstein 1966.

29. Private credit grew about 11.7 percent annually during these years. See Sanderson 1981, 141.

30. For instance, ejido land could not be pledged as loan collateral; ejidatarios were required to organize into credit societies in order to apply for official credit, and each member had to assume legal responsibility for the entire debt.

31. Between 1947 and 1960, 73 percent of newly irrigated land from state projects was located in the north and northwest. See Venezian and Gamble 1969, 100. Irrigation districts were later expanded in central regions of the country where agribusiness development was rapid in the 1960s and 1970s.

32. *LAER* 7, no. 20 (May 25, 1979): 156.

33. These figures, based on data from statistical appendices to the *President's Annual State of the Nation Report*, are not in agreement with the data reported by Elías in Table 4.2. The Elías figures include the massive expenditures of decentralized agencies, which thus reduce the proportion of funds spent on agricultural development. The figures reported here are based on central government expenditures only.

34. During the Echeverría period, the state increased the number of federal employees by 60 percent and the number of federal agencies increased from 782 to 1,019. Federal spending grew at similarly high rates. See Bailey and Link 1980, 6.

35. The confrontations in Sonora and Sinaloa are discussed in Sanderson 1981; Esteva 1980, 50–52; *LAPR* 9, no. 47 (November 28, 1975): 375; ibid. 10, no. 43 (November 5, 1976): 341; ibid. 10, no. 46 (November 26, 1976): 361–62; ibid. 10, no. 47 (December 3, 1976): 369; ibid. 10, no. 48 (December 10, 1976): 381–82; ibid. 10, no. 49 (December 17, 1976): 388–89.

36. See especially Kalmanovitz 1978. For a case study of the modernizing trend in producer organizations, see Valenzuela Ramírez 1978.

37. On the collapse of political authority during La Violencia, see Oquist 1980. According to Solaún (1980, 14), "The problem in Colombia was that the state—the basic formal organizations of government—lacked sufficient autonomy or develop-

ment to withstand party competition. . . . the state was relatively weak to begin with. Therefore, its mediating-control function tended to disappear under party competition. Government agencies and their agents were seen as partisan agents of a political party."

38. In terms of broad policies for economic development, Colombia's history in this period is similar to that of a number of other Latin American countries. Beginning in the 1930s, the country embarked on efforts to stimulate industry through import substitution. Standard instruments—tariffs, specific taxes, import restrictions, and an overvalued peso—were applied. These policies were more firmly regularized with the imposition of a personalist military dictatorship in 1953.

39. See Feder 1971, pt. 3; Grindle 1980. The agrarian reform of 1961 is discussed in detail in Chapter 7 of the present volume.

40. See Solaún 1980 for an important discussion of parties and oligarchic domination in Colombia.

41. Interviews with officials at the Departmento Nacional de Planeación and the Ministry of Agriculture, Bogotá, January 1981.

42. According to government definitions, commercial crops in Colombia include rice, sorghum, soybeans, cotton, African palm, sugarcane, cacao, banana, livestock, flowers, and coffee. The commercial sector is identified as that which has "an entrepreneurial form of exploitation, the relatively intensive use of machinery, the great capacity to absorb technology oriented toward external markets, and the production of raw materials for import substitution industries" (DNP 1980, 2:263–65).

43. In 1973, the Fondo was reorganized and its control over loan funds was centralized. Its name was changed to the Fondo Financiero Agropecuario. Coffee growers, serviced by their own semipublic bank, were not eligible for Fondo loans.

44. DNP 1980, 2:277; Kalmanovitz 1978, 344; Araya and Ossa 1976, 14. These incentives were especially important in the 1950s, in accordance with the dominant perspective of policy makers as to how agricultural modernization should be achieved. In the 1970s, higher tariffs on agricultural machinery were introduced to encourage import substitution in this industry.

45. Araya and Ossa 1976, 15. See also Abercrombie 1972, 20; DNP 1980, 2:271.

46. Interview, Bogotá, January 1981. See also Junguito 1978, 38.

47. On FEDEARROZ, see Valenzuela Ramírez 1978. See also Scobie and Posada 1978, 85–86; *New York Times*, May 4, 1981, 1.

48. See Collier 1982 for an important discussion of the incorporation of lower-class groups into the Brazilian political system and the maintenance of regime stability. See also Malloy 1979.

49. On these developments, see Evans 1979; Foweraker 1981; Stepan 1978; Skidmore 1967.

50. Public expenditures for agriculture declined from 4.7 percent of the total for 1956/60 to less than 3 percent for 1961/65; from there it fell to 2 percent in the second half of the 1960s and to even less in the 1970s (see Table 4.2).

51. The northeast encompasses the states of Maranhão, Piauí, Ceará, Rio Grande do Norte, Paraíba, Pernambuco, and Alagôas. The east includes the states of Sergipe, Bahía, Minas Gerais, Espiritu Santo, and Rio de Janeiro. The south is comprised of the states of São Paulo, Santa Catarinha, Paraná, and Rio Grande do Sul.

52. Hall 1978; *LARR*, RB-81-94 (April 27, 1981), 5.

53. On agricultural credit in Brazil, see Sanders and Ruttan 1978, 278; Adams 1971, 49; *UNESLA* 1978, 112.

54. Rural elites were organized for representation within the policy-making apparatus under the government of Getulio Vargas in 1945. See Collier 1982 for a discussion of the social bases of Brazilian political parties.

55. According to Collier (1982, 66), until 1964 Brazilian politics was marked by an elite consensus that "there would be no land reform, no legalization of rural unions, and the pre-existing pattern of social relations would remain untouched."

56. Pompermayer Malori 1980, 14. A detailed exploration of politics and policy in the Amazon is found in Foweraker 1981. On the conflict between state agencies, see especially ibid., 159–64.

57. *LARR*, RB-80-10 (November 21, 1980), 5–7.

58. Pompermayer Malori 1980, 16. See also Mahar 1979, 24.

CHAPTER 5. Private Advantage and Public Consequences

1. FAO, *The State of Food and Agriculture*, 1978, 2/34. The overall gross domestic product of the region grew at a rate of 5.7 percent annually during this period.

2. In Peru, growth rates in agriculture declined from 4.9 percent annually in the early 1950s to −1.2 percent by the late 1960s. Between 1970 and 1975, production grew by only 0.6 percent a year. In Argentina, agricultural production declined between 1946 and 1955 as state policies effectively transferred resources to the industrial sector. Between 1965 and 1970, it grew by only 1.1 percent a year; and between 1970 and 1975, by 0.9 percent. Ecuadorian agriculture barely managed to keep pace with population growth through the 1960s; after 1966, its growth fell increasingly behind domestic needs. Likewise, agriculture stagnated in Bolivia in the 1950s, grew by only 1.8 percent a year in the 1960s, and by the late 1960s was growing at a rate of only 0.2 percent a year. In 1979, the sector grew by only 2 percent, and this rate was reduced to 1 percent by 1980. In Mexico, rapid growth in the 1940s and 1950s was followed by steadily declining rates in the 1960s and 1970s. Chilean agriculture grew by 2.3 percent a year during the 1960s but declined to 1.1 percent between 1970 and 1975. In most countries, demand for food outstripped rates of growth in food production.

3. Barraclough and Schatten 1973. Some crops that were not widely produced in the 1960s grew at enormous rates in the 1970s: sorghum in Brazil (125.5 percent annually), Colombia (20.4 percent), and Venezuela (68.9 percent); soybeans in Argentina (63.9 percent), Brazil (59.0 percent), and Paraguay (83.3 percent); and palm oil in Ecuador (29.6 percent).

4. Prior to World War II, exports were strongly oriented toward Europe. The war helped strengthen the linkages between the U.S. market and primary-product exporters in Latin America.

5. The distribution of tractors varied greatly, of course, from a mere 726 in Bolivia to 300,000 in Brazil in the late 1970s. In the areas where they were concentrated, the amount of arable land per tractor was far smaller than the 174 hectares calculated for the region as a whole in 1976. See ECLA 1978, 74. For 1961/75, the figure was 267 hectares per tractor. Data are too scarce and unreliable to detail other forms of mechanization, such as the increased use of harvesters / threshers.

6. Abercrombie 1972, 19. In North America, the ratio was 1:40.

7. In this period, the profits of the corporations grew consistently. In 1976, of 482 transnational affiliates in the food sector, 217 were engaged in processing for the export market, 103 for local markets in flour milling and animal feed, and 162 for local markets in dairy products, beverages, and edible oils. See Scott 1980, 4, 10, 18.

8. Del Monte processed tomatoes in Mexico, Minute Maid processed orange juice in Brazil, Quaker Oats processed cereals in Colombia and Brazil, Nabisco produced crackers in Venezuela, and Carnation dominated the market for canned milk in Peru. Heavily involved in a highly concentrated agribusiness industry were Nestlé, Kraft, General Foods, Coca-Cola, Beatrice Foods, and Ralston-Purina. Bananas were exported and marketed by United Brands in Central America, cotton by Anderson Clayton in Brazil, and soybeans by Cargill in Brazil. See Burbach and Flynn 1980; Feder 1978; Barkin and Suárez n.d.; Garreau 1977; Rama and Vigorito 1979; UNCTC 1981.

9. In Venezuela, the production of tobacco and poultry was encouraged in this way, as was the expansion of fruit and vegetable production in Mexico. On Venezuela, see Schuyler 1980, 111. On Mexico, see Burbach and Flynn 1980, chap. 9; Feder 1978.

10. See USDA 1980; Klein 1980, 94. On Costa Rica, see Guess 1979. On livestock expansion in Mexico, see Feder 1981.

11. As noted previously, increased livestock production also stimulated the expansion of feed grain production, often on land that had formerly produced crops for low- and moderate-income groups. In Costa Rica, livestock expansion was related to widespread deforestation and erosion of productive land. See Guess 1979.

12. Abercrombie 1972, 27. With an increase of 16,557 tractors between 1947 and 1978, approximately 50,000 agricultural workers were displaced in Chile; comparable figures for Colombia and Guatemala indicate the displacement of 96,000 and 10,000 workers respectively.

13. FAO, *The State of Food and Agriculture*, 1978, 2/39. On inefficient land use in Argentina, see *LARR*, RS-80-06 (August 1, 1980), 7.

14. In Central America, seasonal migrant labor was estimated to account for 70 percent of the labor force employed in agriculture in the late 1970s. See Miró and Rodríguez 1982, 64. In Honduras, the number of landless workers expanded from about 20 percent of rural families in 1952 to nearly 33 percent in the 1970s. See Ruhl 1984, 49.

15. The transfer of savings from agriculture to industry has been calculated to be as much as 3.1 billion pesos (at 1960 prices) between 1940 and 1960. See Hewitt de Alcántara 1976, 116–17. For an analysis, see Hansen 1971, 58–59; Solís 1971.

16. For example, the support price for corn remained fixed between 1964 and 1972, while the cost of living increased by 38 percent. See Grindle 1977, 87.

17. This was particularly true of the commercial farms that controlled the best of the nonirrigated areas sown in corn.

18. An analysis of 115 rural conflicts indicated that 86 were caused by cattlemen invading ejido and other communal lands. See Esteva 1980, 174–76. See also Feder 1981.

19. If all communal lands are included, the percentage is 49.9 percent of all agricultural land.

20. Hewitt de Alcántara 1976, 313–14. On the state of Morelos, see Warman 1980, 221.

21. *LAER* 7, no. 20 (May 25, 1979): 156–57; ibid. 7, no. 30 (August 3, 1979): 235.

22. DNP 1980, 1:263–65. After 1970, agricultural exports grew more than 17 percent annually. See DNP 1980, 2:289.

23. In 1950, there was one tractor for every 202 hectares of cultivated land; in 1960, the figure was one for every 113 hectares, and by 1975 it was one for every 99 hectares. See Araya and Ossa 1976, 35.

24. *LARR*, RA-79-01 (November 30, 1979), 5; ibid., RA-80-03 (April 4, 1980), 5.

25. This proportion fluctuated widely during the agricultural cycle, however; at peak season only 8.9 percent were unemployed, but during the slack period 43.2 percent were out of work. See Kalmanovitz 1978, 195.

26. Employment in the livestocking subsector grew at only 2 percent a year, even during the period of its most rapid expansion, between 1960 and 1970.

27. A dramatic case is that of soybeans, the production of which increased annually by one and a half to two million tons in the 1970s, thereby increasing its export value from about 27 million dollars to over 180 million dollars in the same period. The production of sugar also expanded substantially under innovative conditions in the rapidly developing São Paulo region. The northeast produced two times more sugar than the southern region in 1950, but by the early 1970s, the latter region was producing more than the northeast, under much more mechanized forms of production. The expansion of cattle, swine, and poultry production strongly stimulated the growth of corn, sorghum, and soybeans for animal feed in the 1970s. In addition, official policies from the mid 1960s encouraged the processing of important export crops in the country, and the food and raw materials processing industries expanded rapidly.

28. *LARR*, RB-81-02 (February 6, 1981), 2.

29. *LAER* 7, no. 10 (March 9, 1979): 76.

30. *LARR*, RB-81-07 (August 7, 1981), 7.

31. Ibid., RB-80-02 (February 8, 1980), 7.

32. See Mahar 1979, 74; *LARR*, RB-82-04 (April 23, 1982), 6.

33. *LARR*, RB-80-07 (August 8, 1980), 2.

34. Ibid., RB-80-10 (November 21, 1980), 5–7. On the development of the Amazon and its effects on ecology, people, and agriculture, see Morán (1982).

35. See Mahar 1979, 23–24. In 1982, it was estimated that there were some 2.4 million smallholders in the Amazon region, most of whom were extremely vulnerable to violent attempts to dispossess them of their land. See *LARR*, RB-82-04 (April 23, 1982), 6.

CHAPTER 6. Poverty and Survival among the Rural Poor

1. Altimir 1981. A study comparing rural incomes in El Salvador in 1961 and 1975 indicated that in real terms incomes had deteriorated by 16 percent for landless peasants and by 20 percent for families that had access to less than one hectare of land. See Klein 1980, 114.

2. See Saint 1980; Goodman and Redclift 1977. See also Burbach and Flynn 1980, 156. An urban agricultural work force is found elsewhere in Latin America. In El Salvador, for instance, twice as many rural laborers were required during the harvest season than at other times, a need that resulted in the recruitment of some urban laborers for the harvest season. See Klein 1980, 114–15. In many cases, women and

children were hired at much less than the average rural wage, making family subsistence even more problematic. See Nairn 1981, 14.

3. In the state of Paraná in southern Brazil, a soybean boom in the 1960s and 1970s led to rapid concentration of landholding, expansion of the agricultural frontier, and extensive mechanization. Small farmers, facing rising land values and declining security at home, were attracted to eastern Paraguay, where fertile soil, favorable policies, and lower land values made the production of soybeans a profitable enterprise. These farmers were frequently able to purchase considerable quantities of land in Paraguay and to buy some machinery. By 1979, 300,000 Brazilians were living in the eastern agricultural zone of Paraguay, doubling the size of its population. Brazilian, U.S., and Japanese corporations followed the colonists into the region. See Nickson 1981.

4. Other peasants were evicted from their land because of their inability to validate uncertain land titles; Paraguayan peasants were evicted from the land by Paraguayan troops, often in defense of Brazilian or other transnational interests.

5. At times, a single individual worked his land and sought wage labor; in other cases, various family members assumed responsibility for one task or the other. As temporary laborers, these workers were not eligible for social security benefits, could not form unions, and were paid lower wages than permanent laborers on the enterprises.

6. From the sixteenth century on, rural life was occasionally punctuated by active resistance on the part of the peasants and frequent repression on the part of the landowners. Periodically, boom conditions encouraged encroachments on peasant landholdings and systems of security, such as that which accompanied the expansion of agrarian capitalism in the nineteenth and early twentieth centuries. As we have seen, this often brought sudden and devastating change in the lives of the rural poor. By and large, however, life changed slowly, in a process that allowed some observers to believe that rural areas enshrined tradition and passivity and exhibited static social, political, and economic relationships.

7. Peasants could approach landowners for small favors that would increase the potential for family survival—a plot of land, a loan, protection, employment—but in doing so they became further indebted to the landowners and simultaneously decreased their capacity for collective class-based action. Patron-client linkages are persistent exchange relationships between two individuals of differing social status. Because they are individual linkages formed in the expectation of acquiring scarce and valued resources, they tend to create or exacerbate tensions and competition among individuals of similar status. See Grindle 1977; Powell 1970; Scott 1972; Van den Berghe and Primov 1977, chap. 6.

8. See Schryer 1980; Seligson 1980. Warman (1980, 230–31) writes of a rural area in central Mexico where the "old bosses, the corn and ox-team lenders . . . appropriated perhaps half of the area's total production of corn" through their power over the livelihood of the local peasantry.

9. See Long and Roberts 1978 for a discussion of the importance of towns and villages in peasant life in highland Peru. See also Van den Berghe and Primov 1977.

10. Hewitt de Alcántara (1980, 31) explains typical rural conditions in Mexico. "For centuries, rural people throughout Mexico had survived by emphasizing microregional self-sufficiency in basic goods, limiting trade with the wider monetary economy, curtailing conspicuous consumption within the village, and enforcing a limited

redistribution of small surpluses through the periodic sponsorship of religious celebrations. The resources of most communities were not great, but neither were their needs, and a web of personal relationships among local families functioned to ensure that no-one would be destitute (unless a catastrophe left the entire village destitute)."

11. Thus, in Panama, in contrast to the 1940s, "In place of thatch, corrugated roofing now is often purchased; for vines, nails are used; metal eating utensils have replaced those fashioned from wood and gourds" (Gudeman 1978, 30). See also Hewitt de Alcántara 1976, 32; Preston 1980. For a useful study of changing patterns of consumption in a rural community in Costa Rica, see Barlett 1982. On Peru, see Mallon 1983.

12. In some cases, small proprietors would have to pay as much as half of their crop to commercial middlemen in order to purchase fertilizer on credit, obtain seeds and chemicals, or rent tractors. Eventually, some became wage laborers on their own land renting it to commercial entrepreneurs. In contrast, large landholders engaged in commercial cropping had both the land available for less-intensive overuse and the resources to acquire productive inputs on better terms. See Pearse 1975, 257–58, 188.

13. Peasant production of barley in Mexico, for example, was encouraged and then controlled by a few large breweries. Coffee production on Indian smallholdings was controlled through credit and inputs by large local producers and transnational firms producing instant coffee until the state stepped in, in the 1970s to displace many of the large exploiters, but only to assume the role of controlling access to credit and markets. A similar situation developed in the peasant-based production of tobacco. See Esteva 1980, 169, 172. Redclift (1978, 68) describes the conditions in a coastal zone of Ecuador where, in response to the demand of an urban market, tenants grew rice in exchange for access to land. In exchange for a loan, the local moneylender acquired the peasants' crops. For lack of title to the land, the tenants were excluded from official sources of credit. "Usually the tenant sold the crops to the landlord, or to a rice-mill, if not to a dealer. Most rice mills were owned by landlords, and the three roles were quite commonly played by one man, or members of the same family. In some circumstances, this monopolization of control over the commercialization process meant that landlords-cum-dealers could charge rates of interest as high as 10 per cent per month to tenants. . . . The multiplicity of cross-cutting ties which bound tenant to landlord made it difficult for the [rice tenant] to free himself from debt, as well as reinforced his moral obligation to his patron."

14. For a useful discussion of literature related to this point, see Ortega 1982, 105–9.

15. Warman 1980, 238. These changes are related to the decline of traditional forms of mutual help and exchange. See Hewitt de Alcántara 1980; Pearse 1975, 256.

16. The expansion of export-oriented agrarian capitalism is analyzed in Duncan and Rutledge 1977; Mallon 1983; Moore 1966; Migdal 1974; Paige 1975; Scott 1976; Wolf 1969. For some smallholders—those who initially had access to better quality land in areas where climatic conditions or irrigation facilities were adequate, and those who qualified for official or private institutional credit programs—increased participation was not necessarily disadvantageous. As indicated previously, many of these "rich" peasants were able to use their greater financial resources to establish control over poor peasants and to exercise the traditional exploitive powers of the intermediary or ca-

cique in the local economy. By and large, however, these peasants were unable to compete easily with the large commercial producers. See Pearse 1975, 258; Hewitt de Alcántara 1976.

17. On this process in Panama, see Gudeman 1978.

18. Redclift 1978. On Chile, see Klein 1980, 107–8.

19. For a description and study of the "peasant bourgeoisie," see Pearse 1975, 225. See also Schryer 1980.

20. Klein 1980, 120. See also Pearse 1970, 26.

21. For a discussion of the sugar plantations expropriated by the state in Peru, see Stepan 1978, 195–229.

22. Considerable consensus has emerged in recent years over the question of the "rationality" of peasant behavior. In general, there is agreement that the behavior of the rural poor can be accounted for most effectively by considering the alternatives available to the peasant household for ensuring family subsistence at acceptable levels of risk. Peasant decision making based on a rational assessment of the costs and benefits of ensuring short- and medium-term subsistence needs is particularly noticeable under deteriorating economic conditions. See note 18, Chapter 2.

23. Gudeman 1978, 93–94. See also Pearse 1975, chap. 6.

24. See Klein 1980, 96–99, for a discussion of how salaried workers in northeast Brazil acquired access to land but at the same time increased their level of insecurity.

25. The discussion of colonization in the Amazon region is taken from *LARR*, RB-80-04 (April 25, 1980); *LAWR*, WR-80-44 (November 7, 1980), 4; *LAER* 7, no. 40 (October 12, 1979); ibid. 7, no. 2 (January 12, 1979): 1; *LAWR* 7, no. 23 (June 15, 1979); *LARR*, RB-80-01 (January 4, 1980). On settlement in Paraguay, see Nickson 1981; *LARR*, RS-80-03 (April 18, 1980), 7.

26. In the northeast, estimates of regionwide unemployment reached 22.5 percent and underemployment topped 25 percent in the late 1970s, figures that were most likely higher for rural areas of the region.

27. The original plan called for settling 10 million northeasterners over a ten-year period. See *LAER* 7, no. 2 (January 12, 1979): 11.

28. Miró and Rodríguez 1982, 65; Feder 1971, 37; Stavenhagen 1975, 178. For Feder (1971, 38), this group of "professional migrants" in rural Latin America represents a "continuous, large-scale 'milling around' of poor farm people in search of jobs or land, and involves annually several million people in the hemisphere." The search for wage labor led to wider use of the labor contractor in many areas, especially in highland zones, where cheap labor was recruited for lowland, plantation-based agriculture. Promising high wages and generous benefits, labor contractors enrolled needy peasants for work in distant areas. With cash advances or charges for transportation and food, the contractor could begin a process of indebtedness which would ensure that the highlander, actually paid very low wages and deprived of all benefits, would retain very little of what he or she earned. See Burbach and Flynn 1980, 154–55.

29. Warman 1980, 228. For a discussion of seasonal movements and intrarural migration, see Miró and Rodríguez 1982; Dinerman 1982.

30. This theme is developed in Rivière d'Arc 1980, 192. See also Klein 1980, 97; Hewitt de Alcántara 1980, 32. A useful discussion of this literature is found in Miró and Rodríguez 1982.

CHAPTER 7.   Agrarian Reform: Ideology and Politics

1. "Agrarian reform" refers to official efforts to modify landowning and tenure relationships in rural areas. The organization of beneficiary holdings into cooperatives, communes, or individual smallholdings may vary. Generally, these efforts include a wide variety of programs whose purpose is to aid beneficiaries and to increase levels of production and productivity among the rural poor. To be classified as an agrarian reform, however, such efforts must include the attempt to alter the structure of landowning toward greater equity for the rural poor.

2. *LARR*, RM-81-05 (June 5, 1981), 7; Volk 1981.

3. See Griffin 1976; *LAER* 5, no. 27 (July 15, 1977): 107; ibid. 6, no. 50 (December 22, 1978): 398; *LAPR* 11, no. 3 (January 21, 1977): 22–23; ibid. 11, no. 17 (May 6, 1977): 130, 132; Redclift 1978.

4. See Grindle 1977; see also *LTCN*, no. 56 (1977), 5–8.

5. See *LAPR* 11, no. 25 (July 1, 1977): 197–98; McClintock 1981, Alberts 1983.

6. See *LARR*, RA-80-10 (December 12, 1980), 2.

7. In 1960, there had been 1.2 million holdings on 27.3 million hectares of agricultural land in Colombia. INCORA's activities thus affected about one-third of one percent of all private agricultural holdings.

8. A fascinating study of the agrarian revolt is found in Womack 1968. On the Revolution of 1910 and its agrarian component more generally, see Esteva 1980; Ronfeldt 1973; Simpson 1937; Whetten 1948; Wolf 1968.

9. On the agrarian reform in Bolivia, see Eckstein 1982, 52–67; Eckstein et al. 1978; Malloy 1970, chap. 10.

10. The process by which such clienteles developed is described in Heath 1972.

11. By 1970, because of population growth, the land reform beneficiaries constituted only 34 percent of all farm families.

12. On the agrarian reform in Cuba, see Eckstein 1982, 52–67; Domínguez 1978.

13. On the agrarian reform in Nicaragua, see Deere 1982, Kaimowitz and Havens 1982; *LAWR*, WR-80-33 (August 22, 1980), 9–10; *New York Times*, July 23, 1980, 2.

14. See Baer 1962. Similar analyses emerged in Alliance for Progress, U.N., and FAO documents.

15. For example, Redclift (1978, 141) claims that "it would be more accurate to see the Ecuadorian agrarian reform as carried out as part of a strategy to create an urban bourgeoisie, a strategy that was made possible by expanding foreign exchange revenues." On Chile, see Lehman 1971.

16. In some countries, such as Brazil, where little real commitment to redistribution existed among policy makers, reform legislation was enacted primarily to stimulate more entrepreneurship among large landowners threatened by expropriation if the performance of their estates did not improve.

17. Quoted in Hirschman 1963, 142. On the impact of the Cuban Revolution generally, see Feder 1971, chap. 18; Petras and LaPorte 1971.

18. This process has been well documented in Chile, Venezuela, Peru, and Bolivia. On Chile, see Kaufman 1972; Lehman 1974; Loveman 1976; Thiesenhusen 1971. On Peru, see Astiz 1969; Paige 1975; Zaldívar 1974. On Venezuela, see Cox 1978; Kirby 1973; Martz 1966; Powell 1971. On Bolivia, see Malloy and Thorn 1971.

19. For a perspective on the New Frontier and the Alliance for Progress, see Schle-

singer 1975. See also Levinson and Onís 1970. For an analysis of the Alliance as an aspect of U.S. ideology, see Packenham 1973. See also Petras and LaPorte 1971, chap. 8.

20. For a readable review of efforts to deal with social and economic problems in Colombia's agricultural sector, see Hirschman 1963.

21. See Campos and McCamant 1972; Dix 1967, chap. 6. Clearly identifying either the Liberals or the Conservatives with specific interests within the class structure of Colombia is problematic. Kline (1980, 61–62) argues that "the Liberals are more welfare-state oriented, more anticlerical, and less private-property oriented than the Conservatives. . . . [E]conomic interests tend to be organized into several groups (as in the case of labor) along party lines, or to have equal access to the membership of all parties, (as in the case of the upper status groups such as the Coffee Growers Federation)."

22. See Hirschman 1963, 141–48, for details of the negotiations between the parties.

23. The impact of these international influences was an article of faith to many who were involved in the debates about agrarian reform. When questioned many years afterward, they stressed the importance of the threat of social unrest, its relationship to the Cuban Revolution, and the pressure exerted by the United States through the Alliance for Progress. The following responses about the origin of the agrarian reform law of 1961 are characteristic. "It wasn't until the external impact of the Cuban Revolution occurred that anything was done. All of a sudden, with the threat of this revolution, the important classes began to say, if we don't make an agrarian reform, the peasants will make it by force." "The 1961 law was a response to a considerable amount of outside pressure—there was much talk of the whole countryside blowing up in the Cuban fashion if it were not done." "Agrarian reform got underway with the Alliance for Progress and the threat of Cuba and revolution all over Latin America. When that threat died down, so did the impetus for agrarian reform." Interviews with INCORA officials, Bogotá, June–July 1977.

24. On the agrarian reform legislation, see Feder 1971, chap. 19; Thome 1971; Vertinsky and Fox 1972.

25. According to one informant, "[Carlos Lleras] was a young man in the 1920s, when there was a considerable amount of agitation over ownership of land, and it was the one time when there was an authentic Communist Party in the country. This agitation seems to have marked him deeply, as experiences in one's youth often do, and doing something about the agrarian problem became a central focus of his political life; it became a mission for him, and when he became President he finally had a chance to do something about it. . . . I won't say he was the only one interested in agrarian reform—he brought much of the Liberal Party with him. But he was certainly a central and energizing figure." Interview with a former minister of state, Bogotá, July 7, 1977.

26. Quoted in Escobar Sierra 1972, 77–78. See also Bagley and Botero 1977, 61–62.

27. Bejarano 1977, 42; Gómez 1975, 62; Bagley and Laun 1977, 32–33. Adoption of the official program of the Pastrana administration, the Four Strategies Plan, indicated that the Conservative government did not see much justification in a major commitment to agrarian reform. This plan, based on recommendations made initially by Lauchlin Currie in the early 1960s and repeated in the 1970s, argued that the solu-

tion to the agrarian problem was to be found not in agriculture but in the provision of alternative sources of employment for peasants who abandoned the land. The movement of peasants from the rural areas was not to be artificially discouraged by government actions; its beneficial consequence would be to stimulate agricultural modernization based on large, heavily capitalized landholding in private hands. According to this perspective, the minifundio, not the latifundio, stood most directly in the way of agricultural commercialization. Thus, urbanization, resulting from increased rural-to-urban migration, could be salutary to both the agricultural and the industrial sector of the economy. See DNP 1972.

28. DNP n.d., 28. See also López Michelsen 1972.

29. *LARR*, RA-80-10 (December 12, 1980), 2.

30. See Clark 1971; McClintock 1980; Seligson 1977; Klein 1980, 107–8.

31. The Nicaraguan Revolution was a significant factor in encouraging support for agrarian reform in El Salvador, but this return to reformism was not generalized to other countries. The Salvadoran reform was directed at estates over 500 hectares in size, which generally belonged to sugar and cotton growers. It left intact estates of 150–500 hectares, where coffee—the basis of the country's export economy—was grown. Thus, it left intact the political power of the landed elite and encouraged the owners of expropriated land to invest their cash compensation in the industrial sector. See Deere 1982.

32. Soon after the initiation of the Alliance for Progress, and certainly after the installation of the Johnson administration, interest in stimulating reform of social, economic, and political structures in Latin America was overshadowed by greater direct concern with the issues of hemispheric and internal security. At the same time, Latin America lost importance for policy makers in Washington as the United States became more intensely involved in Vietnam and as it became apparent that the Cuban Revolution was not igniting similar movements elsewhere. By the late 1960s, U. S. policy toward the region was once again typified by the "low profile" of general disinterest. See Ferguson 1975, 2. Although some pressure was exerted on authoritarian governments in terms of human rights in the late 1970s, the major thrust of U.S. policy in the 1970s was toward ensuring the loyalty and orthodoxy of trading and defense partners, not toward bringing about "reform rather than revolution."

33. In Chile, Lehman reported (1971, 372), the agrarian reform undertaken by the Frei government between 1964 and 1970 "played as much a role in creating instability as it did in integrating and incorporating the rural works into the society, on account of both excluded peasants and discontented landowners."

34. In Ecuador in the early 1970s, many landowners who were threatened by the 1973 land reform of the military government sold their land and expelled from their estates tenants and sharecroppers who were potential reform claimants, and ultimately only a small number of peasants actually benefited from the reform. See Preston 1980, 5; Redclift 1978, 32; Redclift and Preston 1980, 53. On Brazil, see *LAER* 6, no. 3 (January 20, 1978): 18. In Paraguay, the agrarian reform agency was primarily charged by the landowners themselves with resettling squatters and other peasants from the agriculturally rich central zone to areas in the northern and eastern parts of the country. See Nickson 1981, 115.

35. For suggestive evidence of this, see Bagley 1982; Kay 1978; Taussig 1978; Terán

1976; *LARR*, RM-80-06 (July 11, 1980); *LAWR*, WR-80-32 (August 15, 1980), 8. In El Salvador, the agrarian reform of 1980 benefited approximately 38,000 families in its early stages and for a time diminished the support of these peasants for left-wing organizations involved in the war against the regime and entrenched social classes. It also provided the state with the opportunity to move into rural areas and increase its military presence there.

36. Redclift 1978, 166. On Peru, see *LAER* 7, no. 25 (June 29, 1979): 196–97. On Mexico, see Barkin 1978.

CHAPTER 8. Integrated Rural Development: The "New Dualism"

1. On the relationship of food shortages to increased concern for agriculture in Costa Rica and Peru, see USDA 1980, 17, 30–31; *LARR*, RA-81-06 (July 24, 1981). On Mexico, see Grindle 1981a.

2. McNamara's speech in Nairobi, Kenya, in 1973 is generally recognized as a benchmark for redirecting the Bank's efforts toward poverty-alleviating development efforts. See World Bank 1975; Hürni 1980.

3. On the role of the Bank in Latin America, see *LAWR*, WR-81-12 (March 20, 1981), 9.

4. Full descriptions of integrated rural development can be found in Lele 1975; Rondinelli and Ruddle 1978; World Bank 1975; Hürni 1980, 45–62. On the problems of implementing rural development programs, see Grindle 1981b.

5. The concept of integrated rural development is not entirely new. Such thinking was often part of agrarian reform and colonization programs in previous decades. Generally, however, such an approach was too expensive and too complex to implement and sustain. It has become axiomatic that smallholders need more than land in order to produce efficiently and to enjoy at least minimal standards of health, welfare, and education. In some cases, integrated rural development included the colonization of frontier areas, which was expected to bring new or marginal lands into the national economy. This was true of the attempts to develop the *selva* in Peru and the *franja transversal* in Guatemala, although in these cases large commercial interests benefited from the programs more than the colonists did. On Guatemala, see *LAER* 7, no. 4 (January 26, 1979): 27. On Peru, see *LARR*, RA-81-06 (July 24, 1981), 6–7.

6. The rural development approach emphasized that the quality of inputs and the appropriateness of the "package," not the quantity of land, make agriculture productive.

7. For a full discussion of the problems of implementing integrated rural development programs, see Grindle 1981b; Johnston and Clark 1982.

8. PIDER is the acronym for Programa de Inversiones para el Desarrollo Rural Integrado; DRI stands for Desarrollo Rural Integrado; and POLONORDESTE refers to Programa de Desenvolvimento de Areas Integradas do Nordeste.

9. See Cernea 1979; PIDER 1980. Microregions typically covered 2–7 adjacent municipalites in a state, and represented approximately 50,000 people. According to program documents, microregional communities that ranged in population from 500 to 5,000 were PIDER targets. These communities often had inherent productive potential but lacked basic infrastructure and services.

10. See DRI 1980. DRI regions were selected in part because of the concentration of farms of 20 hectares or less and low productivity, but with the potential to expand through the introduction of appropriate technology.

11. These were to be located in humid valley areas, humid mountain ranges, dry farming areas, the coastal tableland, and the pre-Amazonian Maranhão.

12. In interviews, a number of informants mentioned the ties between DRI and the well-known Plan Puebla in Mexico. Plan Puebla focused primarily on the introduction of green revolution technology to an underproductive rural area.

13. Interview with Interamerican Development Bank official, Washington, D.C., June 11, 1980.

14. *LARR*, RA-82-03 (April 2, 1982), 2.

15. Finan and Fox 1980, 17–18. A project to develop tomato production in the region was cited by these authors (ibid., 18) as an example of lack of coordination: "While one agency was attempting to control the supply of tomatoes, another continued to stimulate the supply."

16. Interview with World Bank official, Washington, D.C., June 13, 1980.

17. Interview with World Bank official, Washington, D.C., June 6, 1980; interviews with various officials, Mexico City, September 1980.

18. One PIDER official admitted: "It is rather ironic that we are always telling the ministries that they need better trained people and we can't even get them ourselves because of the low salaries" (interview, Mexico City, September 11, 1980).

19. As stated by one official, "At first there was a great deal of pressure to show results in DRI and as a result, a great deal of waste occurred because there was little idea of exactly what needed to be done" (interview with DRI officials, Bogotá, January 13, 1981).

20. Interview with Ministry of Programming and Budget official, Mexico City, September 11, 1980.

21. Interview with World Bank official, Washington, D.C., June 11, 1980.

22. See Cernea 1979; Swanberg 1980; *LARR*, RA-82-03 (April 2, 1982), 2; Finan and Fox 1980.

23. Mexico 1980; *LAWR*, WR-80-31 (August 8, 1980), 9.

24. Interview with Ministry of Programming and Budget official, Mexico City, September 8, 1980.

25. The official target date for the "end" of agrarian reform in Mexico was January 1, 1980. For a discussion of López Portillo's policies toward the rural sector, see *LAER* 6, no. 23 (June 16, 1978): 180–81; Grindle 1981a. His state of the nation addresses in 1977, 1978, and 1979 all stressed his desire to end agrarian reform. That of 1980 dealt largely with resolving the backlog of land claims and petitions that had resulted from the more active periods of redistribution.

26. *LAER* 7, no 10 (March 9, 1979): 77–78.

27. See Chapter 7. See also DNP n.d.

28. DRI became known in agrarian reformist circles in Colombia as the Desmonte Rapido del Incora (Rapid Dismantling of INCORA) program. The 1979–82 development plan included participation by INCORA in DRI. Its role was limited to aiding technological development.

29. *LAWR*, WR-79-07 (December 14, 1979), 1.

30. Interviews with World Bank officials, Washington, D.C., June 10, 13, 1980.
31. Interview with World Bank official, Washington, D.C., June 11, 1980.

CHAPTER 9. Conclusion: Agrarian Protest and the State

1. Peasant protest against egregious social and economic conditions is not new in the Latin American context. The history of the region is replete with instances of Indian uprisings against the encroachment of colonial institutions, radical organizations demanding an end to exploitation, and revolts whose aim was to reclaim lands lost to large landholders. The revolt of Tupac Amarú in Peru, the wars of the Argentine pampas, the Zapatista revolt in Mexico, the agrarian focus of the Bolivian Revolution, and the widespread land invasions and rural organizations in Peru, Chile, Brazil, and Colombia in more recent history are all part of a long experience of peasant efforts to maintain or acquire control over land and to insist on more equitable economic and political relations with the rest of society. Far from being fatalistic or docile in the face of deteriorating conditions, throughout the four centuries since the Spanish and Portuguese conquest, peasants have repeatedly "come to object" to the conditions imposed on them by the rest of society. See Warman 1980.

2. See Hewitt de Alcántara 1976 and Yates 1981 for discussion of the linkages between the ejido and the state.

3. Early in 1981, for instance, 12,000 peasants protested against the depredation of their crops, livestock, water, and lands caused by the state oil company, PEMEX. While the CNC denounced their activities, PEMEX began procedures for compensating the peasants. Organizational efforts by indigenous groups were effectively countered by the creation of COPLAMAR, a state program to provide specific benefits to marginal groups and areas, often in response to local conditions of unrest. In addition, organizations of peasants were formed that effectively increased conflicts between mestizo peasants and indigenous communites, further dividing the rural poor into competing groups. Repression also was in evidence; 12 peasant deaths were reported in June 1980 following an attack on a peasant village by the military. On these events, see *LAWR*, WR-81-04 (January 23, 1981), 12; ibid., WR-81-05 (January 30, 1981), 2–3; *LARR*, RM-79-01 (November 16, 1979), 6–7; ibid., RM-80-07 (August 15, 1980), 7; *LAWR*, WR-80-27 (July 11, 1980), 12; *LARR*, RA-81-07 (August 28, 1981), 5–6; ibid., RA-80-01 (January 25, 1980), 7.

4. *LARR*, RA-80-04 (May 16, 1980), 6–7; ibid., RA-79-01 (November 30, 1979), 5; ibid., RA-81-04 (May 15, 1981), 3–4. The FARC, which was established in 1966, was built upon the Communist Party's experiences in rural organization and armed conflict in the 1920s and 1930s, when the party helped peasants resist violence at the hands of gunman hired by landlords, and the peasant's experience of violence in the 1960s, when the military attacked communities that had organized themselves into "independent republics" and self-defense areas with the help of the party.

5. The extent of military action was considerable. Air and ground actions by some 5,000 troops were involved in one foray against the FARC in 1980, forcing 1,500–2,000 peasants to flee the area. These same peasants had suffered similar military action in 1964 under a "pacification drive." According to one report, "Many of the peasant refugees were settled on government land following the 1964 'pacification' campaign,

with the promise of generous credits from the Caja Agraria. Very little has been forthcoming, and the campesino leaders complain bitterly of a lack of schools, clinics and even roads in an area that the central government has largely ignored" (*LARR*, RA-80-08 [October 3, 1980], 3–4; see also *LAWR*, WR-80-37 [September 19, 1980], 11; *LARR*, RA-81-06 [July 24, 1981], 3).

6. In 1980, the organization claimed that at least 35 of its leaders had been murdered in the previous decade. See *LARR*, RA-79-01 (November 30, 1979), 5; ibid., RA-80-03 (April 4, 1980), 5; ibid., RA-80-07 (August 29, 1980), 7; ibid., RA-81-04 (May 15, 1981), 3–4.

7. Many squatters had occupied the land for long periods of time; in the Department of Córdoba they were on the land for nearly 20 years before landowners arrived with the local police to evict them. At times, when peasants were not driven off the land, officially sponsored repression caused smallholders to sell out to large landowners interested in producing sugar, bananas, African palm, cotton, and cattle. See ibid., RA-80-03 (April 4, 1980), 5.

8. See Moraes 1970 for a discussion of agrarian movements in Brazil in the post-war period.

9. In the 1940s, the Communist Party had attempted, without great success, to mobilize rural inhabitants around common interests. These efforts ended when the party was declared illegal in 1947.

10. The leagues themselves were named by landowners, who attempted to link them with the leagues established by the Communist Party in the 1940s. See Cehelsky 1979, 41.

11. See Moraes 1970; Cehelsky 1979, 49. This rapid growth created problems of organization for the various movements and often resulted in poor linkages and coordination among a large number of local-level units. Ultimately, lack of coordination and linkages to national political events were to limit the effectiveness of the leagues and allow other organizations, more responsive to government direction, to supersede them.

12. SUDENE was headed by the respected economist and promoter of regional development, Celso Furtado. For a discussion of the origin and early activities of SUDENE, see Hirschman 1963.

13. The same legislation, however, restricted the organizational rights of smallholders, sharecroppers, and tenants.

14. See Moraes 1970, 484–89. By 1966, the Confederation of Rural Workers represented only slightly more than 300,000 of an estimated 25 million rural workers. The organization acted to stimulate modest attempts at agrarian reform and the direction of public resources toward the alleviation of the most immediate problems of its members.

15. *LAWR*, WR-80-49 (December 12, 1980), 8–9.

16. One major rural conflict in 1980 was an important exception to this pattern. In the northeastern state of Pernambuco, more than 160,000 sugarcane cutters and day laborers struck in demand for higher wages. Because the strikers carefully followed legal procedures in the action, the government was unable to deal with it as an illegal strike. The employers and local police, however, did have recourse to violence during the strike. Utimately, a wage increase was agreed upon and the cutters returned to work. See ibid., WR-80-40 (October 10, 1980), 2–3.

17. *LARR*, RB-82-04 (April 23, 1982), 7; ibid., RB-81-03 (March 13, 1981), 3.

18. Ibid., RB-80-01 (January 4, 1980), 6-7.

19. Ibid.

20. Ibid., RB-80-10 (November 21, 1980), 1; *LAWR*, WR-81-42 (October 23, 1981), 9-10.

21. *LAWR*, WR-80-07 (February 15, 1980), 1.

22. Ibid., WR-81-42 (October 23, 1981), 9-10; ibid., WR-80-23 (June 13, 1980), 11; ibid., WR-80-07 (February 15, 1980), 11. The GETAT was also accused by the National Council of Brazilian Bishops of granting plots of insufficient size for subsistence, withholding important assistance, and aiding large landowners in the use of troops and police to drive off the peasant farmers. See *LARR*, RB-81-03 (March 13, 1981), 3.

23. *New York Times*, January 25, 1981, E-7.

24. *LARR*, RB-82-04 (April 23, 1982), 7; ibid., RB-80-01 (January 4, 1980), 6-7. Plots were limited to 20 hectares per family; given the climate and ecological conditions, this was considered insufficient to maintain a peasant family, especially one with little or no access to credit or inputs. See *LAWR*, WR-81-43 (October 30, 1981), 5.

25. Ibid., WR-80-49 (December 12, 1980), 7-9.

26. Protests against opening up the Amazon to colonization and exploitation figured prominently in such demands in Peru, Colombia, Ecuador, and Brazil, as did demands for agrarian reform. Highland Indians also were increasingly active in Andean countries in demanding land and services. In El Salvador, Honduras, and Guatemala, peasant organizations focused primarily on demanding agrarian reform; to give credence to their demands, land invasions were increasingly undertaken in the late 1970s and early 1980s and occupations of churches and embassies occurred frequently. Low prices for agricultural products stimulated protests against the government by an estimated 10,000 peasants in Venezuela in 1980. On these events, see *LARR*, RA-81-07 (August 28, 1981), 5-6; ibid., RA-80-01 (January 25, 1980), 7; ibid., RM-81-05 (June 5, 1981), 7; *LAWR*, WR-80-30 (August 1, 1980), 11; *LARR*, RM-81-03 (March 20, 1981), 34; *LAWR*, WR-80-35 (September 5, 1980), 12; ibid., WR-80-29 (July 25, 1980), 12.

27. When 5,000 banana workers struck a United Brands plantation in Costa Rica in 1981, for example, the state reached an agreement with the workers to assume control of the plantation for a period and to set up a commission to study the issues raised by the worker. In Panama, the object of a 1981 strike by banana workers was legislation that restricted the organization of workers in state-owned companies. In the Dominican Republic, sugar workers went on strike against the state-managed mill for which they worked. And in Honduras, a former Standard Fruit banana plantation-turned-workers'-cooperative was the site of a confrontation between state and workers in 1981. The conflict developed when peasants, supported by the military and backed by the state, took over the cooperative; ultimately, however, the state sent troops to occupy it and used force to end the workers' strike. On these events, see *LAWR*, WR-80-34 (August 29, 1980), 11; ibid., WR-80-43 (October 31, 1980), 2-3; ibid., WR-80-46 (November 21, 1980), 11; *LARR*, RM-81-02 (February 12, 1981), 3; ibid., RM-81-03 (March 20, 1981), 7.

28. In Peru, for instance, conflict between recently recruited colonists and Indian groups over land rights involved not only these two groups but also private colonization companies and the Ministry of Agriculture, which was asked to evict the colonists. Peasant communities excluded from the 1969 agrarian reform also sharply increased

their invasions of the lands of reform beneficiaries in the late 1970s. The state's response to this conflict was to promulgate legislation to cancel or refinance the agrarian debt under certain conditions, and to open up a market in land for landless peasants. On these events, see *LARR*, RA-80-06 (July 25, 1980), 6; *LAWR*, WR-80-06 (February 8, 1980), 12.

Bibliography

Abercrombie, K. C.
1972 "Agricultural Mechanization and Employment in Latin America." *International Labor Review* 106, no. 1 (July): 11–45.

Adams, Dale W.
1971 "What Can Under-Developed Countries Expect from Foreign Aid to Agriculture? Case Study: Brazil, 1950–1970," *Interamerican Economic Affairs* 25, no. 1 (Summer): 47–63.

Adams, Dale W., and G. I. Nehman
1979 "Borrowing Costs and the Demand for Rural Credit." *Journal of Development Studies* 15, no. 2 (January): 165–76.

Adams, Richard N.
1967 *The Second Sowing: Power and Secondary Development in Latin America.* San Francisco: Chandler.

Adie, Robert, and Guy Poitras
1973 *Latin America: The Politics of Immobility.* Englewood Cliffs, N.J.: Prentice-Hall.

Affonso, A.
1972 Papel de los campesinos en la ejecución de la reforma agraria. IICA-CIRA Material Didáctico no. 175. Bogotá: IICA-CIRA.

Alberts, Tom
1983 *Agrarian Reform and Rural Poverty: A Case Study of Peru.* Boulder, Colo.: Westview Press.

Alcântara de Camargo, Aspásia
1979 "Authoritarianism and Populism: Bipolarity in the Brazilian Political System." In Neuma Aguiar, ed., *The Structure of Brazilian Development.* New Brunswick, N.J.: Transaction Books.

Allison, Graham
1971 *Essence of Decision.* Boston: Little, Brown.

Altimir, Oscar
1981 "Poverty in Latin America: A Review of Concepts and Data," *CEPAL Review*, no. 13 April, 65–91.

Amin, Samir
  1976   *Imperialism and Unequal Development.* New York: Monthly Review Press.
Anderson, Charles
  1967   *Politics and Economic Change in Latin America: The Governing of Restless Nations.* New York: Van Nostrand.
ANUC (Asociación Nacional de Usuarios Campesinos)
  1971   "Primer mandato campesino." Bogotá. Mimeo.
Araya, Juan Enrique, and Carlos Ossa
  1976   *La mecanización en la agricultura colombiana.* Bogotá: Adimagro.
Astiz, Carlos A.
  1969   *Pressure Groups and Power Elites in Peruvian Politics.* Ithaca, N.Y.: Cornell University Press.
Austin, James E.
  1974   *Agribusiness in Latin America.* New York: Praeger.
Baer, Werner
  1962   "The Economics of Prebisch and ECLA." *Economic Development and Cultural Change* 10, no. 2, pt. 1 (January): 169–82.
Baer, Werner, Richard Newfarmer, and Thomas Trebat
  1976   "On State Capitalism in Brazil: Some New Issues and Questions." *Latin American Economic Affairs* 30 (Winter): 63–93.
Bagley, Bruce
  1982   "The State and the Peasantry in Contemporary Colombia." Paper prepared for the 1982 meeting of the Latin American Studies Association, Washington, D.C., March 3–6.
Bagley, Bruce, and Fernando Botero
  1977   "Organizaciones campesinas contemporáneas en Colombia: Un estudio de la Asociación Nacional de Usuarios Campesinos (ANUC)." Unpublished paper, Department of Political Science, Universidad de los Andes, Bogotá.
Bagley, Bruce, and Matthew Edel
  1980   "Popular Mobilization Programs of the National Front: Cooptation and Radicalization." In R. Albert Berry, Ronald G. Hellman, and Mauricio Solaún, eds., *Politics of Compromise.* New Brunswick, N.J.: Transaction Books.
Bagley, Bruce, and John I. Laun
  1977   "Political Power and Agricultural Policy Making in Colombia: A Case Study of Laws 4 and 5 of 1973." Unpublished paper, Department of Political Science, Universidad de los Andes, Bogotá.
Bailey, John J.
  1975   "Policymaking in Colombian Decentralized Agencies: Presidential Control versus Agency Autonomy." Paper prepared for the 1975 meeting of the American Political Science Association, San Francisco, Calif., September 2–5.
Bailey, John J., and John Link
  1980   "Statecraft and Agriculture in Mexico, 1980–1982: Domestic and Foreign Policy Considerations." Paper prepared for the 1980 meeting of the Latin American Studies Association, Bloomington, Ind., October 17–19.

Baily, Samuel
1967   *Labor, Nationalism, and Politics in Argentina.* New Brunswick, N.J.: Rutgers University Press.
Barkin, David
1978   *Desarrollo regional y reorganización campesina.* Mexico City: Editorial Nueva Imagen.
Barkin, David, and Blanca Suárez
n.d.   *El complejo de granos en México.* Mexico City: Centro de Ecodesarrollo, Instituto Latinoamericano de Estudios Transnacionales.
Barlett, Peggy F.
1982   *Agricultural Choice and Change: Decision Making in a Costa Rican Community.* New Brunswick, N.J.: Rutgers University Press.
Barraclough, Solon
1973   *Agrarian Structure in Latin America.* Lexington, Mass.: Lexington Books.
Barraclough, Solon, and Arthur L. Domike
1970   "Agrarian Structure in Seven Latin American Countries." In Rodolfo Stavenhagen, ed., *Agrarian Problems and Peasant Movements in Latin America.* Garden City, N.Y.: Doubleday.
Barraclough, Solon, and J. Schattan
1973   "Technological Policy and Agricultural Development." *Land Economics* 29, no. 2:175–94.
Bartra, Roger
1974   *Estructura agraria y clases sociales en México.* Mexico City: Era.
1975   "Sobre la articulación de modos de producción en América Latina." *História y Sociedad* (Mexico City) 5 (Spring): 5–19.
Bauer, Arnold J.
1975   *Chilean Rural Society from the Spanish Conquest to 1930.* Cambridge: Cambridge University Press.
1979   "Rural Workers in Spanish America: Problems of Peonage and Oppression." *Hispanic American Historical Review* 59.
Bejarano, Jesús Antonio
1977   "Contribución al debate sobre el problema agrario." In *El agro en el desarrollo histórico colombiano: Ensayos de economía política.* Bogotá: Editorial Punta de Lanza.
Bennett, Douglas, and Kenneth Sharpe
1980   "The State as Banker and Entrepreneur: The Last Resort Character of the Mexican State's Economic Intervention, 1917–1976." *Comparative Politics* 12, no. 2 (January): 165–90.
Berger, Susan
1982   "The Role of the State in Rural Politics: Guatemala." Paper prepared for the 1982 meeting of the International Political Science Association, Rio de Janeiro, August 9–14.
Berry, R. Albert
1975   "Special Problems of Policy Making in a Technologically Heterogeneous Agriculture: Colombia." In Lloyd G. Reynolds, ed., *Agriculture in Development Theory.* New Haven: Yale University Press.

1978   "Rural Poverty in Twentieth Century Colombia." *Journal of Interamerican Studies and World Affairs* 20, no. 4 (November): 355–76.

n.d.   "The Development of the Agricultural Sector in Colombia." Mimeo.

Berry, R. Albert, and William R. Cline

1979   *Agrarian Structure and Productivity in Developing Countries.* Baltimore: Johns Hopkins University Press.

Blank, David Eugene

1973   *Politics in Venezuela.* Boston: Little, Brown.

Bourque, Susan, and Kay Warren

1981   *Women of the Andes.* Ann Arbor: University of Michigan Press.

Brading, David

1977   "*Hacienda* Profits and Tenant Farming in the Mexican Bajío, 1700–1860." In Kenneth Duncan and Ian Rutledge, eds., *Land and Labour in Latin America.* Cambridge: Cambridge University Press.

1978   *Haciendas and Ranchos in the Mexican Bajío: León, 1700–1860.* Cambridge: Cambridge University Press.

1981   "Population and Agriculture in Colonial Mexico." *Journal of Latin American Studies* 13, pt. 2 (November): 403–13.

Brazil, Ministério do Interior

1979a   *Principais linhas de ação do Ministério do Interior para o período 1979–1985.* Brasília.

1979b   *SUDENE: Vinte Anos.* Recife.

Browning, David

1983   "Agrarian Reform in El Salvador." *Journal of Latin American Studies* 15, pt. 2:269–94.

Bulmer-Thomas, V.

1983   "Economic Development Over the Long Run—Central America Since 1920." *Journal of Latin American Studies* 15, pt. 2:269–94.

Burbach, Roger, and Patricia Flynn

1980   *Agribusiness in the Americas.* New York: Monthly Review Press.

Burns, E. Bradford

1977   *Latin America: A Concise Interpretive History.* 2nd ed. Englewood Cliffs, N.J.: Prentice-Hall.

Butterworth, Douglas, and John K. Chance

1981   *Latin American Urbanization.* Cambridge: Cambridge University Press.

Calder, Bruce J.

1982   "Sugar Estate Expansion and the Creation of a Rural Proletariat in the Dominican Republic, 1870–1925." Paper prepared for the 1982 meeting of the Latin American Studies Association, Washington, D.C., March 3–6.

Campos, Judith Talbot, and John F. McCamant

1972   "Cleavage Shift in Colombia: Analysis of the 1970 Elections." *Sage Professional Paper in Comparative Politics,* no. 01-032. Beverly Hills, Calif.: Sage.

Canak, William L.

1984   "The Peripheral State Debate: State Capitalist and Bureaucratic-Authoritarian Regimes in Latin America." *Latin American Research Review* 19, no. 1:3–36.

Cardoso, Ciro F. S.
1977 "The Formation of the Coffee Estate in Nineteenth Century Costa Rica." In Kenneth Duncan and Ian Rutledge, eds., *Land and Labour in Latin America.* Cambridge: Cambridge University Press.
Cardoso, Fernando E.
1973 "Associated-Dependent Development: Theoretical and Political Implications." In Alfred Stepan, ed., *Authoritarian Brazil: Origins, Policies, and Future.* New Haven: Yale University Press.
1980 "On the Characterization of Authoritarian Regimes in Latin America." In David Collier, ed., *The New Authoritarianism in Latin America.* Princeton: Princeton University Press.
Cardoso, Fernando E. and Enzo Faletto
1979 *Dependency and Development in Latin America.* Berkeley and Los Angeles: University of California Press.
CDIA (Centro de Investigaciones Agrarias)
1974 *Estructura agraria y desarrollo agrícola en México.* Mexico City: Fondo de Cultura Económica.
Cehelsky, Marta
1979 *Land Reform in Brazil: The Management of Social Change.* Boulder, Colo.: Westview Press.
CEPAL (Comisión Económica para América Latina)
1965 *Problemas y perspectivas de la agricultura latinoamericana.* Buenos Aires: Solar/Hachette.
Cernea, Michael
1979 "Measuring Project Impact: Monitoring and Evaluation in the PIDER Rural Development Project—Mexico." World Bank Staff Working Paper no. 332, Washington, D.C.
Chayanov, A. V.
1966 *The Theory of Peasant Economy.* Edited by Daniel Thorner, Basile Kerblay, and R. E. F. Smith. Homewood, Ill.: Richard D. Irwin.
Chevalier, François
1963 *Land and Society in Colonial Mexico: The Great Hacienda.* Berkeley and Los Angeles: University of California Press.
Chile, Ministerio de Agricultura
1970 *Plan de Desarrollo Agropecuario, 1965–1980, Resúmen.* Santiago.
Chonchol, Jacques
1965 "Land Tenure and Development in Latin America." In Claudio Veliz, ed., *Obstacles to Change in Latin America.* London: Oxford University Press.
Clark, Ronald J.
1971 "Agrarian Reform: Bolivia." In Peter Dorner, ed., *Land Reform in Latin America: Issues and Cases.* Land Economics Monograph no. 3. Madison: Land Tenure Center, University of Wisconsin.
Cleaves, Peter S. and Martin J. Scurrah
1980 *Agriculture, Bureaucracy, and Military Government in Peru.* Ithaca, N.Y.: Cornell University Press.

Clements, Harold M., Sr.
  1969   *The Mechanization of Agriculture in Brazil.* Gainesville: University of Florida Press.
Colburn, Forrest D.
  1984   "The Rural Poor in the Nicaraguan Revolution." Paper prepared for the 1984 meeting of the American Political Science Association, Washington, D.C., August 30–September 2.
Collier, David, ed.
  1979   *The New Authoritarianism in Latin America.* Princeton: Princeton University Press.
Collier, Ruth Berins
  1982   "Popular Sector Incorporation and Political Supremacy: Regime Evolution in Brazil and Mexico." In Sylvia Ann Hewlett and Richard S. Weinert, eds., *Brazil and Mexico: Patterns in State Development.* Philadelphia: ISHI.
Colombia, Ministerio de Agricultura
  1980   "Fondo Financiero Agropecuario: Programa de Crédito, 1981." Bogotá. Mimeo.
Cornelius, Wayne A.
  1973   "Nation-building, Participation, and Distribution: The Politics of Social Reform under Cárdenas." In Gabriel Almond and Scott Flanagan, eds., *Developmental Episodes in Comparative Politics: Crisis, Choice and Change.* Boston: Little, Brown.
  1980   "Immigration, Mexican Development Policy, and the Future of U.S.-Mexican Relations." Working Papers in U.S.-Mexican Studies no. 8. San Diego: Center for U.S.-Mexican Studies, University of California.
Cortés Conde, Roberto
  1974   *The First States of Modernization in Spanish America.* New York: Harper and Row.
Cosío Villages, Daniel
  1965   *El porfiriato: La vida económica.* Mexico City: Editorial Hermes.
Cotler, Julio
  1970   "Traditional Haciendas and Communities in a Context of Political Mobilization in Peru." In Rodolfo Stavenhagen, ed., *Agrarian Problems and Peasant Movements in Latin America.* Garden City, N.Y.: Doubleday.
  1979   "State and Regime: Comparative Notes on the Southern Cone and the 'Enclave' Societies." In David Collier, ed., *The New Authoritarianism in Latin America.* Princeton: Princeton University Press.
Cox, Paul
  1978   *Venezuela's Agrarian Reform at Mid-1977.* Land Tenure Center Research Paper no. 71. Madison: University of Wisconsin.
Craig, Ann L.
  1983   *The First Agraristas: An Oral History of a Mexican Agrarian Reform Movement.* Berkeley and Los Angeles: University of California Press.
DANE (Departamento Administrativo Nacional de Estadística)
  1971   *Debate agrario: Documentos.* Bogotá.

Davis, Shelton
    1977   *Victims of the Miracle: Development and the Indians of Brazil.* Cambridge: Cambridge University Press.

Deas, Malcolm
    1977   "A Colombian Coffee Estate: Santa Bárbara, Cundinamarca, 1870–1912." In Kenneth Duncan and Ian Rutledge, eds., *Land and Labour in Latin America.* Cambridge: Cambridge University Press.

Deere, Carmen Diana
    1982   "A Comparative Analysis of Agrarian Reform in El Salvador and Nicaragua." *Development and Change* 13, no. 1 (Winter): 3–41.

Deere, Carmen Diana, and Alain de Janvry
    1979   "A Conceptual Framework for the Empirical Analysis of Peasants." *American Journal of Agricultural Economics* 61, no. 4 (November): 601–11.

de Janvry, Alain
    1975   "The Political Economy of Rural Development in Latin America: An Interpretation." *American Journal of Agricultural Economics* 57, no. 3 (August): 490–99.
    1978   "Social Structure and Biased Technical Change in Argentine Agriculture." In Hans P. Binswanger and Vernon W. Ruttan, eds., *Induced Innovation: Technology, Institutions, and Development.* Baltimore: Johns Hopkins University Press.
    1981   *The Agrarian Question and Reformism in Latin America.* Baltimore: Johns Hopkins University Press.

de Janvry, Alain, and Carlos Garramón
    1977   "The Dynamics of Rural Poverty in Latin America." *Journal of Peasant Studies* 4, no. 3 (April): 206–16.

de Janvry, Alain, and L. Ground
    1978   "Types and Consequences of Land Reform in Latin America." *Latin American Perspectives* 19:90–112.

DeWalt, Billie R.
    1979   *Modernization in a Mexican Ejido.* Cambridge: Cambridge University Press.

Dillon Soares, Glaucio Ary
    1977   "The Web of Exploitation: State and Peasants in Latin America." *Studies in Comparative International Development* 7, no. 3 (Fall).

Dinerman, Ina
    1982   *Migrants and Stay-at-Homes: A Comparative Study of Rural Migration from Michoacan, Mexico.* Research Reports and Monographs in U.S.-Mexican Studies no. 5. San Diego: Center for U.S.-Mexican Studies, University of California.

Dix, Robert H.
    1967   *Colombia: The Political Dimensions of Change.* New Haven: Yale University Press.
    1981   "Political Oppositions under the National Front." In R. Albert Berry, Ronald G. Hellman, and Mauricio Solaún, eds., *Politics of Compromise.* New Brunswick, N.J.: Transaction Books.

DNP (Departmento Nacional de Planeación)
 1960 *Plan Decenal de Desarrollo, 1960–1969*, Bogotá.
 1972 *Las Cuatro Estratégias.* Bogotá.
 1980 *Plan de Integración Nacional, 1979–1982.* 2 vols. Bogotá.
 n.d. *To Close the Gap: Social, Economic and Regional Development Plan, 1975–1978.* Bogotá.
Domínguez, Jorge
 1978 *Cuba: Order and Revolution.* Cambridge, Mass.: Harvard University Press.
Dorner, Peter, ed.
 1971a *Land Reform in Latin America: Issues and Cases.* Land Economics Monograph no. 3. Madison: Land Tenure Center, University of Wisconsin.
Dorner, Peter, and Donald Kanel
 1971b "The Economic Case for Land Reform: Employment, Income Distribution, and Productivity." In Peter Dorner, ed., *Land Reform in Latin America: Issues and Cases.* Land Economics Monograph no. 3. Madison: Land Tenure Center, University of Wisconsin.
Dos Santos, Teotonio
 1970 "The Structure of Dependence." *American Economic Review* 60, no. 5:235–46.
DRI (Desarrollo Rural Integrado)
 1980 *Normas generales sobre la organización del Programa de Desarrollo Rural Integrado.* Bogotá.
Duncan, Kenneth, and Ian Rutledge
 1977 "Introduction: Patterns of Agrarian Capitalism in Latin America." In Kenneth Duncan and Ian Rutledge, eds., *Land and Labour in Latin America.* Cambridge: Cambridge University Press.
Durham, Kathleen Foote
 1977 "Expansion of Agricultural Settlement in the Peruvian Rainforest: The Role of the Market and the Role of the State." Paper prepared for the 1977 meeting of the Latin American Studies Association, Houston, Tex., November 2–5.
Durham, William H.
 1979 *Scarcity and Survival in Central America: Ecological Origins of the Soccer War.* Stanford: Stanford University Press.
ECIEL (*Estudios Conjuntos Sobre Intergración Económica Latinoamericana*)
   Published by the Brookings Institution
Eckstein, Salomon
 1966 *El ejido colectivo en México.* Mexico City: Fondo de Cultura Económica.
Eckstein, Shlomo, Gordon Donald, Douglas Horton, and Thomas Carroll
 1978 "Land Reform in Latin America: Bolivia, Chile, Mexico, Peru, and Venezuela." World Bank Staff Working Paper no. 275, Washington, D.C.
Eckstein, Susan
 1982 "The Impact of Revolution on Social Welfare in Latin America." *Theory and Society* 11:43–94.
ECLA (Economic Commission for Latin America)
 1978 *Statistical Yearbook.*

Edelman, Marc
   1982   "The Hacienda System in Guanacaste Province, Costa Rica, and the Crea-
          tion of a Labor Force, 1880–1950." Paper prepared for the 1982 meeting of
          the Latin American Studies Association, Washington, D.C., March 3–6.
Eisenberg, Peter L.
   1977   "The Consequences of Modernization for Brazil's Sugar Plantations in the
          Nineteenth Century." In Kenneth Duncan and Ian Rutledge, eds., *Land and
          Labour in Latin America.* Cambridge: Cambridge University Press.
Elías, Victor J.
   1981   "Government Expenditures on Agriculture in Latin America." International
          Food Policy Research Institute Research Report no. 23. Washington, D.C.
Emiliani Roman, R.
   1971   "El fracaso ruinoso de la reforma agraria." *Revista Colombiana* (Populibro
          37). Bogotá.
Engels, Friedrich
   1968   *The Origin of the Family, Private Property, and the State.* In Karl Marx and
          Friedrich Engels, *Selected Works.* New York: International Publishers.
Escobar Sierra, H.
   1972   *Las invasiones en Colombia.* Bogotá: Tercer Mundo.
Esteva, Gustavo
   1978   "Y si los campesinos existen?" *Comercio Exterior* 28 (June): 699–732.
   1980   *La batalla en el México rural.* Mexico City: Siglo XXI.
Evans, Peter
   1979   *Dependent Development: The Alliance of Multinational, State, and Local
          Capital in Brazil.* Princeton: Princeton University Press.
Fagen, Richard
   1969   *The Transformation of Political Culture in Cuba.* Stanford: Stanford Uni-
          versity Press.
Fagen, Richard, and Wayne A. Cornelius, Jr.
   1970   "Conclusions." In Richard Fagen and Wayne Cornelius, Jr., *Political Power
          in Latin America: Seven Confrontations.* Englewood Cliffs, N.J.: Prentice-
          Hall.
FAO (Food and Agriculture Organization of the United Nations)
          Production Yearbook. Rome. Published annually.
   1979   *Review and Analysis of Agrarian Reform and Rural Development in Devel-
          oping Countries since the Mid 1960s.* Rome (July).
          The State of Food and Agriculture. Rome. Published periodically.
          Trade Yearbook. Rome. Published annually.
Farrell, Gilda, and Sara da Ros
   1983   *El acceso a la tierra del campesino ecuatoriano.* Quito: Mundo Andino.
Faucher, Philippe
   1981   "The Paradise That Never Was: The Breakdown of the Brazilian Authoritar-
          ian Order." In Thomas C. Bruneau and Philippe Faucher, eds., *Authoritar-
          ian Capitalism: Brazil's Contemporary Economic and Political Develop-
          ment.* Boulder, Colo.: Westview Press.

Feder, Ernest
1971 *The Rape of the Peasantry: Latin America's Landholding System.* Garden City, N.Y.: Doubleday.
1976 "La nueva penetración en la agrícola de los paises subdesarrollados por los paises industriales y sus empresas multinacionales." *El Trimestre Económico* 169 (January).
1977 "Campesinistas y descampesinistas: Tres enfoques divergentes (no incompatibles) sobre la destrucción del campesinado." *Comercio Exterior* 27 (December): 1436–39.
1978 *Strawberry Imperialism.* Mexico City: Editorial Campesina.
1980 "The New Agrarian and Agricultural Change Trends in Latin America." In David Preston, ed., *Environment, Society, and Rural Change in Latin America.* Chichester: John Wiley and Sons.
1981 "Lean Cows, Fat Ranchers: The International Ramifications of Mexico's Beef Cattle Industry." Unpublished paper, distributed by América Latina, London.
Fedesarrollo
1975 *La política agraria en Colombia, 1950–1975.* Bogotá.
Fei, John C. H., and Gustav Ranis
1964 *Development of the Labor Surplus Economy: Theory and Policy.* Homewood, Ill.: Richard D. Irwin.
1975 "Agriculture in Two Types of Open Economies." In Lloyd G. Reynolds, ed., *Agriculture in Development Theory.* New Haven: Yale University Press.
Felstehausen, Herman
1971 "Agrarian Reform: Colombia." In Peter Dorner, ed., *Land Reform in Latin America: Issues and Cases.* Land Economics Monographs no. 3. Madison: Land Tenure Center, University of Wisconsin.
Ferguson, Yale
1975 "Trends in Inter-American Relations, 1972–Mid-1974." In Ronald G. Hellman and H. Jon Rosenbaum, eds., *Latin America: The Search for a New International Role.* New York: John Wiley and Sons.
Finan, Timothy J., and Roger W. Fox
1980 "Integrated Rural Development Programs in Northeast Brazil: The Case of the Ibiapaba Project." Paper prepared for the 1980 meeting of the Latin American Studies Association, Bloomington, Ind., October 17–19.
Fitzgerald, E. V. K.
1976 *The State and Economic Development: Peru Since 1968.* New York: Cambridge University Press.
Flammang, Robert
1979 "Economic Growth and Economic Development." *Economic Development and Cultural Change* 28, no. 1:47–61.
Fletcher, L. B., and W. C. Merrill
1968 "Latin American Agricultural Development and Policies." International Studies in Economics Monograph no. 8, Iowa State University, Mimeo.
Forman, Shepard
1975 *The Brazilian Peasantry.* New York: Columbia University Press.

Foster, George
1967   *Tzintzuntzan: Mexican Peasants in a Changing World.* Boston: Little, Brown.

Foweraker, Joe
1981   *The Struggle for Land: A Political Economy of the Pioneer Frontier in Brazil from 1930 to the Present Day.* Cambridge: Cambridge University Press.

Frankman, Myron T.
1974   "Sectoral Policy Preferences of the Peruvian Government, 1946–1968." *Journal of Latin American Studies* 6, no. 2 (November): 289–300.

Freebairn, Donald K.
1983   "Agricultural Interactions between Mexico and the United States." *Journal of Interamerican Studies and World Affairs* 25, no. 3 (August): 275–98.

Furtado, Celso
1963   *The Economic Growth of Brazil.* Berkeley and Los Angeles: University of California Press.

Gallo, Ezequiel
1977   "The Cereal Boom and Changes in the Social and Political Structure of Santa Fe, Argentina, 1870–95." In Kenneth Duncan and Ian Rutledge, eds., *Land and Labour in Latin America.* Cambridge: Cambridge University Press.

García García, Jorge
1980   "The Impact of Exchange Rate and Commercial Policy on Incentives to Agriculture in Colombia, 1953–1978." Unpublished paper, International Food Policy Research Institute, Washington, D.C.

Garreau, Gerard
1980   *El negocio de los alimentos: Las multinacionales de la desnutrición.* Mexico City: Editorial Nueva Imagen.

Geertz, Clifford
1963   *Agricultural Involution.* Berkeley and Los Angeles: University of California Press.

Gomes, Gerson, and Antonio Pérez
1979   "The Process of Modernization in Latin American Agriculture." *CEPAL Review*, no. 8 August, 55–74.

Gómez, Alcides
1975   "Política agraria de López y ley de aparcería." *Ideología y Sociedad* 14–15 (July–December): 47–63.

González, Michael
1980   "Capitalist Agriculture and Labour Contracting in Northern Peru, 1800–1905." *Journal of Latin American Studies* 12, no. 2:291–315.

Goodman, David, and Michael Redclift
1977   "The 'Boias Frias': Rural Proletarianization and Urban Marginality in Brazil." *International Journal of Urban and Regional Research* 1, no. 2:348–64.

1982   *From Peasant to Proletarian: Capitalist Development and Agrarian Transitions.* New York: St. Martin's Press.

Grieshaber, Erwin P.
1980   "Survival of Indian Communities in Nineteenth Century Bolivia: A Regional

Comparison." *Journal of Latin American Studies* 12, no. 2 (November): 223–69.

Griffin, Keith
1976   *Land Concentration and Rural Poverty*. New York: Holmes and Meier.

Grindle, Merilee S.
1977   *Bureaucrats, Peasants, and Politicians in Mexico: A Case Study in Public Policy*. Berkeley and Los Angeles: University of California Press
1980   *Whatever Happened to Agrarian Reform? The Latin American Experience*. Institute of Latin American Studies Technical Paper no. 23. University of Texas at Austin.
1981a   "Official Interpretations of Rural Underdevelopment: Mexico in the 1970s." Working Papers in U.S.-Mexican Studies no. 20. San Diego: Center for U.S.-Mexican Studies, University of California.
1981b   "Anticipating Failure: The Implementation of Rural Development Programs." *Public Policy* 29, no. 1 (Winter): 51–74.

Grunig, James
1969   "Economic Decision-making and Entrepreneurship among Colombian Latifundistas." *Interamerican Economic Affairs* 23, no. 1 (Summer): 21–46.

Gudeman, Stephen
1978   *The Demise of a Rural Economy: From Subsistence to Capitalism in a Latin American Village*. London: Routledge and Kegan Paul.

Guess, George M.
1979   "Pasture Expansion, Forestry, and Development Contradictions: The Case of Costa Rica." *Studies in Comparative International Development* 14, no. 1 (Spring): 42–55.

Gunder Frank, André
1972   "Economic Dependence, Class Structure, and Underdevelopment Policy." In James D. Cockcroft, André Gunder Frank, and Dale L. Johnson, *Dependence and Underdevelopment*. Garden City, N.Y.: Doubleday.
1976   *Capitalism and Underdevelopment in Latin America*. New York: Monthly Review Press.

Gutelman, M.
1975   *Capitalismo y reforma agraria en México*. Mexico City: Era.
1976   "Reforma agraria y desarrollo del capitalismo." *Cuadernos Agrários* 1 (October–December): 3–13.

Hall, Anthony
1978   *Drought and Irrigation in Northeast Brazil*. Cambridge: Cambridge University Press.

Hamilton, Nora
1982   *The Limits of State Autonomy: Post-revolutionary Mexico*. Princeton: Princeton University Press.

Hansen, Roger D.
1971   *The Politics of Mexican Development*. Baltimore: Johns Hopkins Press.

Haring, C. H.
1947   *The Spanish Empire in America*. New York: Harcourt, Brace, and World.

Harris, Charles H., III
1975   *A Mexican Family Empire: The Latifundio of the Sánchez Navarros, 1765–1867.* Austin: University of Texas Press.
Harris, Richard
1978   "Marxism and the Agrarian Question in Latin America." *Latin American Perspectives* 5, no. 4 (Fall): 2–26.
Havens, A. Eugene, William L. Flinn, and Susana Lastarria-Cornhill
1980   "Agrarian Reform and the National Front: A Class Analysis." In R. Albert Berry, Ronald G. Hellman, and Mauricio Solaún, eds., *Politics of Compromise.* New Brunswick, N.J.: Transaction Press.
Heath, Dwight B.
1972   "New Patrons for Old: Changing Patron-Client Relationships in the Bolivian Yungas." In Arnold Strickon and Sidney Greenfield, eds., *Structure and Process in Latin America: Patronage, Clientage, and Power Systems.* Albuquerque: University of New Mexico Press.
Heaton, Louis E.
1969   *The Agricultural Development of Venezuela.* New York: Praeger.
Hellman, Judith Adler
1978   *Mexico in Crisis.* New York: Holmes and Meier.
1983   "The Role of Ideology in Peasant Politics: Peasant Mobilization and Demobilization in the Laguna Region." *Journal of Interamerican Studies and World Affairs* 25, no. 1:3–30.
Hewitt de Alcántara, Cynthia
1976   *Modernizing Mexican Agriculture: Socioeconomic Implications of Technological Change, 1940–1970.* Geneva: UNRISD.
1980   "Land Reform, Livelihood, and Power in Rural Mexico." In David A. Preston, ed., *Environment, Society, and Rural Change in Latin America.* Chichester: John Wiley and Sons.
Hewlett, Sylvia Ann, and Richard S. Weinert
1982   "Introduction: The Characteristics and Consequences of Late Development in Brazil and Mexico." In Sylvia Ann Hewlett and Richard S. Weinert, eds., *Brazil and Mexico: Patterns in Late Development.* Philadelphia: ISHI.
Heynig, Klaus
1982   "The Principal Schools of Thought on the Peasant Economy." *CEPAL Review,* no. 16 (April), 113–39.
Hirschman, Albert
1963   *Journeys toward Progress.* New York: W. W. Norton.
1979   "The Turn to Authoritarianism in Latin America and the Search for Its Economic Determinants." In David Collier, ed., *The New Authoritarianism in Latin America.* Princeton: Princeton University Press.
Huizer, Gerrit
1972   *The Revolutionary Potential of Peasants in Latin America.* Lexington, Mass.: Lexington Books.
Hunter, John M., and James W. Foley
1975   *Economic Problems of Latin America.* Boston: Houghton Mifflin.

Hürni, Bettina S.
  1980   *The Lending Policy of the World Bank in the 1970s: Analysis and Evaluation.* Boulder, Colo.: Westview Press.
IDB (Interamerican Development Bank)
        Economic and Social Progress in Latin America. Washington, D.C. Published annually.
Iglesias, Enrique V.
  1981   "Development and Equity: The Challenge of the 1980s." *CEPAL Review,* no. 15 (December), 7–46.
ILO (International Labour Organisation)
  1977   *Meeting Basic Needs.* Geneva.
INCORA (Instituto Colombiano de Reforma Agraria)
  1975   *Reforma social agraria: Leyes y decretos reglamentarios.* Bogotá.
  1977   *Realizaciones del Incora, 1962–1977.* Bogotá.
  n.d.   Unpublished data. Sección de Información e Estadística. Bogotá.
Irwin, Howard, and Robert Goodland
  1975   *Amazon Jungle: Green Hell to Red Desert?* Amsterdam: Elsevier Scientific.
Johnson, A. W.
  1971   *Sharecroppers of the Sertão.* Stanford: Stanford University Press.
Johnston, Bruce F., and William C. Clark
  1982   *Redesigning Rural Development: A Strategic Perspective.* Baltimore: Johns Hopkins University Press.
Johnston, Bruce F., and John W. Mellor
  1961   "The Role of Agriculture in Economic Development." *The American Economic Review* 51, no. 4 (September): 565–93.
Johnston, Bruce F., and Soren T. Nielson
  1966   "Agriculture and Structural Transformation in a Developing Economy." *Economic Development and Cultural Change* 14, no. 3 (April): 279–301.
Jonas, Susanne
  1974   "Guatemala: Land of Eternal Struggle." In Ronald H. Chilcote and Joel C. Edelstein, eds., *Latin America: The Struggle with Dependency and Beyond.* Cambridge, Mass.: Schenkman.
Junguito, Roberto
  1978   *Bases para una política agropecuaria.* Bogotá: Biblioteca SAC.
Kaimowitz, David, and A. Eugene Havens
  1982   "Nicaragua in Transition: Agriculture and the State." Paper prepared for the 1982 meeting of the Latin American Studies Association, Washington, D.C., March 4–7.
Kalmanovitz, Salomon
  1978   *Desarrollo de la agricultura de Colombia.* Bogotá: Editorial La Carreta.
Kaufman, Robert R.
  1972   *The Politics of Land Reform in Chile, 1950–1970.* Cambridge, Mass: Harvard University Press.
  1979   "Industrial Change and Authoritarian Rule in Latin America: A Concrete Review of the Bureaucratic-Authoritarian Model." In David Collier, ed.,

The New Authoritarianism in Latin America. Princeton: Princeton University Press.

Kay, Cristobal
  1974   "El sistema señorial europeo y la hacienda latinoamericana." *Revista de México Agrário,* 7:162–69.
  1977   "The Development of the Chilean *Hacienda* System, 1850–1973." In Kenneth Duncan and Ian Rutledge, eds., *Land and Labour in Latin America.* Cambridge: Cambridge University Press.
  1978   "Agrarian Reform and the Class Struggle in Chile." *Latin American Perspectives* 5 (Summer): 117–40.

Keith, Robert G.
  1976   *Conquest and Agrarian Change: The Emergence of the Hacienda System on the Peruvian Coast.* Cambridge, Mass.: Harvard University Press.
  1977   *Haciendas and Plantations in Latin American History.* New York: Holmes and Meier.

Kirby, J.
  1973   "Venezuela's Land Reform: Progress and Change." *Journal of Interamerican Studies and World Affairs* 15 (May): 205–20.

Klarén, Peter F.
  1973   *Modernization, Dislocation, and Aprismo: Origins of the Peruvian Aprista Party, 1870–1932.* Austin: University of Texas Press.
  1977   "The Social and Economic Consequences of Modernization in the Peruvian Sugar Industry, 1870–1930." In Kenneth Duncan and Ian Rutledge, eds., *Land and Labour in Latin America* Cambridge: Cambridge University Press.

Klein, Emilio
  1980   "Pauperización campesina: Empleo e ingresos agrícolas." *Nueva Antropología* 4, nos. 13–14 (May): 87–120.

Laclau, Ernesto
  1971   "Feudalism and Capitalism in Latin America." *New Left Review,* no. 67 (May–June), 19–38.

LAER (Latin America Economic Report)
     Published weekly.

Landsberger, Henry A., ed.
  1969   *Latin American Peasant Movements.* Ithaca, N.Y.: Cornell University Press.

Landsberger, Henry A., and Cynthia N. Hewitt
  1970   "Ten Sources of Weakness and Cleavage in Latin American Peasant Movements." In Rodolfo Stavenhagen, ed., *Agrarian Problems and Peasant Movements in Latin America.* Garden City, N.Y.: Doubleday.

Lappé, Frances Moore, and Joseph Collins
  1977   *Food First: Beyond the Myth of Scarcity.* Boston: Houghton Mifflin.

LAPR (Latin America Political Report)
     Published weekly.

LARR (Latin America Regional Report)
     Published weekly.

Lassen, Cheryl A.
  1980   *Landlessness and Rural Poverty in Latin America: Conditions, Trends, and Policies Affecting Income and Employment.* Ithaca, N.Y.: Center for International Studies, Cornell University.
LAWR (Latin America Weekly Report)
        Published weekly.
Lehman, David
  1971   "Political Incorporation versus Political Stability: The Case of the Chilean Agrarian Reform, 1965–1970." *Journal of Development Studies* 7, no. 4 (July): 365–96.
  1974   "Agrarian Reform in Chile, 1965–1972: An Essay in Contradictions." In David Lehman, ed., *Peasants, Landlords, and Governments.* New York: Holmes and Meier.
Lele, Uma
  1975   *The Design of Rural Development: Lessons from Africa.* Baltimore: Johns Hopkins University Press.
Levinson, Jerome, and Juan de Onís
  1970   *The Alliance That Lost Its Way.* Chicago: Quadrangle Books.
Lewis, W. Arthur
  1954   "Economic Development with Unlimited Supplies of Labour." *Manchester School of Economic and Social Studies* 22, no. 2:139–91.
Lipton, Michael
  1968   "The Theory of the Optimising Peasant." *Journal of Development Studies* 4 (April): 327–51.
Long, Norman
  1980   "Some Concluding Comments: Directive Change and the Question of Participation." In David A. Preston, ed., *Environment, Society, and Rural Change in Latin America.* Chichester: John Wiley and Sons.
Long, Norman, and Brian R. Roberts, eds.
  1978   *Peasant Cooperation and Capitalist Expansion in Central Peru.* Austin: University of Texas Press.
López Córdovez, Luís
  1982   "Trends and Recent Changes in the Latin American Food and Agriculture Situation." *CEPAL Review*, no. 16 (April), 7–42.
López Michelsen, A.
  1972   "El futuro está en el campo: Alternativa: reforma agraria que opere." *Revista Nacional de Agricultura* 66, no. 789:30–41.
Loveman, Brian
  1976   *Struggle in the Countryside: Politics and Rural Labor in Chile, 1919–1973.* Bloomington: Indiana University Press.
LTCN (Land Tenure Center Newsletter)
  1977   "International Seminar: Agrarian Reform, Institutional Innovation, and Rural Development: Major Issues in Perspective." No. 56 (April).
McClintock, Cynthia
  1980   "Reform Governments and Policy Implementation: Lessons from Peru." In Merilee S. Grindle, ed., *Politics and Policy Implementation in the Third World.* Princeton: Princeton University Press.

1981 *Peasant Cooperatives and Political Change in Peru.* Princeton: Princeton University Press.

MacLeod, Murdo
1973 *Spanish Central America: A Socioeconomic History, 1520–1720.* Berkeley and Los Angeles: University of California Press.

Mahar, Dennis J.
1979 *Frontier Development Policy in Brazil: A Study of Amazonia.* New York: Praeger.

Mallon, Florencia E.
1978 "Peasants and Rural Laborers in Pernambuco, 1955–1964." *Latin American Perspectives* 5, no. 4 (Fall): 49–70.
1983 *The Defense of Community in Peru's Central Highlands.* Princeton: Princeton University Press.

Malloy, James M.
1970 *Bolivia: The Uncompleted Revolution.* Pittsburgh: University of Pittsburgh Press.
1974 "Authoritarianism, Corporatism, and Mobilization in Peru." In F. B. Pike and T. Stritch, eds., *The New Corporatism: Socio-Political Structures in the Iberian World.* Notre Dame, Ind.: University of Notre Dame Press.
1977 "Authoritarianism and Corporatism in Latin America: The Modal Pattern." In James M. Malloy, ed., *Authoritarianism and Corporatism in Latin America.* Pittsburgh: University of Pittsburgh Press.
1979 *The Politics of Social Security in Brazil.* Pittsburgh: University of Pittsburgh Press.

Malloy, James M., and R. S. Thorn, eds.
1971 *Beyond the Revolution: Bolivia Since 1952.* Pittsburgh: University of Pittsburgh Press.

Mamalakis, Markos
1969 "The Theory of Sectoral Clashes." *Latin American Research Review* 4, no. 3 (Fall): 9–46.
1971 "The Theory of Sectoral Clashes and Coalitions Revisited." *Latin American Research Review* 6, no. 3 (Fall): 89–126.

Marini, R. M.
1976 "La reforma agraria en América Latina." *Cuadernos Agrarios* 1:14–19.

Martínez-Alier, Juan
1977 *Haciendas, Plantations, and Collective Farms: Agrarian Class Societies— Cuba and Peru.* London: Frank Cass.

Martínez de Hoz, José Alfredo
1967 *La agricultura y la ganadería argentina en el período 1930–1960.* Buenos Aires: Editorial Sudamericana.

Martz, John
1966 *Acción Democrática: Evolution of a Modern Political Party.* Princeton: Princeton University Press.

Marx, Karl
1963 *The Eighteenth Brumaire of Louis Bonaparte.* New York: International Publishers.

Mattos, Carlos A. de
 1979   "Plans versus Planning in Latin American Experience." *CEPAL Review,*
        no. 8 (August), 75–89.
Meade, T.
 1978   "The Transition to Capitalism in Brazil: Notes on a Third Road." *Latin
        American Perspectives* 18:7–26.
Mendonça de Barros, José Roberto, and Douglas H. Graham
 1980   "Brazilian Development and the Problems of Constrained Modernization."
        Paper presented at the Center for Brazilian Studies, SAIS, Johns Hopkins
        University, September 25.
Mexico, Oficina de Asesores del C. Presidente
 1980   *Sistema Alimentario Mexicano: Primer planteamiento de metas de consumo
        y estratégia de producción de alimentos básicos para 1980–1982.* Mexico
        City.
Migdal, Joel S.
 1974   *Peasants, Politics, and Revolution: Pressures toward Political and Social
        Change in the Third World.* Princeton: Princeton University Press.
Miliband, Ralph
 1969   *The State in Capitalist Society.* New York: Basic Books.
Miró, Carmen, A., and Daniel Rodríguez
 1982   "Capitalism and Population in Latin American Agriculture." *CEPAL Re-
        view,* no. 16 (April), 51–71.
Moncayo, Victor M.
 1975   "La ley y el problema agrario en Colombia," *Ideología y Sociedad* 14–15
        (July–December): 7–46.
Montes de Oca, R. E.
 1977   "The State and the Peasants." In José Luís Reyna and Richard S. Weinert,
        eds., *Authoritarianism in Mexico.* Philadelphia: ISHI.
Moore, Barrington
 1966   *Social Origins of Dictatorship and Democracy.* Boston: Beacon Press.
Moraes, Clodomir
 1970   "Peasant Leagues in Brazil." In Rodolfo Stavenhagen, ed., *Agrarian Prob-
        lems and Peasant Movements in Latin America.* Garden City, N.Y.: Dou-
        bleday.
Morán, Emilio
 1982   "Ecological, Anthropological, and Agronomic Research in the Amazon
        Basin." *Latin American Research Review* 17, no. 1:3–41.
Mörner, Magnus
 1967   *Race Mixture in the History of Latin America.* Boston: Little, Brown.
Murmis, Miguel; José Bengoa; and Osvaldo Barsky
 1978   *Terratenientes y desarrollo capitalista en el agro.* Quito: CEPLAES.
NACLA (North American Congress on Latin America)
 1978   "Agribusiness Targets Latin America." *NACLA Report on the Americas* 12,
        no. 1 (January–February): 2–36.
Nairn, Allan
 1981   "Guatemala." *Multinational Monitor* 2, no. 5 (May): 12–14.

Nelson, Richard R., T. Paul Schultz, and Robert Slighton
 1971 *Structural Change in a Developing Economy*. Princeton: Princeton University Press.
Nickson, R. Andrew
 1981 "Brazilian Colonization of the Eastern Border Region of Paraguay." *Journal of Latin American Studies* 13, pt. 1 (May): 111–31.
Nordlinger, Eric
 1981 *On the Autonomy of the Democratic State*. Cambridge, Mass.: Harvard University Press.
OAS (Organization of American States)
 América en Cifras. Published periodically.
O'Donnell, Guillermo
 1973 *Modernization and Bureaucratic Authoritarianism*. Berkeley and Los Angeles: University of California Press.
 1979 "Tensions in the Bureaucratic-Authoritarian State and the Question of Democracy." In David Collier, ed., *The New Authoritarianism in Latin America*. Princeton: Princeton University Press.
Oquist, Paul
 1980 *Violence, Conflict, and Politics in Colombia*. New York: Academic Press.
Ortega, Emiliano
 1982 "Peasant Agriculture in Latin America." *CEPAL Review* no. 16 (April), 75–111.
Packenham, Robert A.
 1973 *Liberal America and the Third World*. Princeton: Princeton University Press.
Page, Joseph A.
 1972 *The Revolution That Never Was: Northeast Brazil, 1955–1964*. New York: Grossman.
Paige, Jeffrey
 1975 *Agrarian Revolution: Social Movements and Export Agriculture in the Underdeveloped World*. New York: Free Press.
Pansini, J. Jude
 1981 "Lake Atitlán: The Seasonal Farm Labor Problem." *ARC Newsletter* 5, no. 2 (June): 5.
Pardo Buelvas, R.
 1972 "Reforma en entredicho." *Revista Nacional de Agricultura* 65, no. 787:24–29.
Paré, Louisa
 1977 *El proletariado agrícola en México*. Mexico City: Siglo XXI.
Paulino, Leonardo A., and Shen Sheng Tseng
 1980 *A Comparative Study of FAO and USDA Data on Production, Area, and Trade of Major Food Staples*. Research Report no. 19. Washington, D.C.: International Food Policy Research Institute.
Pearse, Andrew
 1970 "Agrarian Change Trends in Latin America." In Rodolfo Stavenhagen, ed., *Agrarian Problems and Peasant Movements in Latin America*. Garden City, N.Y.: Doubleday.

1975   *The Latin American Peasant*. London: Frank Cass.
Petras, James
    1969   *Politics and Social Forces in Chilean Development*. Berkeley and Los Angeles: University of California Press.
Petras, James, and Robert LaPorte, Jr.
    1971   *Cultivating Revolution: The United States and Agrarian Reform in Latin America*. New York: Random House.
PIDER (Programa de Inversiones para el Desarrollo Rural Integrado)
    1980   *PIDER*. Mexico.
Pinto, Aníbal
    1980   "The Opening Up of Latin America to the Exterior." *CEPAL Review* no. 11 (August), 31–56.
Poleman, Thomas T.
    1964   *The Papaloapan Project: Agricultural Development in the Mexican Tropics*. Stanford: Stanford University Press.
POLONORDESTE (Programa de Desenvolvimento de Areas Integradas do Nordeste)
    1980   *POLONORDESTE*. Washington, D.C.
Pompermayer Malori, José
    1980   "Agrarian Structure and State Policies in Brazil." Paper presented at the 1980 meeting of the Latin American Studies Association, Bloomington, Ind., October 17–19.
Portes, Alejandro, and William Canak
    1981   "Latin America: Social Structures and Sociology." *Annual Review of Sociology* 7:225–48.
Portes, Alejandro, and John Walton
    1976   *Urban Latin America*. Austin: University of Texas Press.
Poulantzas, Nicos
    1973   *Political Power and Social Classes*. London: New Left Books; Sheed and Ward.
Powell, John D.
    1970   "Peasant Society and Clientelist Politics." *American Political Science Review* 64, no. 2 (June): 411–25.
    1971   *The Mobilization of the Venezuelan Peasant*. Cambridge, Mass.: Harvard University Press.
Prebisch, Raúl
    1950   *The Economic Development of Latin America and Its Principal Problems*. New York: United Nations.
    1951   *Theoretical and Practical Problems of Economic Growth*. New York: United Nations.
Preston, David A., ed.
    1980   "Rural Emigration and the Future of Agriculture in Ecuador." In David A. Preston, ed., *Environment, Society, and Rural Change in Latin America*. Chichester: John Wiley and Sons.
Purcell, Susan Kaufman
    1981   "Business-Government Relations in Mexico: The Case of the Sugar Industry." *Comparative Politics* 13, no. 2 (January): 211–33.

Rama, Ruth, and Raúl Vigorito
1979   *Transnacionales en América Latina: El complejo de frutas y legumbres en México.* Mexico City: Editorial Nueva Imagen.
Redclift, Michael R.
1978   *Agrarian Reform and Peasant Organization on the Ecuadorian Coast.* London: Athlone Press.
Redclift, Michael R., and David A. Preston
1980   "Agrarian Reform and Rural Change in Ecuador." In David A. Preston, ed., *Environment, Society, and Rural Change in Latin America.* Chichester: John Wiley and Sons.
Rello, Fernando
1976   "Modo de producción y clases sociales." *Cuadernos Políticos* 8:100–105.
Reyna, José Luís
1970   "Movilización y participación política: Discusión de algunas hipótesis para el caso mexicano." In Jorge Martínez Rios et al., *El perfil de México*, vol. 3. Mexico: Siglo XXI.
Reynolds, Lloyd G.
1975   "Agriculture in Development Theory: An Overview." In Lloyd G. Reynolds, ed., *Agriculture in Development Theory.* New Haven: Yale University Press.
Rivière d'Arc, Hélène
1980   "Change and Rural Emigration in Central Mexico." In David A. Preston, ed., *Environment, Society, and Rural Change in Latin America.* Chichester: John Wiley and Sons.
Rondinelli, Dennis, and Kenneth Ruddle
1978   *Urbanization and Rural Development.* New York: Praeger.
Ronfeldt, David
1973   "Atencingo: The Politics of Agrarian Struggle in a Mexican Ejido. Stanford: Stanford University Press.
Ruhl, J. Mark
1984   "Agrarian Structure and Political Stability in Honduras." *Journal of Interamerican Studies and World Affairs* 26, no. 1:33–68.
Saint, William S.
1981   "The Wages of Modernization: A Review of the Literature on Temporary Labor Arrangements in Brazilian Agriculture." *Latin American Research Review* 16, no. 3:91–110.
SALA (Statistical Abstract for Latin America)
        Published annually by the Latin American Center, University of California at Los Angeles.
Samper, A.
1971   *La reforma agraria en la encrucijada.* IICA-CIRA Material Didáctico no. 167. Bogatá: IICA-CIRA.
Sanders, J. H. and V. W. Ruttan
1978   "Biased Choice of Technology in Brazilian Agriculture." In H. P. Binswanger and V. W. Ruttan, eds., *Induced Innovation: Technology, Institutions, and Development.* Baltimore: Johns Hopkins University Press.

Sanders, Thomas
  1982   *The Problems of Nutrition in Brazil.* AUFS Reports no. 16 (South America). Hanover, N.H.: AUFS.
Sanderson, Steven
  1981   *Agrarian Populism and the Mexican State.* Berkeley and Los Angeles: University of California Press.
Schlesinger, Arthur
  1975   "The Alliance for Progress: A Retrospective." In Ronald G. Hellman and H. Jon Rosenbaum, eds., *Latin America: The Search for a New International Role.* New York: John Wiley and Sons.
Schryer, Frans J.
  1980   *The Rancheros of Pisaflores: The History of a Peasant Bourgeoisie in Twentieth Century Mexico.* Toronto: University of Toronto Press.
Schuh, Edward
  1970   *The Agricultural Development of Brazil.* New York: Praeger.
Schultz, T. W.
  1964   *Transforming Traditional Agriculture.* New Haven: Yale University Press.
  1968   *Economic Growth and Agriculture.* New York: McGraw-Hill.
Schuyler, George W.
  1980   *Hunger in a Land of Plenty.* Cambridge, Mass.: Schenkman.
Scobie, Grant M., and Rafael Posada T.
  1978   "The Impact of Technical Change on Income Distribution: The Case of Rice in Colombia." *American Journal of Agricultural Economics* 60, no. 1 (February): 85–92.
Scobie, James R.
  1964   *Revolution on the Pampas: A Social History of Argentine Wheat, 1860–1910.* Austin: University of Texas Press.
  1971   *Argentina: A City and a Nation.* 2nd ed. New York: Oxford University Press.
Scott, Christopher D.
  1980   "Transnational Corporations and the Food Industry in Latin America: An Analysis of the Determinants of Investment and Divestment." Working Paper no. 64, Latin American Program, Woodrow Wilson Center, Washington, D.C. Mimeo.
Scott, James C.
  1972   "Patron-Client Politics and Political Change in Southeast Asia." *American Political Science Review* 66, no. 1 (March): 91–113.
  1976   *The Moral Economy of the Peasant: Rebellion and Subsistence in Southeast Asia.* New Haven: Yale University Press.
Seligson, Mitchell
  1977   "Agrarian Policies in Dependent Societies: Costa Rica." *Journal of Interamerican Studies and World Affairs* 19 (May): 201–32.
  1980   *Peasants of Costa Rica and the Development of Agrarian Capitalism.* Madison: University of Wisconsin Press.
  1982   "Cooperative Participation among Agrarian Reform Beneficiaries in Costa Rica." Paper prepared for the 1982 meeting of the Latin American Studies Association, Washington, D.C., March 4–6.

Simpson, Eyler N.
1937   *The Ejido: Mexico's Way Out*. Chapel Hill: University of North Carolina Press.

Skidmore, Thomas E.
1967   *Politics in Brazil, 1930–1964: An Experiment in Democracy*. London: Oxford University Press.
1973   "Politics and Economic Policy Making in Authoritarian Brazil, 1937–1971." In Alfred Stepan, ed., *Authoritarian Brazil: Origins, Policies, and Future.* New Haven: Yale University Press.
1977   "The Politics of Economic Stabilization in Postwar Latin America." In James M. Malloy, ed., *Authoritarianism and Corporation in Latin America.* Pittsburgh: University of Pittsburgh Press.

Skocpol, Theda
1979   *States and Social Revolutions.* Cambridge: Cambridge University Press.

Smith, Gordon W.
1969   "Brazilian Agricultural Policy, 1950–1967." In Howard S. Ellis, ed., *The Economy of Brazil.* Berkeley and Los Angeles: University of California Press.

Smith, Peter H.
1969   *Politics and Beef in Argentina: Patterns of Conflict and Change.* New York: Columbia University Press.
1974   *Argentina and the Failure of Democracy: Conflict among Political Elites, 1904–1955.* Madison: University of Wisconsin Press.

Solaún, Mauricio
1980   "Colombian Politics: Historical Characteristics and Problems." In R. Albert Berry, Ronald G. Hellman, and Mauricio Solaún, eds., *Politics of Compromise.* New Brunswick, N.J.: Transaction Books.

Soles, Roger E.
1974   *Rural Land Invasions in Colombia.* Land Tenure Center Research Paper no. 59. Madison: University of Wisconsin.

Solís, Leopoldo
1971   "Mexican Economic Policy in the Post-war Period: Views of Mexican Economists." *American Economic Review* 61, no. 3, pt. 2, suppl. (June): 1–67.

Sorj, B.
1980   "Agrarian Structure and Politics in Present Day Brazil." *Latin American Perspectives* 24:23–34.

Spaulding, Rose
1981   "State Power and Its Limits: Corporatism in Mexico." *Comparative Political Studies* 14, no. 2 (July): 139–61.

Stallings, Barbara
1978   *Class Conflict and Economic Development in Chile, 1958–1973.* Stanford: Stanford University Press.

Stavenhagen, Rodolfo, ed.
1970   *Agrarian Problems and Peasant Movements in Latin America.* Garden City, N.Y.: Doubleday.

1975   *Social Classes in Agrarian Societies.* Garden City, N.Y.: Doubleday.
Stein, Stanley J., and Barbara H. Stein
1970   *The Colonial Heritage of Latin America: Essays on Economic Dependence in Perspective.* New York: Oxford University Press.
Stepan, Alfred
1978   *The State and Society: Peru in Comparative Perspective.* Princeton: Princeton University Press.
Stinchcombe, Arthur
1961–   "Agricultural Enterprise and Rural Class Relations." *American Journal of*
62   *Sociology* 67:165–67.
Swanberg, Kenneth
1981   "The Caquezá Rural Development Model: Implications for National Development." Unpublished paper, Harvard Institute for International Development, Cambridge, Mass.
Taussig, Michael
1977   "The Evolution of Rural Wage Labour in the Cauca Valley of Colombia, 1700–1970." In Kenneth Duncan and Ian Rutledge, eds., *Land and Labour in Latin America.* Cambridge: Cambridge University Press.
1978   "Peasant Economies and the Development of Capitalist Agriculture in the Cauca Valley, Colombia." *Latin American Perspectives* 18:62–91.
Taylor, William B.
1972   *Landlord and Peasant in Colonial Oaxaca.* Stanford: Standford University Press.
Terán, S.
1976   "Formas de consciencia social de los trabajadores del campo." *Cuadernos Agrarios* 1:20–36.
Thiesenhusen, William C.
1971   "Agrarian Reform, Chile." In Peter Dorner, ed., *Land Reform in Latin America: Issues and Cases.* Land Economics Monograph no. 3. Madison: Land Tenure Center, University of Wisconsin.
Thirsk, Wayne R.
1976   "Price Policy and Agricultural Development in Ecuador." Program of Development Studies Paper no. 76, Rice University, Houston, Tex. Mimeo.
Thome, Joseph R.
1971   "Agrarian Reform Legislation: Chile." In Peter Dorner, ed., *Land Reform in Latin America: Issues and Cases.* Land Economics Monograph no. 3. Madison: Land Tenure Center, University of Wisconsin.
Thorn, Richard S.
1971   "The Economic Transformation." In James M. Malloy and Richard S. Thorn, eds., *Beyond the Revolution: Bolivia Since 1952.* Pittsburgh: University of Pittsburgh Press.
Topik, Steven
1982   "The Defense of Coffee." Paper presented at the 1982 meeting of the Latin American Studies Association, Washington, D.C., March 4–7.
Trimberger, Ellen
1978   *Revolution from Above: Military Bureaucrats and Development in Japan, Turkey, Egypt, and Peru.* New Brunswick, N.J.: Transaction Books.

Tucker, Robert C.
1969 *The Marxian Revolution Idea.* New York: W. W. Norton.
UNCTC (United Nations Centre on Transnational Corporations)
1981 *Transnational Corporations in Food and Beverage Processing.* New York.
UNESLA (United Nations Economic Survey of Latin America)
New York. Published annually.
USDA (United States Department of Agriculture)
Agricultural Situations: Western Hemisphere. Washington, D.C. Published quarterly.
Valderrama, M.
1978 "Reforma agraria y acumulación capitalista en el Perú: El modelo, sus limites, y sus contradicciones." *Estudios Rurales Latinoamericanos* 1:97–110.
Valenzuela Ramírez, Jorge
1978 *Producción arrocera y clientelismo.* Bogotá: Editorial CINEP.
Vallejo Morillo, Jorge
1977 "Problemas de método en el estudio de la cuestión agraria." In F. Leal Buitrago et al., *El agro en el desarrollo histórice colombiano.* Bogotá: Editorial Punta de Lanza.
Van den Berghe, Pierre, and George Primov
1977 *Inequality in the Peruvian Andes: Class and Ethnicity in Cuzco.* Columbia: University of Missouri Press.
Veliz, Claudio
1980 *The Centralist Tradition in Latin America.* Princeton: Princeton University Press.
Venezian, Eduardo L., and William K. Gamble
1969 *The Agricultural Development of Mexico.* New York: Praeger.
Vergara, Pilar
1980 "Las transformaciones del estado chileno bajo el régimen militar." Paper prepared for a workshop entitled "Six Years of Military Rule in Chile," Woodrow Wilson Center, Washington, D.C., May 15–17.
Vertinsky, I. G. D., and S. Fox
1972 "A Perspective of Land Reform Law in Colombia: Choice of Strategy for Change." *Land Economics* 48, no. 4:367–76.
Villareal, J.
1978 *El capitalismo dependiente: estudio sobre la estructura de clases en Argentina.* Mexico: Siglo XXI.
Volk, Steven
1981 "Honduras: On the Border of War." *NACLA Report on the Americas* 15, no. 6 (November–December): 2–30.
Wallerstein, I.
1974 *The Modern World-System: Capitalist Agriculture and the Origins of the European World Economy in the Sixteenth Century.* New York: Academic Press.
Warman, Arturo
1972 *Los campesinos, hijos predilectos del régimen.* Mexico City: Nuestro Tiempo.

1980   *"We Come to Object": The Peasants of Morelos and the National State.*
        Translated by Stephen K. Ault. Baltimore: Johns Hopkins University Press.
Weber, Max
1948   "Politics as a Vocation." In H. H. Gerth and C. Wright Mills, eds., *From
        Max Weber: Essays in Sociology.* New York: Oxford University Press.
Weinstein, Martin
1975   *Uruguay: The Politics of Failure.* Westport, Conn.: Greenwood Press.
Weisskoff, Richard, and Adolfo Figueroa
1976   "Transversing the Social Pyramid: A Comparative Review of Income Dis-
        tribution in Latin America." *Latin American Research Review* 11, no.
        2:71–112.
Wennergren, E. Boyd, and Morris D. Whitaker
1975   *The Status of Bolivian Agriculture.* New York: Praeger.
Whetten, Nathan
1948   *Rural Mexico.* Chicago: University of Chicago Press.
Whitaker, Arthur P.
1964   *Argentina.* Englewood Cliffs, N.J.: Prentice-Hall.
Whitehead, Lawrence
1980   "La política económica del sexenio de Echeverría: Que salió mal y por qué?"
        Foro Internacional, no. 79, 484–513.
Wilkie, James W.
1971   "Public Expenditure Since 1952." In James M. Malloy and Richard S.
        Thorn, eds., *Beyond the Revolution: Bolivia Since 1952.* Pittsburgh: Univer-
        sity of Pittsburgh Press.
Winson, A.
1978   "Class Structure and Agrarian Transition in Central America." *Latin Ameri-
        can Perspectives* 19:27–48.
Wolf, Eric R.
1968   *Peasant Wars of the Twentieth Century.* New York: Harper and Row.
Wolf, Eric R., and Sidney W. Mintz
1957   "Haciendas and Plantations in Middle America and the Antilles." *Social and
        Economic Studies* 6:386–412.
Womack, John, Jr.
1968   *Zapata and the Mexican Revolution.* New York: Vintage Books.
Woodward, Ralph
1976   *Central America: A Nation Divided.* New York: Oxford University Press.
World Bank
1975   *The Assault on World Poverty: Problems of Rural Development, Educa-
        tion, and Health.* Baltimore: Johns Hopkins University Press.
1978   *Guatemala: Economic and Social Position and Prospects.* Washington,
        D.C.: World Bank.
1979   *Ecuador: Development Programs and Prospects.* Washington, D.C.: World
        Bank.
1980a   *World Development Report.* Washington, D.C.: World Bank.
1980b   *World Tables.* 2nd ed. Baltimore: Johns Hopkins University Press.
1984   *World Development Report.* Washington, D.C.: World Bank.

Wynia, Gary
    1978   *The Politics of Latin American Development*. Cambridge: Cambridge University Press.
Zaldívar, Ramon
    1974   "Agrarian Reform and Military Reformism in Peru." In David Lehman, ed., *Peasants, Landlords, and Governments*. New York: Holmes and Meier.
Zuleta, E.
    1973   *La tierra en Colombia*. Bogotá: La Oveja Negra.

Index

Agrarian change, 1, 11, 21–22, 23–24, 189–90; and capitalist agriculture, 79–111; in colonial period, 26–34, 209n.6; in Depression of 1930s, 44–46; in nineteenth century, 34–44; role of state in, 47–78, 89. *See also* Agrarian reform; Agriculture

Agrarian reform, 1–2, 3, 8, 10, 15, 18, 20–21, 112, 119–20, 133–59, 160, 163, 174, 175, 187; in Brazil, 75–76, 173, 183, 184, 186, 212n.16; in Colombia, 67, 68, 105, 133–59, 172, 180, 181, 182; definition of, 212n.1; institutes of, 52, 191; in Mexico, 61–62, 63, 176, 179

Agribusiness, 173; in Brazil, 173, 184; transnational, 20, 85, 207nn.7, 8; transnational, in Brazil, 108, 110–11, 117, 185; transnational, in Mexico, 103, 123, 135

Agricultural prices, 123, 125, 167; in Brazil, 73, 75, 76; in Colombia, 68, 69; control of, 89; for export crops, 83; in Mexico, 101, 117

Agricultural research, 58–59, 173, 187; in Brazil, 74; in Colombia, 71, 105; in Mexico, 58–59, 64, 100, 101

Agriculture: capitalist, 1–5, 6, 11, 19–22, 25, 79–111, 117, 124–25, 131, 151–53, 160, 162; in colonial period, 25–34; contract, 86, 89, 103, 123; and export production, 83, 89, 91–92; modernization of, 8, 15, 21, 133, 160, 171, 202n.8; in national development, 4, 8, 25, 47, 48–50, 54, 89, 131, 140–41, 152, 187; in nineteenth century, 34–44; productivity in, 6–7, 9, 31, 42, 79–88, 163; role of state in, 1, 3–4, 6–9, 11–12, 19–21, 47–78, 163, 164; subsistence, 6, 7, 8, 21, 22, 25, 101, 105, 120, 125, 128, 131, 162. *See also* Agrarian change; Agrarian reform; Modernization of agriculture; Peasants

Alemán, Miguel, 63

Allison, Graham, 17

Amazon: destruction of ecology in, 109; migration to, 128, 185, 186, 208n.27; policies to develop, 76–77, 108, 172; and transnational capital, 111; violence in, 110, 184

Anderson, Charles, 16

ANUC (Asociación Nacional de Usuarios Campesinos, Colombia), 147–48, 152

Argentina: access to land in, 120; agricultural development in, 79; beef production in, 35, 86; distribution of income in, 113; export promotion in, 54; exports from, 36, 83; food processing in, 85; foreign investment in, 37; immigrant labor in, 38; import substitution in, 53; regime in, 156; use of technology in, 42, 60

Autonomy of the state, 4, 5, 6, 10, 12–19, 189; constraints on, in Mexico, 67. *See also* State; State elites

Balance of payments, 3, 54

Balance of trade, 91–93

Bananas, export of, 83, 104, 159

Basic crops. *See* Staple crops

Basic needs, 3, 113, 122. *See also* Poverty

Beans, production of, 89, 99, 106, 108, 126, 131, 171

Beef, export of, 83, 172. *See also* Livestock production

Bolivia: agrarian reform in, 137, 138, 142, 153, 155, 156; agricultural development in, 79; credit in, 58; Indian communities in, 38; infrastructure in, 59–60; migration in, 98

Brazil: agrarian reform in, 134–35; agriculture in, 81, 90, 107–11, 114, 131, 191; *boias frias* in, 117, 128; coffee in, 35, 38–39; in colonial period, 28, 32; distribution of income in, 113; distribution of landholdings in, 41, 95, 117, 120; exports from, 41, 83; food

249

Brazil (*continued*)
processing in, 85; frontier in, 98, 128, 135; and import substitution, 53; integrated rural development in, 8, 164–74; in 1930s, 44–46; northeast, 73, 74, 76, 107, 110, 128; regime in, 5, 10, 134–35, 156, 157, 170–71, 183, 184; rural protest in, 43, 175, 182–86; state policies in, 6, 10, 72–77; use of machinery in, 42, 60. *See also* Amazon; POLONOR-DESTE
Bureaucracy, 15, 17, 162, 163, 167, 179, 187
Bureaucratic politics perspective, 16, 17–18

Cacao, export of, 28, 32–33
Campesinos. See Peasants
Capital: accumulation of, 13; foreign, 6–7, 13, 17, 34, 76, 85–86, 89, 103, 161; national, 17; use of, in colonial period, 27–34; use of, in nineteenth century, 34–44
Cárdenas, Lázaro, 62, 63, 65, 138, 176–77, 189, 195n.5
Caribbean: agricultural development in, 32, 45; plantations in, 28; population decline in, 26
Castro, Fidel, 144
Catholic Church: in Brazil, 183, 185, 186; in colonial period, 27; and liberal reforms, 36
CCI (Independent Peasants' Confederation, Mexico), 177–78, 179
Central America, agricultural development in, 26, 32, 35, 39, 45, 83, 86
Chicorral Agreement, 150, 172
Chile: agrarian reform in, 134–35, 142, 154, 155, 156–57, 158, 214n.33; agricultural development in, 79, 81, 191; distribution of income in, 113; exports from, 28, 35, 83; food policies in, 52, 91; import substitution in, 53; land concentration in, 38, 39, 41; regime in, 134–35; use of technology in, 42, 93, 98
Clientele: partisan, 180; of the state, 4, 24, 126, 131, 133, 137, 158, 160, 163, 174, 176
CNC (National Confederation of Peasants, Mexico), 177–79, 204n.24
Cochineal, 33
Coffee: in Brazil, 72, 107, 108; in Colombia, 69, 71, 104, 152, 172, 180; export of, 33, 35, 83, 89, 99
Colombia: access to land in, 95, 119, 120; agrarian reform in, 8, 10, 67, 68, 134–37, 142, 143–53, 156, 158; agricultural development in, 40, 60, 83, 90, 93, 104–7, 131; coffee in, 35, 39, 68; credit in, 58; distribution of income in, 113; elites in, 7, 67; export promotion in, 54; import substitution in, 53; integrated rural development in, 8, 125–26, 164–74, 181; liberal reforms in, 38; migration in, 98; in 1930s, 45; regime in, 5,

10, 157, 170, 181; rural protest in, 43, 175, 180–82; state policies in, 6, 10, 67–72
Colombian Agricultural Society. *See* SAC
Colonial period, 25–34
Colonization, 130, 135, 159, 163; in Brazil, 76–77, 128, 135, 173, 184, 185; in Colombia, 136, 144, 150
Commerce: in colonial period, 31; in nineteenth century, 36
Communication channels, 35, 36
Conflict, 16; in Colombia, 68; management of, 160; in Mexico, 62, 64; in nineteenth and early twentieth centuries, 43; rural, 5, 9, 12, 22–24, 123, 154, 175–86. *See also* Co-optation; Protest; Repression; Violence
Co-optation, 16; of rural dissent, 9, 24, 158, 174, 179, 180–81, 182, 189
Corn: import of, 102, 164; production of, 89–90, 99, 106, 126, 131, 171
Corporatist theory, 16–17
Costa Rica: coffee in, 35, 39; in colonial period, 31; crops in, 89, 90; exports from, 41, 83; land values in, 42; wage labor in, 39, 98
Cotton: export of, 83, 89, 99, 104, 172; production of, 38, 98, 151
Credit, agricultural, 6, 24, 126, 154, 155, 159, 161, 165, 173, 179, 187, 192; in Brazil, 73, 74, 75, 76, 105, 173; in Colombia, 68–69, 70–71, 126, 144; in Ecuador, 135; and international lending agencies, 164, 168, 190; for mechanization, 60; in Mexico, 62, 63–64, 86, 100, 101, 125; and moneylenders, 122, 123; in nineteenth century, 36; in Peru, 155; state investment in, 51, 153, 188, 191; unequal access to, 57–58
CRIC (Regional Council of Cauca Indians, Colombia), 182
Crisis, 15, 16; Depression of 1930s, 44–46, 201n.2; in Mexico, 66
Crop substitution, 89–91, 101–2
Cuba: foreign investment in, 37; revolution in, 137, 138–39, 141, 144, 192, 193, 213n.23; sugar in, 35–36

Debt: foreign, 161; among peasants, 112, 121–27, 191. *See also* Peonage
Debt bondage. *See* Peonage
de Janvry, Alain, 2–4
Demographic change. *See* Population; Urbanization
Dependency, 197nn.15, 20, 24; efforts to reduce, 45, 54, 89, 187; increased, in Mexico, 103; on state, 158, 159, 191; theory of, 13–15, 16, 20
Depression of 1930s, 44–46
Development ideology, 3–4, 5, 6, 15, 16, 17, 18, 19–21, 87–88, 177; agrarian reform as,

Index

PIDER (Mexico), 8, 164–73
Planners, 8, 17, 161, 162, 164–67. *See also*
State elites
Plantations, 127, 219n.27; in colonial period,
28–34, 200n.36; in Colombia, 119, 126; in
Guatemala, 129; in Peru, 37–38
Pluralist analysis, 16
Policy, 3, 4, 5, 13, 188; for agrarian reform,
133–59; for agricultural development, 18,
21, 47–78, 187; for cheap food, 52–53, 73,
83, 100, 160, 203n.16; formulation of, 5, 17,
61, 143, 161; implementation of, 5, 12, 17,
61, 146, 155, 163, 167–71, 191; in nineteenth century, 42–43; origin of, 12–19; redistributive, 4; revolutionary, 9. *See also*
Agriculture; Development ideology; State
elites
Policy makers. *See* State elites
Policy reform, 2–4, 5, 8, 9, 12, 195n.1. *See
also* Agrarian reform
Political parties: and agrarian reform,
141–42, 154, 156, 160; in Brazil, 182–83,
184; in Colombia, 134–37, 143–53, 168,
180–81, 213n.21; in Mexico, 177, 178; and
rural poor, 125, 131
POLONORDESTE, 8, 164–73
Population: decline of, 26, 28, 30, 34; growth
of, 2, 11, 22, 79, 90, 102, 104, 114, 117, 120,
173; in nineteenth century, 36. *See also* Migration; Urbanization
Poverty: in Brazil, 164, 173; in Mexico, 61;
rural, 1–5, 7, 8, 21, 23, 112–32, 161, 163,
167, 171, 174, 187, 193; urban, 112–15. *See
also* Peasants
Prebisch, Raúl, 47–48
PRI (Party of the Institutionalized Revolution, Mexico), 177, 178, 204n.24
Private sector, 21; in Brazil, 73, 76–77; in
Colombia, 143–53. *See also* Elites
Proletariat: rural, 21–24, 98, 127, 130,
197n.18; urban, 22
Protest, 43; rural, 5, 9, 23, 158, 172, 174,
175–86, 188, 190, 217n.1, 219nn.26, 28. *See
also* Conflict; Peasant mobilization; Peasant
organizations; Repression; Violence

Ranching. *See* Livestock production
Reforms, 133–59, 160, 189–92; liberal, 36,
38; state as beneficiary of, 188–89. *See also*
Agrarian reform; Integrated rural
development
Regime, 8, 9, 18, 36, 44–45, 134–35, 156,
170, 171, 176; in Brazil, 5, 72, 73, 74, 75,
169, 183, 184, 186; in Colombia, 5, 69, 180;
in Cuba, 139; definition of, 18; in Mexico,
5, 10, 61, 138, 176–79, 181–82; in Nicaragua, 138; in Peru, 141

Repression, in rural areas, 24, 32, 175; in
Brazil, 173, 184; in Colombia, 69, 153, 172,
181, 182; in Honduras, 135; in Mexico, 178
Resource allocation, 5–6, 17, 21, 24, 25,
56–61, 122, 163, 165, 168–69; in Brazil,
72–77; in Colombia, 70–72; in Mexico,
61–64
Revolution, 14, 154, 160, 183, 192–94; and
agrarian reform, 135–36, 137–39, 142,
213n.23; Bolivian, 138; Cuban, 24, 137,
138–39, 141, 144, 156; Mexican, 43, 61,
137–38, 172, 176; Nicaraguan, 137, 139
Rice, production of, 89, 98, 99, 104, 106, 108,
152, 171
Rockefeller Foundation, 58–59, 71
Rural poor. *See* Peasants

SAC (Colombian Agricultural Society), 67,
68, 150
SAM (Mexican Food System), 171–72
Self-sufficiency, 31, 69, 70, 121, 122, 209n.10
Sharecroppers, 20, 21, 22, 31, 46, 93, 98, 130,
155, 175; in Brazil, 110, 183; in Colombia,
134, 147, 180; in Cuba, 138; demands on,
36, 41, 119; in Nicaragua, 139, in Peru, 37.
See also Agrarian reform; Peasants; Rural
poor; Smallholders; Tenants
Skocpol, Theda, 15–16
Slavery, 28, 32, 34, 39
Smallholders, 2, 11, 22, 46, 120, 125, 127,
130, 131, 141, 155, 175, 180, 190, 191; in
Brazil, 183, 185; in Colombia, 134; in colo-
nial period, 27, 29, 32; in Mexico, 171. *See
also* Agrarian reform; Peasants; Share-
croppers; Tenants
Social security, 24, 190, 209n.5
Social unrest. *See* Conflict; Peasant mobili-
zation; Peasant organizations; Protest
Social welfare programs, 45, 98, 190. *See also*
Social security
Sorghum, 83, 90; in Brazil, 81, 107; in Colombia, 104; in Mexico, 101–2, 125
Soybeans: in Brazil, 107–8, 117; in Colombia, 104, 126; in Paraguay, 81
Squatters, 27, 119, 191; in Brazil, 185, 186; in
Colombia, 148, 182; in Cuba, 138
Staple crops: 89–91, 93, 131, 154, 155, 191;
in Colombia, 106; in Mexico, 100
State: as beneficiary of reform policies,
157–59, 174; control over, 12–19; definition
of, 5, 13, 15–16, 195n.4, 196n.7; expansion
of, 4–5, 6, 8, 17–18, 45, 46, 51–52, 133, 174,
175, 180, 186–87, 189, 202n.13; interests of,
5, 9, 16, 17–18, 186–94, 196n.11; and rural
protest, 9, 12, 122, 175–86. *See also* Bureaucracy; Policy; State agencies; State
elites

Books in the Series

MERILEE S. GRINDLE is a research associate at the Harvard
Institute for International Development. She is author of
*Bureaucrats, Politicians, and Peasants in Mexico: A Case
Study in Public Policy* and editor of *Politics and Policy
Implementation in the Third World.*

1- 617- 495 - ~~1000~~

~~3161~~

- 1872